WORKSHOPS IN COMPUTING
Series edited by C. J. van Rijsbergen

 KW-326-309

Also in this series

Algebraic Methodology and Software Technology (AMAST'93)
Proceedings of the Third International Conference on Algebraic Methodology and Software Technology, University of Twente, Enschede, The Netherlands, 21–25 June 1993
M. Nivat, C. Rattray, T. Rus and G. Scollo (Eds.)

Logic Program Synthesis and Transformation
Proceedings of LOPSTR 93, International Workshop on Logic Program Synthesis and Transformation, Louvain-la-Neuve, Belgium, 7–9 July 1993
Yves Deville (Ed.)

Database Programming Languages (DBPL-4)
Proceedings of the Fourth International Workshop on Database Programming Languages – Object Models and Languages, Manhattan, New York City, USA, 30 August–1 September 1993
Catriel Beeri, Atsushi Ohori and Dennis E. Shasha (Eds.)

Music Education: An Artificial Intelligence Approach, Proceedings of a Workshop held as part of AI-ED 93, World Conference on Artificial Intelligence in Education, Edinburgh, Scotland, 25 August 1993
Matt Smith, Alan Smaill and Geraint A. Wiggins (Eds.)

Rules in Database Systems
Proceedings of the 1st International Workshop on Rules in Database Systems, Edinburgh, Scotland, 30 August–1 September 1993
Norman W. Paton and M. Howard Williams (Eds.)

Semantics of Specification Languages (SoSL)
Proceedings of the International Workshop on Semantics of Specification Languages, Utrecht, The Netherlands, 25–27 October 1993
D.J. Andrews, J.F. Groote and C.A. Middelburg (Eds.)

Security for Object-Oriented Systems
Proceedings of the OOPSLA-93 Conference Workshop on Security for Object-Oriented Systems, Washington DC, USA, 26 September 1993
B. Thuraisingham, R. Sandhu and T.C. Ting (Eds.)

Functional Programming, Glasgow 1993
Proceedings of the 1993 Glasgow Workshop on Functional Programming, Ayr, Scotland, 5–7 July 1993
John T. O'Donnell and Kevin Hammond (Eds.)

Z User Workshop, Cambridge 1994
Proceedings of the Eighth Z User Meeting, Cambridge, 29–30 June 1994
J.P. Bowen and J.A. Hall (Eds.)

6th Refinement Workshop
Proceedings of the 6th Refinement Workshop, organised by BCS-FACS, London, 5–7 January 1994
David Till (Ed.)

Incompleteness and Uncertainty in Information Systems
Proceedings of the SOFTEKS Workshop on Incompleteness and Uncertainty in Information Systems, Concordia University, Montreal, Canada, 8–9 October 1993
V.S. Alagar, S. Bergler and F.Q. Dong (Eds.)

Rough Sets, Fuzzy Sets and Knowledge Discovery
Proceedings of the International Workshop on Rough Sets and Knowledge Discovery (RSKD'93), Banff, Alberta, Canada, 12–15 October 1993
Wojciech P. Ziarko (Ed.)

Algebra of Communicating Processes
Proceeedings of ACP94, the First Workshop on the Algebra of Communicating Processes, Utrecht, The Netherlands, 16–17 May 1994
A. Ponse, C. Verhoef and S.F.M. van Vlijmen (Eds.)

Interfaces to Database Systems (IDS94)
Proceedings of the Second International Workshop on Interfaces to Database Systems, Lancaster University, 13–15 July 1994
Pete Sawyer (Ed.)

Persistent Object Systems
Proceedings of the Sixth International Workshop on Persistent Object Systems, Tarascon, Provence, France, 5–9 September 1994
Malcolm Atkinson, David Maier and Véronique Benzaken (Eds.)

continued on back page...

Kevin Hammond, David N. Turner and
Patrick M. Sansom (Eds)

Functional Programming, Glasgow 1994

Proceedings of the 1994 Glasgow
Workshop on Functional Programming,
Ayr, Scotland, 12–14 September 1994

Published in collaboration with the
British Computer Society

Springer

London Berlin Heidelberg New York
Paris Tokyo Hong Kong
Barcelona Budapest

Kevin Hammond, PhD
David N. Turner, BSc
Patrick M. Sansom, BSc, PhD

Department of Computing Science,
Glasgow University, Glasgow G12 8QQ, Scotland

ISBN 3-540-19914-4 Springer-Verlag Berlin Heidelberg New York

British Library Cataloguing in Publication Data
Functional Programming, Glasgow 1994: Proceedings of the 1994 Glasgow Workshop on
Functional Programming, Ayr, Scotland, 12–14 September 1994. – (Workshops in
Computing Series)
    I. Hammond, Kevin   II.   Series
    005.1
ISBN 3-540-19914-4

Library of Congress Cataloging-in-Publication Data
Glasgow Workshop on Functional Programming (1994: Ayr, Scotland)
    Functional programming, Glasgow 1994 : proceedings of the 1994
Glasgow Workshop on Functional Programming, Ayr, Scotland, 12–14 September 1994 /
Kevin Hammond, David N. Turner, and Patrick M. Sansom.
        p.   cm. – (Workshops in computing)
    "Published in collaboration with the British Computer Society."
    Includes bibliographical references and index.
    ISBN 3-540-19914-4
    1.   Functional programming (Computer science)–Congresses.
I.   Hammond, Kevin.   II.   Turner, David N. (David Neil), 1968–   .
III   Sansom, Patrick.   IV.   British Computer Society.   V.   Title.
VI.   Series.
QA76.62.G58 1995   94-44476
005.1'1– dc20   CIP

Apart from any fair dealing for the purposes of research or private study, or criticism or
review, as permitted under the Copyright, Designs and Patents Act 1988, this publication
may only be reproduced, stored or transmitted, in any form, or by any means, with the
prior permission in writing of the publishers, or in the case of reprographic reproduction
in accordance with the terms of licences issued by the Copyright Licensing Agency.
Enquiries concerning reproduction outside those terms should be sent to the publishers.

© British Computer Society 1995
Printed in Great Britain

The use of registered names, trademarks etc. in this publication does not imply, even in the
absence of a specific statement, that such names are exempt from the relevant laws and
regulations and therefore free for general use.

The publisher makes no representation, express or implied, with regard to the accuracy of
the information contained in this book and cannot accept any legal responsibility or
liability for any errors or omissions that may be made.

Typesetting: Camera ready by contributors
Printed by Athenæum Press Ltd., Gateshead
34/3830-543210 Printed on acid-free paper

Preface

This is the proceedings of the seventh annual workshop held by the Glasgow Functional Programming Group. The purpose of the workshop is to provide a focus for new research, to foster research contacts with other functional language researchers, and to provide a platform for research students to develop their presentation skills.

As in previous years, we spent three days closeted together in a pleasant seaside town, isolated from normal work commitments. We were joined by colleagues from other universities (both UK and abroad) and from industry. Workshop participants presented a short talk about their current research work, and produced a paper which appeared in a draft proceedings. These papers were then reviewed and revised in the light of discussions at the workshop and the referees' comments. A selection of those revised papers (the majority of those presented at the workshop) appears here in the published proceedings.

The papers themselves cover a wide span, from theoretical work on algebras and bisimilarity to experience with a real-world medical application. Unsurprisingly, given Glasgow's track record, there is a strong emphasis on compilation techniques and optimisations, and there are also several papers on concurrency and parallelism.

Each year many people make significant contributions to organising the workshop, and without their efforts we would not be able to hold the workshop at all. We would particularly like to thank John O'Donnell (General Chair), Sigbjørn Finne, Andy Gill, Cordy Hall, David King, Andrew Partridge, and Simon Peyton Jones for all their hard work this year. We would also like to thank all the reviewers who have devoted their time to help improve the papers which are published here.

This year's workshop was generously sponsored by Canon UK, Harlequin, ICL Ltd., and Software AG. We are very grateful for their continued support over the years that this workshop has been running.

Glasgow University   Kevin Hammond
December 1994   David N. Turner
                                                   Patrick Sansom

Contents

List of Contributors

Bunkenberg, A.   Department of Computing Science, Glasgow University, 17 Lilybank Gardens, Glasgow, G12 8QQ.

Charleston, D.   MRC Human Genetics Unit, Crewe Rd., Edinburgh, EH4 2XU.

Clenaghan, K.   Department of Computing Science, Glasgow University, 17 Lilybank Gardens, Glasgow, G12 8QQ.

Duponcheel, L.   Vakgroep Informatika, Rijks Universitaet Utrecht, Utrecht, The Netherlands.

Finne, S.O.   Department of Computing Science, Glasgow University, 17 Lilybank Gardens, Glasgow, G12 8QQ.

Flynn, S.   Department of Computing Science, Glasgow University, 17 Lilybank Gardens, Glasgow, G12 8QQ.

Foubister, S.P.   Institute for Computer Based Learning, Heriot-Watt University, Riccarton, Edinburgh, EH14 4AS.

Gordon, A.D.   University of Cambridge Computer Laboratory, New Museums Site, Cambridge, CB2 3QG.

Hall, C.V.   Department of Computing Science, Glasgow University, 17 Lilybank Gardens, Glasgow, G12 8QQ.

Hammond, K.   Department of Computing Science, Glasgow University, 17 Lilybank Gardens, Glasgow, G12 8QQ.

Johnsson, T.   Department of Computer Science, Chalmers University of Technology, S-412 96 Göteborg, Sweden.

King, D.J.   Department of Computing Science, Glasgow University, 17 Lilybank Gardens, Glasgow, G12 8QQ.

Loidl, H.W.   RISC-LINZ Research Institute for Symbolic Computation, Johannes Kepler University, A-4040, Linz, Austria.

Meijer, E.   Vakgroep Informatika, Rijks Universitaet Utrecht, Utrecht, The Netherlands.

Mintchev, S.   Department of Computer Science, Victoria University of Manchester, Manchester, M13 9PL.

O'Donnell, J.T.   Department of Computing Science, Glasgow University, 17 Lilybank Gardens, Glasgow, G12 8QQ.

Partridge, A. Department of Computer Science,
               University of Tasmania, Australia.

Peyton Jones, S.L. Department of Computing Science, Glasgow
               University, 17 Lilybank Gardens, Glasgow, G12 8QQ.

Poole, I.   MRC Human Genetics Unit,
               Crewe Rd., Edinburgh, EH4 2XU.

Rünger, G.   FB 14 Informatik, Universität des Saarlandes,
               PF 151150, 66041 Saarbrücken, Germany.

Runciman, C.   Department of Computer Science,
               University of York, Heslington, York, YO1 5DD.

Sansom, P.M.   Department of Computing Science, Glasgow
               University, 17 Lilybank Gardens, Glasgow, G12 8QQ.

Santos, A.   Department of Computing Science, Glasgow
               University, 17 Lilybank Gardens, Glasgow, G12 8QQ.

Trinder, P.W. Department of Computing Science, Glasgow
               University, 17 Lilybank Gardens, Glasgow, G12 8QQ.

Wallace, M.   Department of Computer Science,
               University of York, Heslington, York, YO1 5DD.

Expression Refinement: Deriving Bresenham's Algorithm

Alexander Bunkenburg* and Sharon Flynn*

Computing Science Department, University of Glasgow, Scotland

{bunkenba,sharon}@dcs.glasgow.ac.uk

http://www.dcs.glasgow.ac.uk/~{bunkenba,sharon}

Abstract

This paper illustrates a method of transforming an initial specification expression, which is not necessarily algorithmic, into an efficient functional implementation using a refinement calculus for expressions. In doing this, we benefit from the ease of manipulation that state-less expressions allow. However, implementations of functional algorithms are not as cheap as imperative implementations. We further show how an imperative program can be derived from a functional expression using algebraic transformations based on the state monad model. The example used to illustrate the method is Bresenham's line drawing algorithm.

1 Introduction

In this paper we show how a simple specification expression can be refined to an efficient functional program and then further transformed into an imperative program which is cheaper to implement than its functional equivalent.

For the purpose of derivation, expressions are easier to manipulate than statements. This can be seen, for example, in the Bird-Meertens formalism [Mee86, Bir86, Bac89], 'Squiggol', where obviously correct functional programs are transformed into more efficient programs using derivation steps which are equalities and which preserve correctness. Moreover, it is often the case that problems can be specified more naturally and elegantly using expressions rather than imperative commands. The refinement calculus for expressions used in this paper, based on the refinement calculus for imperative programming [Mor90, Mor89], is being developed to allow the refinement of possibly non-algorithmic specification expressions to executable expressions of a functional programming language, using a set of refinement laws.

Unfortunately, implementations of functional algorithms are not as cheap as imperative implementations, where cheap means fast and using predictably little memory. The use of the state monad [Wad92, PJW93, Lau93] permits the capture of imperative programming in a functional language, which guarantees a safe imperative evaluation. This paper illustrates a method of deriving a correct imperative program from a certain form of functional specification, making use of the state monad.

*Supported by a postgraduate research studentship from the Engineering and Physical Sciences Research Council.

This paper describes an approach to program derivation using the example of Bresenham's line drawing algorithm [SS87, Bre65].

In [Spr82] this example is used to demonstrate program derivation by program transformation, using a form of Pascal extended with real numbers (as opposed to floating point numbers). The transformation steps are justified informally.

In [Sne93] the derivation is also presented in an imperative guarded-command language. Its semantics is given by Hoare-triples.

Our aim in this paper is to derive the algorithm formally, using expression refinement. An imperative program is then derived algebraically using the state monad model for imperative programs.

1.1 Outline of the paper

Section 2 describes the expression language FSL used to specify the problem, and some laws of the refinement calculus which are used later in the derivation of Bresenham's line drawing algorithm. The higher-order functions *map* and *iterate* are defined and two theorems are introduced which allow expressions involving *map* to be transformed into expressions involving *iterate*. Section 3 introduces the line drawing problem, and an initial specification is given. This is then transformed into an efficient functional implementation of Bresenham's algorithm involving the *iterate* function, using laws from the refinement calculus for expressions. Section 4 describes how an 'imperative' style of programming can be achieved in a functional language using the state monad and, in particular, how a correct imperative program can be derived from a functional expression involving *iterate*. Section 5 applies this derivation style to the functional description of Bresenham's algorithm, resulting in an imperative implementation.

2 Expression Refinement

2.1 The Expression Language and Refinement Laws

In the first half of this paper we shall use the notation of FSL (Functional Specification Language), a language of expressions which is based on familiar mathematical notation. The language is intended to form part of a refinement calculus for functional programs, with a refinement relation between expressions and a set of refinement laws to allow the formal derivation of programs from specifications. We do not intend to give a full description of FSL here[1]. We introduce new notation alongside a small selection of laws of the refinement calculus which are used in the derivation in section 3. We simply state these laws, though they have been proved formally.

Although all steps in the derivation presented here are equalities, we give an intuitive notion of refinement. Ultimately, we have that a specification is refined by the program that implements it, written '$S \sqsubseteq P$'. On a smaller scale, and since the process of refinement is stepwise, we have that expression E is refined by expression F, '$E \sqsubseteq F$', if every possible evaluation of F is a possible

---

[1] The interested reader should apply to sharon@dcs.gla.ac.uk

evaluation of E. In general, F is more algorithmic, or its evaluation is more efficient, than E.

In the following, we will use the equivalence sign '$\equiv$' as a meta-equivalence, *ie.* a relation between expressions. We have the property that if $E \sqsubseteq F$ and $F \sqsubseteq E$, then $E \equiv F$.

Almost all constructs of FSL are monotonic with respect to refinement. For example, we have the following law for function application

Law 1 (mono replacement) *If $E \sqsubseteq F$ then $f\ E \sqsubseteq f\ F$*

In the example of Bresenham's line drawing algorithm, definedness is not a problem: all expressions are well-defined. In addition, almost all expressions are deterministic. However, the choice operator for non-determinacy is used, as we shall see, to build conditional expressions.

The *non-deterministic choice* between two expressions E and F of the same type, written $E \mathbin{[\!]} F$, can evaluate to the result of evaluating E or to the result of evaluating F and we don't know, or care, which. Choice enjoys the properties of idempotency, commutativity and associativity and it has an identity which is the empty expression, **empty**. In terms of refinement we have the basic law for reducing non-determinacy in a specification:

Law 2 (reduce non-det) $E \mathbin{[\!]} F \sqsubseteq E$

A *guarded expression* is of the form $B \to E$, where B, the guard, is an expression of type Bool and E is an expression of some type T. The meaning of a guarded expression can be given by the following equivalences:

$$
\begin{aligned}
\textbf{true} \to E &\equiv E \\
\textbf{false} \to E &\equiv \textbf{empty} \\
\perp_{Bool} \to E &\equiv \perp_T
\end{aligned}
$$

where $\perp_T$ is the undefined element of type T. We will insist that guards are deterministic.

Guard information can be used in the refinement of an expression:

Law 3 (guard info) *If B implies that $E \sqsubseteq F$, then $(B \to E) \sqsubseteq (B \to F)$.*

Guarded expressions can be combined using the choice operator resulting in *alternation expressions* of the form

$$\textbf{if}\ B_1 \to E_1 \mathbin{[\!]} \ldots \mathbin{[\!]} B_n \to E_n\ \textbf{fi}$$

When all guards are well-defined, this chooses an E_i for which the corresponding B_i evaluates to **true**. If none of the B_i evaluates to **true** then the expression is undefined.

For convenience we define a *conditional expression*

$$\textbf{if}\ B\ \textbf{then}\ E_1\ \textbf{else}\ E_2 \mathbin{\;\hat{=}\;} \textbf{if}\ B \to E_1 \mathbin{[\!]} \neg B \to E_2\ \textbf{fi}$$

A conditional expression is introduced in a refinement by the law:

Law 4 (if intro) *For B well-defined, $E \equiv \textbf{if}\ B\ \textbf{then}\ E\ \textbf{else}\ E$.*

and can be refined using:

Law 5 (if refinement) (**if** B **then** E_1 **else** E_2) $\sqsubseteq$ (**if** C **then** F_1 **else** F_2)
if $(B \wedge C)$ *implies* $E_1 \sqsubseteq F_1$, $(B \wedge \neg C)$ *implies* $E_1 \sqsubseteq F_2$, $(\neg B \wedge C)$ *implies* $E_2 \sqsubseteq F_1$
and $(\neg B \wedge \neg C)$ *implies* $E_2 \sqsubseteq F_2$.

Function application distributes through conditional expressions:

Law 6 (app thru if) *For B well-defined,*

$$f(\textbf{if } B \textbf{ then } E \textbf{ else } F) \equiv (\textbf{if } B \textbf{ then } f\,E \textbf{ else } f\,F)$$

The 'let' construct is used to introduce local names into specifications. We define

$$\textbf{let } x = E \textbf{ in } F \textbf{ ni} \;\;\hat{=}\;\; (\textbf{fun } x \in T : F)E$$

where T is the type of E. The 'let' expression cannot be used to introduce recursion or any new expressive power to the language. It is used to add clarity to specification.

Function application distributes through **let**:

Law 7 (app thru let) f (**let** $x = E$ **in** F **ni**) $\equiv$ **let** $x = E$ **in** $f\,F$ **ni**
if the variable x is not free in f.

2.2   Preliminaries

The types of the expression language FSL include lists, which can be considered as sequences. We assume that the higher order function *map* is familiar and note the following properties:

Law 8 (functor *map*)

$$map\,(f \circ g) \equiv map\,f \circ map\,g$$
$$map\,id \equiv id$$

where *id* is the identity of function composition '∘'.

Our aim is to transform programs of the shape *map* $f\,[i..k]$ into more iterative programs, where calculation of $f(j+1)$ can re-use some of the work that went into calculating $f\,j$, for integer j such that $i \leq j < k$. Suppose that calculating $f(j+1)$ from $f\,j$ is performed by applying a (simple) function, called *next* say, to $f\,j$, ie.

$$(\forall j \bullet i \leq j < k \Rightarrow f(j+1) = next(f\,j)$$

then we would only have to apply f once, namely to i, the first integer in the range $[i..k]$. After that, we could simply keep applying *next*. We stop if we have a result for each integer in the range $[i..k]$. We can express this idea formally using the functions *iterate* and *take*, which are found in the standard Haskell prelude [Haskell report], and can be defined in any lazy functional language. They are defined as:

Definition 1

$$take : N \to [a] \to [a]$$
$$take\ 0\ as \qquad \hat{=} \quad []$$
$$take\ n\ [] \qquad \hat{=} \quad []$$
$$take\ (n+1)\ (a:as) \quad \hat{=} \quad a:take\ n\ as$$

Definition 2

$$iterate : (a \to a) \to a \to [a]$$
$$iterate\ f\ a \quad \hat{=} \quad a:iterate\ f\ (fa)$$

The function *take* receives a natural number n, say, and a list, and returns a list of the first n elements of the list. If the list has fewer than n elements, the whole list is returned. The function *iterate* receives a function f with equal domain and range type, and a value a of that type. It returns the infinite list $[a, fa, f(fa), f(f(fa)), ...]$. Although this list is infinite, in a lazy language it is only calculated on a need-to-know basis. Typically one applies *take* n to the infinite result of *iterate* f a, and receives a well-defined finite result. In the expression *take* n (*iterate* f a) laziness allows us to separate the loop, represented by *iterate* f, from the halting condition of the loop, represented by *take* n.

Finally, $\#xs$ stands for the length of the list xs. The length of an integer range is, of course, trivial to calculate: $\#[x..y] = max(0, y - x + 1)$. We are now ready to formalise the transformation described above.

Lemma 1 (Map to iterate)

$$map\ f\ [x..y] \equiv (take\#[x..y] \circ iterate\ next)(f\ x)$$

if $x \le i < y$ implies $f(i+1) = next(f\ i)$

The proof is by induction on the length of the list.

To make this a little more general, we need another lemma:

Lemma 2 (Map and take commute)

$$map\ f \circ take\ n \equiv take\ n \circ map\ f$$

These two functions on lists are the same. The proof is by induction on their argument list.

Now we generalise lemma 'map to iterate' by precomposing both sides with *map use*, and using the previous lemma:

Theorem 1 (Map to iterate)

$$map(use \circ make)[x..y] \equiv (take\#[x..y] \circ map\ use \circ iterate\ next)(make\ x)$$

if $x \le i < y$ implies $make(i+1) = next(make\ i)$.

This theorem says that to map a function f over an integer range, all we have to do is find three functions, here called *make*, *use* and *next*, such that *use* composed with *make* is our original function f, and *next* captures a recurrence relation on *make*. Typically *make* will do what f does, and some extra work, whereas *use* is usually a simple function like a projection from a tuple. Naturally this theorem only reduces work if the function *next* is simpler than f.

3 Line drawing

Given two integer pairs, $(x1, y1)$ and $(x2, y2)$, the line drawing problem is to find the pixels which best approximate the line segment between them. The mathematical representation of the (infinite) line is defined by the equation

$$f\, x \,\hat{=}\, y1 + m * (x - x1) \tag{1}$$

where m is the slope of the line, and can be calculated from

$$m \,\hat{=}\, (y2 - y1)/(x2 - x1)$$

For convenience, we use the following abbreviations $d_y \hat{=} y2 - y1$ and $d_x \hat{=} x2 - x1$. However, the points of a mathematical line are given by pairs of real numbers, while pixels are pairs of integers. We would like to calculate those pixels which are nearest to the mathematical line.

Let us assume, for simplicity, that the value of the slope of the line is between 0 and 1, $0 \leq m \leq 1$. Other line segments can easily be obtained by symmetry. The problem is to find, for the list of integer x-values $[x1..x2]$, those y-values which best approximate the mathematical line given by (1). Bresenham's line drawing algorithm [Bre65] solves this problem using only integer arithmetic. We aim to derive this algorithm formally.

Since $0 \leq m \leq 1$, the line segment will be represented well if every $x \in Z$ between $x1$ and $x2$ is paired with some $y \in Z$ closest to $f\, x$. For convenience we define $n \hat{=} \#[x1..x2]$. Thus our initial specification is given by the expression

$$map\ (round \circ f)\ [x1..x2] \tag{2}$$

which computes the integer y-values for $[x1..x2]$. The function $round : \mathrm{I\!R} \to Z$, which is total on the Real numbers and is deterministic, is defined by

$$round\ x \quad \hat{=} \quad \textbf{if}\ x - \lfloor x \rfloor > 0.5\ \textbf{then}\ \lfloor x \rfloor + 1\ \textbf{else}\ \lfloor x \rfloor \tag{3}$$

The floor of $x \in \mathrm{I\!R}$, denoted $\lfloor x \rfloor$, satisfies the usual properties

$$\lfloor x \rfloor \leq x < \lfloor x \rfloor + 1 \tag{4}$$

There are two problems with our initial specification. The first is that it uses real arithmetic, but takes as input and output only integers. We would prefer to use integer arithmetic only. Secondly, the algorithm is inefficient, since f is being applied to each member of the list $[x1..x2]$. From the discussion in section 2.2, we can use the 'Map to iterate' theorem 1 to transform the expression to a more efficient implementation if we can find a recurrence relation for f. Fortunately, such a relation exists, from simple mathematics:

$$f(x + 1) \quad \equiv \quad f\, x + m \tag{5}$$

Since this holds, in particular for $x1 \leq x < x2$ we can apply the theorem with:

$$
\begin{aligned}
next &\quad \hat{=} \quad (\textbf{fun}\, x \in Z : x + m) \\
make &\quad \hat{=} \quad f \\
use &\quad \hat{=} \quad id
\end{aligned}
$$

So, we get:

$map(round \circ f)[x1..x2]$
$\equiv$ law 8 'functor map'
$map\ round\ (map\ f[x1..x2])$
$\equiv$ 'Map to iterate' theorem 1, $f\ x1 = y1$
$map\ round\ ($let $next = ($fun $x \in Z : x + m)$ in
$\qquad\qquad\qquad (take\ n \circ map\ id \circ iterate\ next)y1$ ni$)$
$\equiv$ law 7 'app thru let', law 8 'functor map'
let $next = ($fun $x \in Z : x + m)$ in
$\qquad\qquad (map\ round \circ take\ n \circ iterate\ next)y1$ ni
$\equiv$ 'Map and take commute' lemma
let $next = ($fun $x \in Z : x + m)$ in
$\qquad\qquad (take\ n \circ map\ round \circ iterate\ next)y1$ ni

which is an implementation of specification (2). Unfortunately this algorithm uses real arithmetic, calculating with real numbers which are not needed in the final solution. We aim to derive Bresenham's line drawing algorithm [Bre65], which uses integer arithmetic only.

If we define $r : Z \to Z$ as follows:

$$r\ i \mathrel{\hat{=}} round(f\ i) \tag{6}$$

then our initial specification (2) looks like

$$map\ r\ [x1..x2] \tag{7}$$

We can use the 'Map to iterate' theorem 1 if we can find a recurrence relation for r, preferably using integer arithmetic only. Consider:

$r(x + 1)$
$\equiv$ definition of r (6)
$(round \circ f)(x + 1)$
$\equiv$ definition of $round$ (3)
if $f(x + 1) - \lfloor f(x + 1) \rfloor > 0.5$ then $\lfloor f(x + 1) \rfloor + 1$ else $\lfloor f(x + 1) \rfloor$
$\sqsubseteq$ law 5 'if-refinement', proof requirements below
if $f(x + 1) - r\ x > 0.5$ then $r\ x + 1$ else $r\ x$
$\equiv$ for a suitable e, see below
if $e\ x < 0$ then $r\ x + 1$ else $r\ x$

Law 5 may be applied in the above derivation only if the four proof requirements are satisfied. These are of the following form:

$f(x + 1) - \lfloor f(x + 1) \rfloor > 0.5 \wedge f(x + 1) - r\ x > 0.5$
$\Rightarrow$
$\lfloor f(x + 1) \rfloor + 1 \equiv r\ x + 1$

There are four such proof requirements, one for each of the four alternatives. These can be proved using the properties of floor (4) and arithmetic. This step of the derivation, involving law 5, was initially motivated by knowledge of Bresenham's algorithm. Basically, since the slope of the line is between 0 and 1, the next y-value, $r(x + 1)$, must be either the same as the previous value, $r\ x$, or its successor, $r\ x + 1$. This step can be justified by noting the movement towards a recurrence relation for r.

So, we have a recurrence relation for r, but it depends on the value of $e\ x$. We find a suitable expression for $e\ x$:

$e \; x < 0$

$\equiv \quad$ from above derivation

$f(x+1) - r \; x > 0.5$

$\equiv \quad$ definition (1) of f

$y1 + m * (x + 1 - x1) - r \; x > 0.5$

$\equiv \quad m = d_y/d_x$, multiply by d_x

$d_x * y1 + d_y * (x + 1 - x1) - d_x * r \; x > 0.5 * d_x$

$\equiv \quad$ arithmetic

$2 * d_x * r \; x + d_x - 2 * d_x * y1 - 2 * d_y * (x + 1 - x1) < 0$

So, we define

$$e \; x \; \hat{=} \; 2 * d_x * r \; x + d_x - 2 * d_x * y1 - 2 * d_y * (x + 1 - x1) \qquad (8)$$

The function e, as for f, also satisfies a recurrence relation:

$$e(x+1) \quad = \quad e \; x + 2 * d_x * (r(x+1) - r \; x) - 2 * d_y \qquad (9)$$

Note that this expression for e uses integer arithmetic only. We can now eliminate r from the recurrence relation for e. We have already seen that the difference between $r(x+1)$ and $r \; x$ is always either 0 or 1. This information is used in the following:

$e(x+1)$

$\equiv \quad$ recurrence definition (9)

$e \; x + 2 * d_x * (r(x+1) - r \; x) - 2 * d_y$

$\equiv \quad$ law 4 'if intro'

if $e \; x < 0$ **then** $e \; x + 2 * d_x * (r(x+1) - r \; x) - 2 * d_y$
$\qquad\qquad$ **else** $e \; x + 2 * d_x * (r(x+1) - r \; x) - 2 * d_y$

$\sqsubseteq \quad$ law 3 'guard info', and previous observations

if $e \; x < 0$ **then** $e \; x + 2 * d_x - 2 * d_y$ **else** $e \; x - 2 * d_y$

and we know from definition (8) that $e \; x1 = d_x - 2 * d_y$.

Now we have that the calculation of the next y-value, $r(x+1)$, depends on the previous y-value, $r \; x$, and the difference value $e \; x$. Therefore, at each iteration, we would want to calculate $r(x+1)$ and the next difference value $e(x+1)$. Let us define a function $k : Z \to Z \times Z$ forming the pair:

$$k \; x \; \hat{=} \; (r \; x, e \; x) \qquad (10)$$

and combine the two recurrence relations into one:

$(r(x+1), e(x+1))$

$\equiv \quad$ recurrence relations

(**if** $e \; x < 0$ **then** $r \; x + 1$ **else** $r \; x$,

if $e \; x < 0$ **then** $e \; x + 2 * d_x - 2 * d_y$ **else** $e \; x - 2 * d_y$)

$\equiv \quad$ 'product formation thru if', variation of law 6

if $e \; x < 0$ **then** $(r \; x + 1, e \; x + 2 * d_x - 2 * d_y)$ **else** $(r \; x, e \; x - 2 * d_y)$

Now we can use the 'Map to iterate' theorem 1 with:

$next \quad \hat{=} \quad$ (**fun** $r, e \in Z :$ **if** $e < 0 \quad$ **then** $(r+1, e + 2 * d_x - 2 * d_y)$
$\qquad\qquad\qquad\qquad\qquad\qquad\qquad$ **else** $(r, e - 2 * d_y))$

$make \quad \hat{=} \quad$ (**fun** $x \in Z : (r \; x, e \; x))$

$use \quad \hat{=} \quad$ **fst**

which gives us, from our first specification (2):

$$map(round \circ f)[x1..x2]$$
$$\equiv \quad \text{definitions of } r \text{ (6) and } k \text{ (10)}$$
$$map(\mathbf{fst} \circ k)[x1..x2]$$
$$\equiv \quad \text{'Map to iterate' theorem 1}$$
$$\mathbf{let} \; next = (\mathbf{fun} \, r, e \in Z : \mathbf{if} \; e < 0 \; \mathbf{then} \; (r+1, e+2*d_x - 2*d_y)$$
$$\mathbf{else} \; (r, e - 2*d_y)) \; \mathbf{in}$$
$$(take \; n \circ map \; \mathbf{fst} \circ iterate \; next)(y1, d_x - 2*d_y) \; \mathbf{ni}$$

This implementation of specification (2) is efficient and uses only integer arithmetic. It corresponds to Bresenham's line drawing algorithm [Bre65].

4 Imperative Expressions

4.1 Language and Laws

Our approach to imperative programs is a simplified form of that used in [PJW93, Lau93, LPJ94], based on the state monad [Wad92]. We simplify because we are interested in program derivation, and not so much in semantics.

We regard the *state* as a mapping from references to values. A *reference* to a value is the address of, or a pointer to, a value. We can change the value to which a reference points, *ie.* change what the state maps the reference to, and still the reference itself stays unchanged. If a reference has type *Ref A*, then the value it references has type A.

The state may be changed by special expressions called *state transformers*. Apart from delivering a value, like all expressions, these special expressions also take a state and deliver a state, so their type is $State \to A \times State$, which will be abbreviated by $ST\,A$, where A is the type of the value. We say a state transformer of type $ST\,A$ *returns* a value of type A. We are not concerned with the precise meaning of $State$, but rather rely on intuition. In a program, the state cannot be bound to a formal variable. In the definitions below, we allow the state to be bound, but only to the unusual identifier σ to emphasize that this is for definitions only, and illegal in a program.

These four primitives make state transformers that create a *new* reference, *put* a value into the place to which the reference points, *get* the value to which a reference points, and *return* a value without using the state:

Definition 3

$$
\begin{aligned}
\mathbf{new} \quad &: \quad A \to ST(\text{Ref } A) \\
\mathbf{new}\, a \quad &\hat{=} \quad \mathbf{fun} \; \sigma \in State : \mathbf{let} \; v \in \text{Ref } A \setminus \mathbf{dom}\, \sigma \; \mathbf{in} \; (v, \sigma[v \mapsto a]) \; \mathbf{ni} \\
\mathbf{put} \quad &: \quad \text{Ref } A \to A \to ST\, 1 \\
\mathbf{put}\, v\, a \quad &\hat{=} \quad \mathbf{fun} \; \sigma \in State : ((), \sigma[v \mapsto a]) \\
\mathbf{get} \quad &: \quad \text{Ref } A \to ST\, A \\
\mathbf{get}\, v \quad &\hat{=} \quad \mathbf{fun} \; \sigma \in State : (\sigma\, v, a) \\
\mathbf{return} \quad &: \quad A \to ST\, A \\
\mathbf{return}\, a \quad &\hat{=} \quad \mathbf{fun} \; \sigma \in State : (a, \sigma)
\end{aligned}
$$

The new reference returned by **new** a must be of type *Ref A*, where $a : A$. Any reference of that type will do, as long as it is not already used in the state

σ, *ie.* it is not in the domain of σ. (The backslash in the definition denotes set subtraction.) Therefore the definition of **new** a contains nondeterminacy. In the definitions of **new** and **put** , $\sigma[v \mapsto a]$ is the state that maps reference v to a and otherwise coincides with σ. The state transformer **put** $v\ a$ changes the state, but has nothing interesting to return. So we'll just let it return the empty tuple () of type 1.

Two state transformers may be composed in sequence by the (infix) primitive semicolon, often called *bind*:

Definition 4

$$(;) \quad : \quad ST\ A \to (A \to ST\ B) \to ST\ B$$
$$m; k \quad \hat{=} \quad \textbf{fun } \sigma.\textbf{let } (a, \sigma') = m\ \sigma \textbf{ in } k\ a\ \sigma' \textbf{ ni}.$$

A word about strictness: We assume that **new** , **get** , and **put** are strict in the state, and in the references, but lazy in the values stored. The combinators **return** and semicolon are lazy in all arguments.

The triple $(ST, \textbf{return} , (;))$ is the state monad of [Wad92], and thus we may immediately conclude the *monad laws*:

Law 9 (monad laws)

$$\textbf{return } E; F \quad \equiv \quad F\ E$$
$$E; \textbf{return} \quad \equiv \quad E$$
$$(E; \textbf{fun } x.F); G \quad \equiv \quad E; \textbf{fun } x.(F; G),$$

where x may be free in F, but not in G.

Notice that the scope of a **fun** extends 'as far as possible' and so the brackets on the right side of the third formula are superfluous. The monad laws form the start of a collection of algebraic laws about state transformers.

As an example of composing state transformers, the definition of the combinator *modify*, which applies a function to the contents of a reference is:

$$modify \quad : \quad (A \to A) \to Ref\,A \to ST\ 1$$
$$modify\ f\ v \quad \hat{=} \quad \textbf{get } v; \textbf{fun } a.\textbf{put } v\ (f\ a).$$

The programmer may only use state implicitly via combinations of semicolon and the primitive state transformers. This ensures that the state cannot be duplicated, and thus it may be implemented directly using the memory of the machine. The state monad is nothing more than a convenient abstract data type.

A convenient combinator of state transformers is *for*. It takes a natural number n, and a state transformer k, and delivers a state transformer that is the composition of n copies of k, and returns the list of their results. The definition of *for* is:

Definition 5 (*for*)

$$for \quad : \quad I\!N \to ST\ A \to ST\ [A]$$
$$for\ 0\ k \quad \hat{=} \quad \textbf{return } []$$
$$for\ (n+1)\ k \quad \hat{=} \quad k; \textbf{fun } x.for\ n\ k; \textbf{fun } xs.\textbf{return } (x : xs).$$

A state transformer may be made into a state-less expression by applying **run** to it:

Definition 6 (run)

$$\mathbf{run} \quad : \quad ST\,A \to A$$
$$\mathbf{run}\,k \;\; \hat{=} \;\; \mathbf{let}\,\sigma \in State\,\mathbf{in}\,\mathbf{fst}(k\,\sigma)\,\mathbf{ni}.$$

The state σ is arbitrary. The expression **run** k applies the state transformer k to an arbitrary state, thereby obtaining a value-state pair. The state is discarded, and the value is the outcome of **run** k. We say that **run** *encapsulates* the state.

It is immediate that **run** composed with **return** is the identity function:

Law 10 (run-intro) $E \equiv \mathbf{run}(\mathbf{return}\,E)$.

This is the first step in making a functional program imperative.

The second step is to introduce a reference:

Law 11 (new -intro) **run** $E \equiv \mathbf{run}(\mathbf{new}\,F; \mathbf{fun}\,v.E)$, *where v is not free in state transformer E.*

A function applied to the result of a **run** can be pushed into the **run**:

Law 12 (function into run) $f(\mathbf{run}\,E) \equiv \mathbf{run}(E; \mathbf{fun}\,x.\mathbf{return}\,(f\,x))$.

This law is used to move algorithmic work from the 'functional' to the 'imperative' part of the program.

Another simple law that moves algorithmic work into the imperative part is:

Law 13 (let /return) $\mathbf{let}\,x = E\,\mathbf{in}\,F\,\mathbf{ni} \equiv \mathbf{return}\,E; \mathbf{fun}\,x.F$, *where F is a state transformer.*

Two further simple laws are:

Law 14 (new generates put) $\mathbf{new}\,E; \mathbf{fun}\,v.\mathbf{put}\,v\,F; \mathbf{return}\,v \equiv \mathbf{new}\,F$

and

Law 15 (new generates get) $\mathbf{new}\,E; \mathbf{fun}\,v.\mathbf{get}\,v \equiv \mathbf{new}\,E; \mathbf{fun}\,v.\mathbf{return}\,E$.

The first says that initialising a new reference to E and then overwriting it by F is the same as initialising it to F immediately. The second says that putting a value into a new reference and retrieving it is the same as just putting it into a new reference and returning it.

Many laws are concerned with changing the order of two state transformers that don't interfere with each other, for example:

Law 16 (get , put commute)

$$\mathbf{get}\,v; \mathbf{fun}\,x.\mathbf{put}\,w\,E; \mathbf{fun}\_.\mathbf{return}\,x \equiv \mathbf{put}\,w\,E; \mathbf{fun}\_.\mathbf{get}\,v,$$

where x must not be free in E, and v and w are distinct.

So far all proofs are straightforward from the definitions. The laws mentioned could be used directly to derive an imperative program from a functional one. An imperative program part is introduced via '**run**-intro', work is moved into the imperative part via 'function into **run**' and '**let** /**return** ', and from the trivial state transformer '**return** ' to real use of the state via '**new** generates **get** ' and '**new** generates **put** ', after new references have been introduced via '**new** intro'.

We don't use this strategy directly, but rather derive an imperative implementation for the higher order function *iterate*, and then use that as a standard translation from functional programs built with *iterate* to imperative ones.

4.2 Imperative implementation of *iterate*

Recall the definition of iterate:

Definition 7 (iterate)

$$iterate \quad : \quad (A \to A) \to A \to [A]$$
$$iterate \; f \; a \quad \hat{=} \quad a : iterate \; f \; (f \; a).$$

Typically *take n* for some natural n is used to extract a finite prefix of the infinite result of *iterate f a*.

Lemma 3 (imperative *iterate*) *The imperative implementation of (take n ∘ iterate f) a is:*

run(new a; **fun** v.
$\quad$ **for** n
$\quad\quad$ **get** v; **fun** a.
$\quad\quad$ **put** v $(f \; a)$; **fun** _.
$\quad\quad$ **return** a
$\quad$).

The proof is by induction on n. In each step, we will refer to the laws used, except for the monad laws, which will be used often, without mention.

Base case $n = 0$

$\quad$ $(take \; 0 \circ iterate \; f) \; a$
$\equiv$ $\quad\quad$ def. *take*
$\quad$ []
$\equiv$ $\quad\quad\quad$ **run**-intro, **new** -intro
$\quad$ **run(new** a; **fun** v.**return** [])
$\equiv$ $\quad\quad\quad$ def. *for*
$\quad$ **run(new** a; **fun** v.*for* 0 (**get** v; **fun** a.**put** v $(f \; a)$; **fun** _.**return** a))

The inductive hypothesis is $\exists n \in \mathbb{N}.\forall a$.:

$$(take \; n \circ iterate \; f) \; a$$

$\quad \equiv$

$$\textbf{run(new } a; \textbf{fun } v.for \; n \; (\textbf{get } v; \textbf{fun } a.\textbf{put } v \; (f \; a); \textbf{fun } \_.\textbf{return } a)).$$

Step case $n + 1$

$(take\ (n + 1) \circ iterate\ f)\ a$
$\equiv$ def. *iterate*
$take\ (n + 1)\ (a : iterate\ f\ (f\ a))$
$\equiv$ def. *take*
$a : ((take\ n \circ iterate\ f)\ (f\ a))$
$\equiv$ inductive hypothesis, abbreviating
$a : \textbf{run}(\textbf{new}\ (f\ a); \textbf{fun}\ v.for\ n\ (...))$
$\equiv$ function into **run**
$\textbf{run}(\textbf{new}\ (f\ a); \textbf{fun}\ v.for\ n\ (...); \textbf{fun}\ xs.\textbf{return}\ (a : xs))$
$\equiv$ **new** generates **put**
$\textbf{run}(\textbf{new}\ a; \textbf{fun}\ v.\textbf{put}\ v\ (f\ a); \textbf{fun}\ \_.for\ n\ (...); \textbf{fun}\ xs.\textbf{return}\ (a : xs))$
$\equiv$ let -intro, let /return
$\textbf{run}(\textbf{new}\ a; \textbf{fun}\ v.\textbf{return}\ a; \textbf{fun}\ x.\textbf{put}\ v\ (f\ x); \textbf{fun}\ \_.$
$for\ n\ (...); \textbf{fun}\ xs.\textbf{return}\ (x : xs))$
$\equiv$ **new** generates **get** , expanding abbreviation
$\textbf{run}(\textbf{new}\ a; \textbf{fun}\ v.\textbf{get}\ v; \textbf{fun}\ x.\textbf{put}\ v\ (f\ x); \textbf{fun}\ \_.$
$for\ n\ (\textbf{get}\ v; \textbf{fun}\ a.\textbf{put}\ v\ (f\ a); \textbf{fun}\ \_.\textbf{return}\ a); \textbf{fun}\ xs.\textbf{return}\ (x : xs))$
$\equiv$ monad laws, def. *for*
$\textbf{run}(\textbf{new}\ a; \textbf{fun}\ v.for\ (n + 1)\ (\textbf{get}\ v; \textbf{fun}\ a.\textbf{put}\ v\ (f\ a); \textbf{fun}\ \_.\textbf{return}\ a))$

Lemma proven by induction.

We require another lemma:

Lemma 4 (*map/for*)

$for\ n\ K; \textbf{fun}\ as.\textbf{return}\ (map\ f\ as)\quad \equiv\quad for\ n\ (K; \textbf{fun}\ a.\textbf{return}\ (f\ a))$

. The proof is by induction on n.

Combining the lemmata 'imperative *iterate*' and '*map/for*', we derive an imperative translation for an expression of the form delivered by theorem '*map to iterate*' 1, namely $(take\ n \circ map\ use \circ iterate\ next)\ init$, for some $n, use, next$, and *init*:

Theorem 2
     $(take\ n \circ map\ use \circ iterate\ next)\ init$
$\equiv$

     $\textbf{run}(\textbf{new}\ init; \textbf{fun}\ v.$
        $for\ n$
           $\textbf{get}\ v; \textbf{fun}\ x.$
           $\textbf{put}\ v\ (next\ x); \textbf{fun}\ \_.$
           $\textbf{return}\ x$
        $).$

We will use this theorem to translate the functional program into an equivalent imperative one.

14

5 Line drawing

The functional program that calculates the vertical coordinates of the line from $(x1, y1)$ to $(x2, y2)$ is:

$$(take \ \#[x1..x2] \circ map \ \mathbf{fst} \circ iterate \ next) \ (y1, d_x - 2 * d_y),$$

where $next$ is defined

$$next \quad : \quad Z \times Z \to Z \times Z$$
$$next \ (r, e) \quad \hat{=} \quad \mathbf{if} \ e < 0 \ \mathbf{then} \ (r + 1, e + 2 * d_x - 2 * d_y) \ \mathbf{else} \ (r, e - 2 * d_y).$$

We use the theorem to derive:

$\mathbf{run}(\mathbf{new} \ (y1, d_x - 2 * d_y); \mathbf{fun} \, v.$
    $for \ \#[x1..x2]$
        $\mathbf{get} \ v; \mathbf{fun} \ (r, e).$
        $(\mathbf{if} \ e < 0 \ \mathbf{then}$
            $\mathbf{put} \ v(r + 1, e + 2 * d_x - 2 * d_y)$
        $\mathbf{else}$
            $\mathbf{put} \ v(r, e - 2 * d_y)$
        $); \mathbf{fun} \, \_.$
        $\mathbf{return} \ r$
    $).$

We have moved the function **put** v into the conditional expression for clarity, using law 6 ('function into **if**').

Further improvements would be to replace the reference v to a pair of values by two references to single values. This improvement is a data refinement, and won't be discussed here, however the result is given below.

$\mathbf{run}(\mathbf{new} \ y1; \mathbf{fun} \, vr.\mathbf{new} \ (d_x - 2 * d_y); \mathbf{fun} \, ve.$
    $for \ \#[x1..x2]$
        $\mathbf{get} \ vr; \mathbf{fun} \, r.\mathbf{get} \ ve; \mathbf{fun} \, e.$
        $(\mathbf{if} \ e < 0 \ \mathbf{then}$
            $\mathbf{put} \ vr(r + 1); \mathbf{fun} \, \_.\mathbf{put} \ ve(e + 2 * d_x - 2 * d_y)$
        $\mathbf{else}$
            $\mathbf{put} \ ve(e - 2 * d_y)$
        $); \mathbf{fun} \, \_.$
        $\mathbf{return} \ r$
    $).$

The state in this program is encapsulated by **run**, and the whole program delivers a list of integers, being approximate vertical coordinates for $[x1..x2]$. But we would probably want to display the line on a screen rather than just calculate a list of points. The state of the screen cannot be encapsulated. Therefore we rewrite the program so that the whole program itself is one state transformer returning nothing interesting (the empty tuple), but affecting the state of the screen. Let's assume the state transformer $out : Z \times Z \to S \ 1$ displays a pixel on the screen. We also add a reference to keep track of the horizontal coordinate x.

new $x1;$ **fun** $vx.$**new** $y1;$ **fun** $vr.$**new** $(d_x - 2 * d_y);$ **fun** $ve.$
for $\#[x1..x2]$
    get $vx;$ **fun** $x.$**put** $vx\ (x + 1);$ **fun** _.
    get $vr;$ **fun** $r.$**get** $ve;$ **fun** $e.$
    (**if** $e < 0$ **then**
        put $vr(r + 1);$ **fun** _.**put** $ve(e + 2 * d_x - 2 * d_y)$
    else
        put $ve(e - 2 * d_y)$
    ); **fun** _.
    $out(x, r);$ **fun** _.
return ()

This is the final program, an imperative version of Bresenham's line drawing algorithm that displays the line on a screen.

6 Conclusions

In this paper we have shown, using the example of Bresenham's line drawing algorithm, how a non-algorithmic mathematical specification expression can be transformed into an efficient functional program, using expression manipulation, and then further to a correct imperative program, using algebraic methods and the state monad.

The specification language of expressions, FSL, and the associated refinement calculus for expressions are used for the first part of this process. Much of the transformation is guided by knowledge of the algorithm itself, but each step is justified by refinement laws or theorems. In deriving the functional program from the specification, we benefit from the ease of manipulation that state-less expressions allow.

Because manipulating imperative programs is more cumbersome than manipulating state-less expressions, we translate the functional program built from *iterate* into an imperative program by appealing to a theorem. Other combinators suitable for this method are *until*, the *scan*-family [Lau93, O'D93], and the *fold*-family.

But is the final program really an imperative program? After all, the definitions and transformations use laziness, whereas traditional imperative languages are strict, thereby guaranteeing the desired predictably small usage of memory. Before we execute the derived program in a strict manner, we had better make sure that it doesn't give non-termination. Fortunately for the current program there is no problem, but in general we haven't addressed that question.

The state monad seems a reasonably practical model for imperative programs in a language of expressions. It provides a good integration of functional and imperative features in the language, allowing the programmer to use state where necessary without compromising the full expressiveness of a functional language.

16

Acknowledgments

Thanks to Joe Morris, Muffy Thomas, and Campbell Fraser for reading drafts (on weekends) and suggesting improvements. Thanks to Satnam Singh for suggesting Bresenham's *circle* drawing algorithm - which brought us on to Bresenham's *line* drawing algorithm.

References

[Bac89] Roland Backhouse. An exploration of the Bird-Meertens Formalism. *International Summerschool on Constructive Algorithmics, Ameland 1989*, September 1989.

[Bir86] Richard S. Bird. An introduction to the theory of lists. In M. Broy, editor, *Logic of Programming and Calculi of Discrete Design*, volume F36 of *NATO ASI Series*. Springer Verlag, 1986.

[Bre65] J. E. Bresenham. An algorithm for computer control of a digital plotter. *IBM Syst. J.*, 4(1):25 – 30, 1965.

[Lau93] John Launchbury. Lazy imperative programming. *ACM SigPlan Workshop on State in Prog. Langs.*, June 1993.

[LPJ94] John Launchbury and Simon Peyton Jones. Lazy functional state threads. In *Programming Languages Design and Implementation*, 1994.

[Mee86] Lambert Meertens. Algorithmics - towards programming as a mathematical activity. *Mathematics and Computer Science*, 1, 1986. CWI Monographs (J. W. de Bakker, M. Hazewinkel, J. K. Lenstra, eds.) North Holland, Puhl. Co.

[Mor89] J.M. Morris. Programs from Specifications. In Edsger W. Dijkstra, editor, *Formal Development of Programs and Proofs*, University of Texas at Austin Year of Programming Series, chapter 9, pages 81–115. Addison-Wesley, 1989.

[Mor90] C. Morgan. *Programming from Specifications*. Prentice Hall, U.K., 1990.

[O'D93] John T. O'Donnell. Bidirectional fold and scan. In John T. O'Donnell and Kevin Hammond, editors, *Functional Programming, Glasgow 1993*, Workshops in Computing Science, pages 193 – 200. Springer Verlag, July 1993. Proceedings of the 1993 Glasgow Workshop on Functional Programming, Ayr, Scotland, 5 - 7 July 1993.

[PJW93] Simon L. Peyton Jones and Philip Wadler. Imperative functional programming. *Principles of Programming Languages*, January 1993.

[Sne93] Jan L. A. Snepscheut. *What computing is all about*. Texts and Monographs in Computer Science. Springer Verlag, 1993.

[Spr82]   Robert F. Sproull. Using program transformations to derive line-drawing algorithms. *ACM Transactions on Graphics*, 1(4):259 – 273, October 1982.

[SS87]   Rod Salmon and Mel Slater. *Computer Graphics, Systems and Concepts*. Addison Wesley, 1987.

[Wad92]   Philip Wadler. The essence of functional programming. January 1992. Presented at 19th Annual Symposium on Principles of Programming languages, Albuquerque, New Mexico.

Dynamic Algebra for Calculating Algorithms *

Kieran Clenaghan

Department of Computing Science, The University of Glasgow

Glasgow, Scotland

Abstract

One concern in making the calculation of algorithms a formal mathematical activity is succinctness of notation and proof. Here we consider two recent contributions to this concern that we believe to be valuable. The contributions show how matrix algebra and relation algebra, respectively, enhance succinctness in the formal calculation of algorithms for path problems (amongst others) in graphs. The contributions are independent, and use different notations and proof strategies. However, the differences can be reconciled. Here we show how to make this reconciliation. The reconciliation is valuable for two reasons. First, it provides a straightforward synthesis of overlapping aspects of the two independent pieces of work, revealing the common ground behind superficially different appearances. Second, it prompts consideration of a unifying abstract framework as the basis for further algorithm calculations. An appropriate unifying framework is shown to be *dynamic algebra*.

1   Introduction

The recent independent papers [Möl93] and [BEG94] illustrate succinct derivations of algorithms for path problems by algebraic calculation. [Möl93] uses a relation algebra based on formal language concepts, and [BEG94] uses matrix algebra. The seeming distinctiveness of the characterisations is superficial. The goal of this paper is to show, in a precise sense, how the two approaches relate. This is achieved by showing that Möller's calculations can be translated and carried out in the matrix algebra setting of [BEG94]. To do this, it is natural to ask what abstract algebraic framework unites the relation and matrix algebras which are used. It turns out to be the *dynamic algebra* of [Pra90].

We start by setting out the matrix algebra of [BEG94] as a dynamic algebra. Next, we choose one algorithm from [Möl93], the graph reachability algorithm, and we express its calculation using the matrix dynamic algebra. Then we compare this to the relation-algebra calculation of [Möl93], showing that Möller's calculations can be reinterpreted in the matrix dynamic algebra setting[1]. A nice by-product is that one of Möller's proofs can be shortened by adapting the calculations of [BEG94]. The paper concludes with a few remarks on the potential for further work based on applications of dynamic algebra. An extended version of this paper is in preparation as a CWI technical report.

---

*This work was carried out while on leave during 1994 at CWI, Amsterdam. The author gratefully achknowledges the support of the CWI.

[1]We should stress that we choose just one simple algorithm for comparison, and that both papers contain other algorithms.

1.1 Background

The body of this paper is brief and sharply focussed. Here we comment on some background to provide additional motivation for the less well acquainted with algebraic algorithm calculation and the algebraic structures special to path problems in graphs.

Formal algorithm calculation concerns the specification of an object that we wish to compute, and the manipulation of this specification by mathematical laws into a form that is recognisably an algorithm. [Möl93] and [BEG94] choose some graph problems that admit succinct specification, and enjoy good support from established algebra. Much of their calculation is concerned with equational reasoning. This is in contrast to the more usual reasoning about graph algorithms, e.g. [Kin90], and should be more amenable to machine assistance. [Möl93] sticks primarily to recursive equations (i.e. functional programs), whilst [BEG94] uses imperative loop contructs with equational invariants. [Möl93] is concerned with showing how relation algebra yields succinct formal developments, and is widely applicable. It does not dwell on the passage from recursive equations to imperative programs. [BEG94] is concerned with showing how algebraic terms and laws can guide the derivation steps. Like [Möl93] it is concerned with compactness of expressions and derivations, but unlike [Möl93], it tackles deeper stages of algorithm refinement, producing imperative program code.

The overlap of [Möl93] and [BEG94] is their treatment of path problems in graphs. The simplest overlap is the reachability problem that we use as a comparative vehicle in the paper. In general, path problems are a nice choice, because of the generality of certain algorithms that exist [Car79], [GM84], and because the underlying pure algebra (semiring theory) has been enjoying recent active research [Gol92]. Much of the established literature on algebra applied to path problems has been in establishing generic algorithms, and cataloguing their instantiation to a diversity of problems. A generic algorithm typically solves a fixed-point equation based on a kind of semiring, and its instantiation is obtained by nominating a particular semiring. [Car79] and [GM84] contain extensive examples of this.

The work of [Möl93] and [BEG94] is distinctive in that it advances the formalisation of proofs of algorithms for path problems. A key feature is the algebraicisation of (finite) quantification by exploiting products with (finite) sets (or selector vectors), as illustrated in $S \cdot R$, where S is a set (or vector) and R is a relation (or matrix). This has a history in automata theory, as recently highlighted in that subject by Kozen [Koz94], and its abstract setting is the theory of semimodules [KS86]. It also has a history in relation algebra where sets may be disguised as special relations [SS93].

Both [Möl93] and [BEG94] are clear about their use of Kleene algebra (a special kind of semiring), but neither identifies an abstract semimodule algebra which governs their calculations. [Möl93] adds sets as a special kind of relation, but then has to qualify some laws to account for the two kinds of relation that may be involved. [BEG94] just uses the specific matrix algebra that one gets over an underlying Kleene algebra, and points out the special rôle of so-called *selector* vectors for representing sets. It is easy to see that dynamic algebra [Pra90] is a unifying semimodule algebra. We believe that this observation should, at least, be useful in encouraging a convergence of notation.

2 Matrix algebra as dynamic algebra

The basic calculational methods of [Möl93] and [BEG94] can be conveyed by considering the calculation of a simple algorithm for the graph reachability problem. We review this problem now in order to motivate our choice of matrix algebra. Throughout, we assume that graphs are finite (i.e. the node set is finite).

Definition 1 (Graph Reachability)   Let $G = (V, E)$ be a graph where $E \subseteq V \times V$ is the edge relation between nodes. The graph reachability problem is to find, for a given set of nodes, $S \subseteq V$, all nodes reachable from any node in S by reflexivity and transitivity of E. In other words, it is the problem of finding the image of S through the reflexive transitive closure of E. Treating S as the constant relation $\mathbb{1} \times S$ the problem is succinctly captured as the computation of $S ; E^*$, where E^* is the reflexive transitive closure of E defined as usual by:

$$(2) \quad E^* \triangleq \bigcup_{n \in \mathbb{N}} E^n \ where \ E^0 \triangleq I \ and \ E^{n+1} \triangleq E^n ; E$$

Similarly, we can represent relations by Boolean matrices, and sets by Boolean vectors, in which case relational composition becomes matrix product, and taking the image of a set through a relation is vector-by-matrix product. The graph reachability problem can be rewritten as $S \cdot E^*$, where $\cdot$ is matrix product, and E^* is the sum of all positive powers of E. We shall adopt the matrix viewpoint because it easily generalises to the non-Boolean case which is important for many problems on edge-weighted graphs.

□

Definition 3 (Paths)   Let $G = (V, E)$ be a graph. A path from node i_1 to node j is a sequence of nodes $i_1 i_2 ... i_n j$ such that there is an edge in E from node i_k to i_{k+1} for $1 \leq k \leq n-1$, and there is an edge from i_n to j. The nodes in a path preceding the last node are called the *antecedent* nodes (of the path). An A-path, for $A \subseteq V$, is a path whose set of antecedent nodes is contained in A. The A-path relation between nodes can be denoted by $(I_A \cdot E)^*$ where I_A is a partial identity matrix, introduced in the next section. We shall say that a node, j, is A-*reachable* from a node i if there is an A-path, from i to j. Similarly, an m-path is a path with m antecedent nodes.

□

2.1 A matrix algebra

In the interests of general applicability it is useful to develop matrix algorithms in terms of general (or abstract) matrix algebra. It is well-known that matrix algebra can be presented abstractly using module theory, or more generally, semimodule theory. Recall that a module, $\langle M, S, \bullet \rangle$, combines a group M and a ring S with a multiplication, $\bullet : M \times S \to M$ that satisfies natural distributivity, unit, and zero laws. Roughly, a semimodule is a module without subtraction and division, and as such M is required only to be a monoid, and S a semiring. The semimodule treatment is particularly useful in computing science, see for example [KS86].

Vector-matrix algebra is based on the semimodule $\langle S^V , S^{V \times V} , \cdot \rangle$ where V is an index set, S is a semiring, and multiplication is matrix multiplication. In interesting special cases, S is a semiring with a unary * operator that extends uniformally to matrices. For example, we may stipulate that S is countably complete [Heb90] and define * to be the sum of all positive powers (countable completeness means that addition extends to the summation of countable subsets, and associativity, commutativity, and distributivity generalise accordingly). Alternatively, we may stipulate that S is a Kleene algebra [Koz94] which is an idempotent semiring (addition is idempotent) with an axiomatisation of * that generalises countable completeness (in the case of idempotent semirings). There are interesting non-idempotent examples (e.g. counting paths), but idempotency is often satisfied, e.g. Boolean and min-max algebras [GM84].

A semimodule $\langle M , S , \bullet \rangle$ in which M is a Boolean algebra, and S is a Kleene algebra has been called a dynamic algebra in [Pra90]. If S is a Kleene algebra with $\{0 , 1\} \subseteq S$, then it is straightforward to construct a dynamic algebra $\langle \{0 , 1\}^V , S^{V \times V} , \cdot \rangle$. This is particularly useful because $\{0 , 1\}^V \cong \mathbb{P}V$ and for a set $A \in \{0 , 1\}^V$, and an S-valued relation or matrix $E \in S^{V \times V}$, $A \cdot E$ denotes the image of A through E. This is exploited in [BEG94] for the calculation of Dijkstra's single-source shortest paths algorithm.

For our purposes, we use just two special dynamic algebras, these are: $\langle \mathbb{B}^V , \mathbb{B}^{V \times V} , \cdot \rangle$ and $\langle I(\mathbb{B}^V) , \mathbb{B}^{V \times V} , \cdot \rangle$, where $I(\mathbb{B}^V)$ is the set of partial identity matrices (i.e. $I_A \in I(\mathbb{B}^V)$ is a matrix which is everywhere 0 except for a 1 in each position (a , a) for $a \in A$). We shall use the standard set notation for elements of $\mathbb{B}^V$ and matrix notation for elements of $I(\mathbb{B}^V)$. We illustrate this in completing the picture of I as a morphism $\mathbb{B}^V \to I(\mathbb{B}^V)$:

(4) $\quad I_{A \cup B} = I_A + I_B$

(5) $\quad I_{A \cap B} = I_A \cdot I_B$

(6) $\quad I_\emptyset = 0 \text{ and } I_V = 1$

It is important to recognise the following relational interpretations. Let $A , B \in \mathbb{B}^V$ and $R \in \mathbb{B}^{V \times V}$:

- $I_A \cdot R$ is the domain-restriction of R to A.

- $R \cdot I_B$ is the range-restriction of R to B.

- $A \cdot R$ is the image of A through R.

Here are some elementary properties that we shall use:

(7) $\quad 1 = I_V = I_{\overline{A} \cup A} = I_{\overline{A}} + I_A \quad$ (identity decomposition)

(8) $\quad M = I_{\overline{A}} \cdot M + I_A \cdot M \quad$ (matrix decomposition)

(9) $\quad B \cdot I_A = B \cap A \quad$ (partial image)

2.2   The * operator

For our example of graph reachability, we want the star operator on relations to be the transitive, reflexive closure, i.e. the sum of all positive powers (where multiplication is relational composition). The main work in deriving an algorithm from the specification $S \cdot E^*$ is the decomposition of the work performed by * so that we arrive at a recursive formulation in which * no longer applies (or becomes trivial).

We need not spell out the axiomatisation of Kleene algebra, nor the formal definition of countably complete semirings, but instead we just list the following properties of * which we use in our calculations (and which happen to be common to both kinds of algebra):

(10) $a^* = 1 + a \cdot a^* = 1 + a^* \cdot a$ (*-fixpoint)

(11) $(a+b)^* = (a^* \cdot b)^* \cdot a^*$ (*-decomposition)

(12) $a \cdot (b \cdot a)^* = (a \cdot b)^* \cdot a$ (*-leapfrog)

Variants of the *-decomposition law are easily obtained by using *-leapfrog and commutativity of addition.

A useful further law derived from those above is the following which enables one to "unfold" occurrences of summands out of a starred sum. Let $c = a+b$.

(13) $c^* = (1 + c^* \cdot b) \cdot a^*$ (*-unfold)

The proof is a straightforward algebraic calculation. We give it here to illustrate our proof style which is borrowed from [BEG94]. Note, in particular, that an assumption used in a proof step is highlighted by a bullet.

$$
\begin{aligned}
&c^* \\
=\quad &\{ \quad \bullet \quad c = a+b \ \} \\
&(a+b)^* \\
=\quad &\{ \quad \text{*-decomposition} \ \} \\
&(a^* \cdot b)^* \cdot a^* \\
=\quad &\{ \quad \text{*-fixpoint} \ \} \\
&(1 + (a^* \cdot b)^* \cdot a^* \cdot b) \cdot a^* \\
=\quad &\{ \quad \text{*-(de)composition} \ \} \\
&(1 + (a+b)^* \cdot b) \cdot a^* \\
=\quad &\{ \quad \bullet \quad c = a+b \ \} \\
&(1 + c^* \cdot b) \cdot a^*
\end{aligned}
$$

The following elementary propositions, specific to certain dynamic algebras, will also be used.

Proposition 14 (Guarded *)   Let S be a semiring and consider the dynamic algebra $\langle I(\{0\,,1\}^V)\,,S^{V\times V}\,,\cdot\rangle$. If $A\cap B\,=\,\emptyset$ then $A\cdot(I_B\cdot M)^*\,=\,A$, where $A\,,B\in\{0\,,1\}^V$, $M{\in}S^{V\times V}$.

Proof

$$A\cdot(I_B\cdot M)^*$$
$$=\qquad\{\qquad \text{*-recurrence, distributivity}\quad\}$$
$$A+A\cdot I_B\cdot M\cdot(I_B\cdot M)^*$$
$$=\qquad\{\qquad A\cdot I_B\,=\,A\cap B\,=\,\emptyset\quad\}$$
$$A$$

$\square$

Proposition 15 (*-Reflexivity)   Let $A\,,B\in\mathbb{B}^V$ and $E{\in}\mathbb{B}^{V\times V}$ in the dynamic algebra $\langle I(\mathbb{B}^V)\,,\mathbb{B}^{V\times V}\,,\cdot\rangle$. If $A\subseteq B$ then $B\cdot E^*\cdot I_A\,=\,A$.

Proof

$$B\cdot E^*\cdot I_A$$
$$=\qquad\{\qquad\text{*-fixpoint and distributivity}\quad\}$$
$$B\cdot 1\cdot I_A\cup B\cdot E\cdot E^*\cdot I_A$$
$$=\qquad\{\qquad A\subseteq B\quad\}$$
$$A\cup B\cdot E\cdot E^*\cdot I_A$$
$$=\qquad\{\qquad X\cdot I_A\subseteq A\quad\}$$
$$A$$

$\square$

We have borrowed a lot from the notation and calculations in [BEG94]. There are some minor differences, the main one being our use of I_A for the $\underline{A}$ of [BEG94] . We choose I_A because it is standard (I being a natural transformation), and because it strikes a good balance between the quality of the identity relation and its restriction to A. Our silent transfer between sets and their characteristic vectors is not present in [BEG94] but is consistent with the pursuit of conciseness expounded in that paper; so too is our use of context to distinguish vector-valued and matrix-valued variables.

3 Reachability: a matrix approach

There is an easy solution to the reachability problem. To compute $S \cdot E^*$ we take the nodes in S (since they are reachable by reflexivity), and we (recursively) solve the problem for the immediate successors of S in E. This is given by the algebra in just two steps. Define $r_B = B \cdot E^*$, (so that r_B represents the problem at some intermediate point, the whole problem being distinguished as r_S). We calculate:

$$r_B$$

$$= \qquad \{ \qquad \text{definition of } r \quad \}$$

$$B \cdot E^*$$

$$= \qquad \{ \qquad \text{*-fixpoint} \quad \}$$

$$B \cdot (1 + E \cdot E^*)$$

$$= \qquad \{ \qquad \text{algebra} \quad \}$$

$$B \cup (B \cdot E) \cdot E^*$$

$$= \qquad \{ \qquad \text{definition of } r \quad \}$$

$$B \cup r_{B \cdot E}$$

This leads to the following recursive definition that will solve the reachability problem for acyclic graphs.

$$r_\emptyset = \emptyset \text{ and } r_B = B \cup r_{B \cdot E}$$

Termination is guaranteed because finiteness and acyclicity ensure that, for some n, there are no m-paths (i.e. $E^m = \emptyset$), for all $m > n$.

To obtain a definition that terminates for cyclic graphs, a little thought tells us that the recursive case can be restricted to a smaller graph, E restricted by removing edges leading from B. Edges are used only for the nodes to which they lead, and once we have these the edges can be deleted. The deletion of edges leading from B is obtained by restricting the domain of E to nodes outside B. This is $I_{\overline{B}} \cdot E$. Thus we arrive at the following definition.

$$R(\emptyset, E) = \emptyset \text{ and } R(B, E) = B \cup R(B \cdot E, I_{\overline{B}} \cdot E)$$

We need to show that this is correct and terminates. Correctness obliges us to show that R is consistent with the assumption $R(B, E) = B \cdot E^*$. The base case is easy, and we are left to show the recursive case, i.e.:

$$B \cdot E^* = B \cup R(B \cdot E, I_{\overline{B}} \cdot E) = B \cup (B \cdot E) \cdot (I_{\overline{B}} \cdot E)^*$$

This equation succinctly captures (a variant of) the breadth-first strategy for traversing graphs, so we shall give it the status of a lemma.

Lemma 16 (Breadth-first decomposition)

$$B \cdot E^* = B \cup (B \cdot E) \cdot (I_{\overline{B}} \cdot E)^*$$

Proof

$$B \cdot E^*$$

= { matrix decomposition (8) }

$$B \cdot (I_{\overline{B}} \cdot E + I_B \cdot E)^*$$

= { *-unfold (13) }

$$B \cdot (1 + E^* \cdot I_B \cdot E) \cdot (I_{\overline{B}} \cdot E)^*$$

= { algebra }

$$(B \cup B \cdot E^* \cdot I_B \cdot E) \cdot (I_{\overline{B}} \cdot E)^*$$

= { $B \cdot E^* \cdot I_B = B$ (Prop. 15) }

$$(B \cup B \cdot E) \cdot (I_{\overline{B}} \cdot E)^*$$

= { algebra }

$$B \cdot (I_{\overline{B}} \cdot E)^* \cup B \cdot E \cdot (I_{\overline{B}} \cdot E)^*$$

= { $B \cdot (I_{\overline{B}} \cdot E)^* = B$ (Prop. 14) }

$$B \cup B \cdot E \cdot (I_{\overline{B}} \cdot E)^*$$

□

Now we must justify termination. Clearly, $I_{\overline{B}} \cdot E \subseteq E$, and if $I_{\overline{B}} \cdot E = E$ then $B \cdot E = \emptyset$. So, either E is strictly reduced or we reach the termination case. Since E is finite there can be no infinite sequence of strict reductions, and $E = \emptyset$ leads directly to the terminating case.

A variation on the above solution is easily derived. Instead of successively removing edges leading from visited nodes, we can accummulate the visited nodes, as say, C. Then, $I_{\overline{C}} \cdot E$ (E domain-restricted to nodes outside C) is equal to E with all the edges leading from visited nodes deleted. Now, instead of taking the successors of B in (the reduced) E, we take the successors of B in $I_{\overline{C}} \cdot E$. This is captured by the following equations.

$$R'(\emptyset , C) = \emptyset \text{ and } R'(B , C) = B \cup R'(B \cdot I_{\overline{C}} \cdot E , B \cup C)$$

The intuition behind R' is that it computes the nodes which are $\overline{C}$-reachable from B. This is formalised as $B \cdot (I_{\overline{C}} \cdot E)^*$ (cf. Defn. 3). The whole reachability problem is the case $C = \emptyset : R'(S , \emptyset) = S \cdot (I_{\overline{\emptyset}} \cdot E)^* = S \cdot E^*$. We now verify that R' is consistent with $R'(B , C) = B \cdot (I_{\overline{C}} \cdot E)^*$. The base case, $B = \emptyset$, is easy. For the recursive case, we calculate:

$$B \cdot (I_{\overline{C}} \cdot E)^*$$

= { breadth-first decomposition: lemma 16 }

$$B \cup (B \cdot I_{\overline{C}} \cdot E) \cdot (I_{\overline{B}} \cdot I_{\overline{C}} \cdot E)^*$$

= { $I_{\overline{B}} \cdot I_{\overline{C}} = I_{\overline{B} \cap \overline{C}} = I_{\overline{B \cup C}}$ }

$$B \cup (B \cdot I_{\overline{C}} \cdot E) \cdot (I_{\overline{B \cup C}} \cdot E)^*$$

$$= \qquad \{ \qquad \bullet \quad R'(B\,,C) \ = \ B \cdot (I_{\overline{C}} \cdot E)^* \quad \}$$
$$B \cup R'(B \cdot I_{\overline{C}} \cdot E\,,\,B \cup C)$$

Here is the termination argument. The set of visited nodes is non-decreasing: $B \cup C \supseteq C$, and if $B \cup C = C$ then $B \subseteq C$ and $B \cdot I_{\overline{C}} = B \cap \overline{C} = \emptyset$, so the terminating case is reached. Termination is guaranteed since the set of visited nodes is bounded by V , and $I_{\overline{V}} = 0$.

Notice that $B \cdot I_{\overline{C}} \cdot E = (B \cap \overline{C}) \cdot E = (B-C) \cdot E$ (which is the term used in [Möl93]).

4 Reachability: a relational approach

The definition of R' which we derived is essentially the same as the definition derived in [Möl93]. The derivation is different for three main reasons. First, Möller uses an algebra of relations based on sets of words rather than sets of pairs. This enables ordinary sets, i.e. sets of singleton words, and ordinary relations, i.e. sets of words of length 2, to be treated as the same sort, and handled uniformly under composition (but with qualified associativity). Second, Möller employs a path algebra which is closely related to his algebra of relations. Third, Möller proves lemma 16 (his corollary 5) by direct appeal to a closure induction principle. We now review Möller's approach and examine the significance of these differences.

Definition 17 (Words and languages)   Given an alphabet, V , a *word* over V is a sequence of symbols drawn from V . The empty word is denoted ε. The set of all words over V is denoted V^*. A symbol $a \in V$ also denotes a singleton word $a \in V^*$. A language over V is a subset of V^*. A word $w \in V^*$ also denotes a singleton language $w \in PV^*$. The set of non-empty words over V , $V^* - \varepsilon$, is denoted V^+. We note that Möller brackets * and + to make a distinction with the * and + as applied to relations. Here, we get away with overloading these symbols.

□

Definition 18 (Language, Relation, and Path algebras)   The following algebras are exploited in [Möl93].

$$LAN \triangleq \langle PV^*\,,\ \cup\ ,\ \bullet\ ,\ \emptyset\,,\ \varepsilon \rangle$$

$$REL \triangleq \langle P(V \bullet V)\,,\ \cup\ ,\ ;\ ,\ \emptyset\,,\ I_V \rangle$$

$$PAT \triangleq \langle PV^+\,,\ \cup\ ,\ \bowtie\ ,\ \emptyset\,,\ V \rangle$$

Each of these algebras is obtained by lifting the following set-valued (remember, elements also stand for singleton sets) operations on words pointwise to operations on languages.

$$
\begin{aligned}
u \bullet v &= uv \\
ua \ ; \ bv &= \begin{cases} uv & \text{if } a = b \\ \emptyset & \text{otherwise} \end{cases} \\
ua \bowtie bv &= \begin{cases} uav & \text{if } a = b \\ \emptyset & \text{otherwise} \end{cases}
\end{aligned}
$$

It is easy to check that each of LAN , REL , and PAT is a Kleene algebra when * is added as the sum of all positive powers.

□

Möller points out that for $E \subseteq V \bullet V$, and $S \subseteq V$, $S \ ; E$ and $E \ ; S$ denote the image and inverse image, respectively, of S through E . So the reachability problem is captured by $S \ ; E^*$. But, of course, this set-by-relation composition, ;, is just our (Boolean) vector-by-matrix product, $\cdot$. More precisely, $\langle PV , \mathrm{P}(V \bullet V) , ; \rangle$ is isomorphic to $\langle \mathbb{B}^V , \mathbb{B}^{V \times V} , \cdot \rangle$. Moreover, all of Möller's calculations use dynamic algebra specialised to relations, and they translate faithfully into our notation. His few uses of $\bowtie$ are easily eliminated by his own law (8), which states:

$$
S \bowtie R = I_S \ ; R \ and \ R \bowtie S = R \ ; I_S
$$

With this translation we can see that lemma 16 is Möller's corollary 5, and that the proof given here offers a shorter alternative.

5 Concluding remarks

In this paper we have highlighted the connection between two recent independent approaches to the formal calculation of graph algorithms, represented by [Möl93] and [BEG94]. That there is a connection is fairly obvious at an informal level, but since both approaches are concerned with formality, it is natural to ask for a formal explanation of the connection. We hope to have provided this explanation. In so doing we have appealed to the abstract setting of dynamic algebra. Dynamic algebra is more general than is needed to bring the two approaches together, but it encourages a convergence of terminology, and ties the work more deeply into established literature.

One might remark that path problems are priveledged among the huge volume of graph-oriented problems since they enjoy good algebraic support. The algebraic calculation of algorithms for most other graph problems is still very much an open area of research. We propose, as might be expected, that this offers a fine test bed for further adventures with dynamic algebra. In particular, one wonders whether a useful body of re-usable lemmas and theorems might be established that progressively extends the applicability of dynamic algebra in graph algorithmics. Furthermore, the algebraic proofs are at a level of sufficient detail that they could be checked by machine, and this surely provides some motivation for using dynamic algebra as a test case for mechanised proof systems.

Acknowledgements I am grateful to Lambert Meertens for providing valuable feedback on an early (extended) version of this paper. Akihiko Takano supplied crucial encouragement. Many thanks also to Andy Gordon and David King for their comments.

This document was prepared using the MathSpad editing system developed at The University of Eindhoven, The Netherlands.

References

[BEG94] Roland C. Backhouse, J.P.H.W. van den Eijnde, and A.J.M. van Gasteren. Calculating path algorithms. *Science of Computer Programming*, 1994.

[Car79] Bernard Carré. *Graphs and Networks*. Clarendon Press, Oxford, 1979.

[GM84] Michel Gondran and Michel Minoux. *Graphs and Algorithms*. Wiley-Interscience, New York, 1984.

[Gol92] Jonathon S. Golan. *The Theory of Semirings with Applications in Mathematics and Computer Science*. Longman Scientific and Technical, 1992.

[Heb90] Udo Hebisch. The Kleene theorem in countably complete semirings. *Bayreuther Mathematische Schriften*, 31:55–66, 1990.

[Kin90] Jeffrey H. Kingston. *Algorithms and Data Structures: Design, Correctness, and Analysis*. Addison-Wesley, 1990.

[Koz94] Dexter Kozen. A completeness theorem for Kleene algebras and the algebra of regular events. *Information and Computation*, 110(2), 1994.

[KS86] Werner Kuich and Arto Salomaa. *Semirings, Automata, Languages*. EATCS Monographs on Theoretical Computer Science. Springer Verlag, 1986.

[Möl93] Bernhard Möller. Derivation of graph and pointer algorithms. Technical report, Institut fur Mathematik, Augsburg, 1993.

[Pra90] V.R. Pratt. Dynamic algebras as a well-behaved fragment of relation algebras. In D.L. Pigozzi C.H. Bergman, R.D. Maddux, editor, *Algebraic Logic and Universal Algebra in Computer Science (Iowa 1988)*, LNCS 425, 1990. Springer-Verlag.

[SS93] Gunther Schmidt and Thomas Strölein. *Relations and graphs*. Springer-Verlag, 1993.

On the expressive power of Constructor Classes

Luc Duponcheel

Vakgroep Informatika, Rijks Universiteit Utrecht
Utrecht, The Netherlands luc@cs.ruu.nl

Erik Meijer

Vakgroep Informatika, Rijks Universiteit Utrecht
Utrecht, The Netherlands erik@cs.ruu.nl

December 9, 1994

Abstract

The aim of this paper is to explore the expressive power of constructor classes, a generalisation of type classes. We present a categorical `prelude` for `Gofer`, a programming environment which supports constructor classes. The `prelude` contains much more code than the one which is dealt with in the paper. We do not go into all the details of the `prelude`. We explain *why* we wrote it and *how* certain language constructs have made it possible to do so.

1 Introduction

Every programming language comes with its standard libraries. If a new release of a programming language introduces new constructs, then it is challenging to make these libraries more useful by making use of the expressive power of those constructs. The introduction of *type classes* in `Haskell` (see [3]) has had an influence on the design of its standard `prelude`. The `prelude` contains, among others, type classes `Text`, `Eq` and `Num` which make it possible to overload standard function and operator notation for a variety of type class instances. `Gofer` is the first programming language which supports *constructor classes* (see [4]). Constructor classes are a generalisation of type classes. Thus, as stated above, it is challenging to make use of the expressive power offered by them. This paper tries to give an idea about which kind of things are possible.

In the paper we show how to write an categorical `prelude` for `Gofer` from scratch. It turns out that a considerable amount of useful concepts from category theory can be encoded in `Gofer` by making use of its constructor classes. Such an encoding makes it possible to use of a uniform notation for a variety of similar programming problems. Well-known general purpose functions like `map` and `foldr` (plus a whole range of functions which are defined in terms of them) can be used in different (but similar) situations. The categorical encoding also encourages a modular approach to solving programming problems.

Non-trivial pieces of code can be obtained by combining and/or transforming other, conceptually simpler, pieces of code.

The main part of the paper simply consists of a thourough study of (part of) the categorical `prelude`. The style of the paper is sometimes a little bit unusual: some (sub)sections start with a piece of code. Do not try to understand the code at once: the aim of the (sub)section is precisely to explain that piece of code. The `prelude` contains much more code than the one which is explained in the paper. The number of classes (and the corresponding categorical concepts) which occur in the `prelude` may, at first reading, be a little bit overwhelming. Therefore we decided *not* to go into the details of all of them. In the introduction we explain *why* these classes are introduced, i. e. which constructs they are generalisations of. In the main part of the paper we show *how* to introduce the classes. We concentrate on the language features of `Gofer` which make it possible to encode categorical concepts in a convenient way. For more details we refer to a forthcoming report [2]. In that report we show (among other things) how to write a generic categorical lambda-calculus interpreter. It is based upon the following standard result: any reflexive object of any cartesian closed category can be used as a denotational model for lambda-calculus. Specific reflexive objects can be chosen to obtain call-by-value, call-by-name resp. call-by-need semantics. The forthcoming report does not explain all the details either ; explaining all the details of the `prelude` would probably lead to a book rather than a report or a paper. In fact, many researchers have suggested us that we write a book, similar to the one of Burstall and Rydeheard (see [1]), about the contents and usage of the categorical `prelude`.

1.1   Functions

Functional programming is based upon lambda-calculus. This means that, if we start `Gofer` with a minimal non-empty `prelude` e. g.

```
> bottom = bottom
```

then we can:

- *define* functions (lambda-abstraction), and

- *use* functions (lambda-application).

One of the main ideas of the paper is to generalise functions by defining a `Category` class which introduces morphisms[1]. Functional programs use functions as first class citizens. We model this fact in our categorical framework by

---

[1]The possibility to encode a `Category` class in `Gofer` was first recognised by Mark P. Jones. A first definition of such a class appeared in the file `fancycat` of the `demo` directory the `Gofer` `2.28` release.

defining a `FunCategory` class which introduces internal functions. A considerable amount of useful code dealing with functions can be generalised to the framework of morphisms and internal functions.

1.2 Data Definitions

Data types can be introduced in `Gofer` by making use of `data` definitions. Lists can, for example, be defined as follows:

```
> data List a = Nil | Cons a (List a)
```

Even a simple example like this one makes use of three important data structuring facilities:

- **Products** : the `Cons` data constructor constructs compound data out of constituents `a` and `List a`.

- **Sums** : the `|` construct splits up the `List a` data type in two parts: a `List a` expression is either `Nil` or an expression of the form `Cons a as`, where `as` is a `List a` expression.

- **Recursion** : `List a` occurs both at the left and at the right hand side of its definition. This means that `List a` is defined recursively (in terms of itself).

One of the main ideas of the paper is to generalise data definitions by defining a class `ProdCategory` which introduces internal products, a class `SumCategory` which introduces internal sums and a class `RecCategory` which introduces internal recursion.

By the way, in [6] yet another useful data structuring facility is introduced: the subtyping mechanism. Subypes can e. g. be defined as follows:

```
> class SubTypeOf sup sub where
>    inj :: sub -> sup
>    prj :: sup -> sub
```

Any type is a subtype of itself.

```
> data Only x = Only x

> instance SubTypeOf (Only x) x where
>    inj x = Only x
>    prj (Only x) = x
```

We have introduced a dummy data constructor `Only` to avoid overlapping instances. By making use of the `|` construct, it is possible to define an important range of `SubType` instances as follows:

```
> data AddTo x y = Old x | New y

> msg = "don't know where to go to"

> instance SubTypeOf sup sub
>          => SubTypeOf (AddTo sup any) sub where
>   inj x = Old (inj x)
>   prj (Old x) = prj x
>   prj (New _) = error msg
```

In other words: adding any data to sup preserves the SubTypeOf relation with sub. Given types One, Two, Three, ..., one can now construct towers of types:

```
type First  = Only  One
type Second = AddTo First  Two
type Third  = AddTo Second Three
...
```

Subtyping is one of the facilities which are used in [6] for writing complex programs such as interpreters in a modular way. The facilities (subtyping, monad transformers, ...) which are used are precisely the ones which we have tried to implement in our categorical prelude.

1.3   Restricted Type Synonyms

As explained in 1.2, one of the main ideas of the paper is to replace data definitions by appropriate class definitions. But how can we define data types if we are not allowed to use any data definitions at all? Gofer offers an alternative to data definitions: restricted type synonyms. Type synonyms are (as the name suggests) aliases for other type expressions[2]. Restricted type synonyms are aliases only for a particular list of functions. Outside the scope of those functions they behave as (untagged) data definitions. Restricted type synonyms can be used to define abstract data types (adts). The particular list of functions contains the functions which are allowed to access the internal repesentation of the adt. Here is a (simplified) typical example:

```
> class EuclidSpace v where
>   (<*>) :: v -> v -> Float

> angle :: EuclidSpace v => v -> v -> Float
> angle v w = acos (v<*>w / sqrt (v<*>v + w<*>w))

> type Vector = [Float] in inprod
```

---

[2]Constructor synonyms would be a better name since they can also be used to define aliases for constructor expressions.

```
> inprod :: Vector -> Vector -> Float
> xs 'inprod' ys = sum (zipWith (*) xs ys)

> instance EuclidSpace Vector where
>    (<*>) = inprod
```

The inprod function is allowed to access the internal representation of the
Vector adt. One can now define Vector as an instance of the EuclidSpace class
and, as a consequence, use the angle function for computing the angle between
two vectors. Adts can, of course, also be introduced using data definitions:

```
> data Vector = Vec [Float]

> instance EuclidSpace Vector where
>    Vec xs <*> Vec ys = sum (zipWith (*) xs ys)
```

However, there is an important difference. Suppose that the source code of an
adt is included in a library package as a *read-only* file. If the adt code is written
using a restricted type synonym, then it is not possible to access the internals
of the adt since the list of access-functions cannot be extended in another file.
If the adt code is written using a data definition, then one can, in any other
file, make use of the data constructor to open the adt. Here is the adt-opening
code for vectors:

```
> openVec :: Vector -> [Float]
> openVec (Vec xs) = xs
```

As can be seen from the Vector example, there is a (minor) programming in-
convenience related to the usage of restricted type synonyms when defining class
instances: one has to introduce auxiliary access-functions. When working with
data definitions, class instances can be defined without introducing auxiliary
functions. One final remark about restictd type synonyms: it is often needed
to associate an access-function with more than one adt (this corresponds to the
friend construct in C^{++}) . Here is an example:

```
> class Apply m v where
>    (#) :: m -> v -> v

> type Matrix = [[Float]] in app

> app :: Matrix -> Vector -> Vector
> xss 'app' ys = [ xs <*> ys | xs <- xss ]

> instance Apply Matrix Vector where
>    (#) = app
```

The types of this code are correct only if `app` is added to the list of access-functions of `Vector`.

1.4 Constructor Classes

Constructor classes are a generalisation of type classes. Constructor classes were introduced in `Gofer` starting from release `2.28` (see [4]). We have already presented a type class `EuclidSpace` in subsection 1.3. In this subsection we present a typical example of a constructor class.

```
> class Stack s where
>    empty :: s a
>    push :: a -> s a -> s a
>    pop :: s a -> s a
>    top :: s a -> a
```

In contrast with the example of subsection 1.3, where we defined a class of types, the example of this subsection defines a class of constructors. A (unary) constructor `s` is a `Stack` instance if the usual operations are defined on *any* type `s a`. Lists can be defined as `Stack` instances as follows:

```
> instance Stack List where
>    empty = Nil
>    push = Cons
>    pop (Cons _ xs) = xs
>    top (Cons x _) = x
```

Constructor classes are, in our opinion, one of the most important tools for structuring functional programs. One of the main ideas of the `prelude` is to make use of constructor classes to encode data type structuring facilities.

1.5 Squiggol Syntax

Squiggol syntax is introduced as a notation for supporting the Bird-Meertens programming style. We have chosen the syntax of the class members of the categorical `prelude` in such a way that it is possible to make use of Squiggol-like syntax in `Gofer`. To give an idea about the kind of notation that will enter the picture in the main body of the paper, we now show how one can quickly introduce Squiggol notation in `Gofer` (in the main body of the paper we will do this in a more structured way).

```
> type Mor = (->)
> type Prod = (,)
```

```
> infixl 8 <*>, >*<
> infixr 7 <+>, >+<

> exl (x,y) = x
> exr (x,y) = y

> f <*> g = \x -> (f x,g x)
> f >*< g = \(x,y) -> (f x,g y)

> data Sum x y = L x | R y

> inl x = L x
> inr y = R y

> f <+> g = \s -> case s of L x -> f x ; R y -> g y
> f >+< g = \s -> case s of L x -> L (f x) ; R y -> R (g y)

> data RecR f x = InR (f x (RecR f x))

> isoR x = InR x
> osiR (InR x) = x

> class FunctorR f where
>    mapR :: Mor u v -> Mor (f x u) (f x v)

> cataR :: FunctorR f => Mor (f a x) x -> Mor (RecR f a) x
> cataR phi = phi . mapR (cataR phi) . osiR
```

The Sum and RecR data definitions are generic. The idea is to define *all* other data definitions in terms of them (and, of course, also Mor and Prod). The function cataR can be used to define a whole range of recursive functions on recursive types RecR f a. This function generalises the foldr function on lists. Using recursion in a structured way (i. e. via cata) makes it possible to write reusable programs.

1.5.1 Binary Trees

In this subsection we show how trees can be defined using the Bird-Meertens formalism (lists are defined in a similar way). In subsection 2.11.2 we will show how to define trees in our categorical framework without using any data definitions at all.

```
> type T a x = Sum a (Prod x x) in leafT, nodeT,
>                                   mapRT, mapLT, revT
```

```
> type Tree = RecR T

> leafT :: Mor a (T a x)
> leafT = inl

> nodeT :: Mor (Prod x x) (T a x)
> nodeT = inr

> leaf :: Mor a (Tree a)
> leaf = isoR . leafT

> node :: Mor (Prod (Tree a) (Tree a)) (Tree a)
> node = isoR . nodeT
```

Notice that we have started with a binary (non-recursive) constructor T and ended up with a unary (recursive) constructor Tree. The type Tree a is essentially the same as the one which is defined using the data definition:

```
> data Tree a = Leaf a | Node (Tree a) (Tree a)
```

Up to now we have only given the code for functions leaf and node which can be used to construct trees. Next we turn T into a FunctorR instance. This makes it possible to define recursive functions on trees using cataR.

```
> mapRT :: Mor x y -> Mor (T a x) (T a y)
> mapRT g = id >+< g >*< g

> instance FunctorR T where
>    mapR = mapRT
```

Here comes a simple example of a recursive function on trees: the function revTree which reverses a tree.

```
> revT :: Mor (T a (Tree a)) (Tree a)
> revT = leaf <+> node . (exr <*> exl)

> revTree :: Mor (Tree a) (Tree a)
> revTree = cataR revT
```

The function revT swaps the top level subtrees (if any). The full power of revTree comes from cataR which, when going down into the subtrees, recursively keeps on swapping the top level subtrees. It is also possible to make Tree an instance of useful classes. A typical example is the Functor class which makes it possible to overload the map notation when iterating through a tree:

```
> mapLT :: Mor a b -> Mor (T a x) (T b x)
> mapLT g = g >+< id >*< id

> instance Functor Tree where
>    map g = cataR (isoR . mapLT g)
```

2 The prelude

Now we are ready for the main part of the paper: the actual code of the
prelude. The code contains a lot of restriced type synonyms. The access-
functions for those restricted type synonms will (just as in the tree example
of subsection 1.5.1) be introduced gradually. Therefore we will often write ...
after their list of access-functions to indicate that there may be other access-
functions following.

2.1 Identity and Composition

Together with abstraction and application, composition and identity are perhaps the most important concepts one can make use of when writing functional
programs. Composition and identity are so essential for functional programming that it is worth the pain to generalise them from functions to morphisms.
For example: in many programmig problems substitutions and/or transformations play a central role. A substitution and/or transformation from x to y is
not really a function from x to y[3]. However, substitutions and/or transformations *do* have an identity and *can* be composed. The experimental prelude
establishes a programming environment in which one can, to a large extent,
treat substitutions and/or transformations as if they are functions. This does
not only simplifies our perception of programming problems which make use
of them, it also offers us notational convenience for programming with them.
The situation is very similar to the one we encounter when writing technical
documents. If we write a document which deals with substitutions and/or
transformations, then we deliberately overload the words identity and composition (notice that we actually did so a few lines ago!). This is just a convenient
abuse of notation: the context in which we use the words makes it evident
which kind of identity and composition we are talking about.

2.2 Categories

```
> class Category mor where
```

---

[3]Substitutions are functions from x to Term x, where Term is a unary constructor which
constructs terms of type Term x having variables of type x. Transformations are functions
from x to Maybe(y,x). An input of type x *may* be transformed to an output of type y (and
the rest of the input, of type x).

```
>    id :: mor x x
>    (.) :: mor y z -> mor x y -> mor x z
```

In this subsection we deal with the basic properties of the function space constructor (->) and generalise these properties to `Category` instances. A binary constructor `mor` (standing for morphism) is a `Category` instance if an appropriate identity morphism `id` and composition meta-operator (.) on morphisms are defined. Notice that the objects of a category necessarily correspond to types. The morphims from x to y, however, do not necessarily need to correspond to functions from x to y. The most important `Category` instance is, of course, the category of funtions:

```
> type Mor = (->)
```

```
> instance Category Mor where
>    id = \x -> x
>    g . f = \x -> g (f x)
```

The identity function does nothing with its argument. Function composition is defined by making explicit use of association to the right (application associates to the left). Notice that, when dealing with functions, we have introduced `Mor` as a type synonym for (->). We will use (->) as a meta-notation: morphism composition associates with a morphism from y to z and a morphism from x to y a morphism from x to z. The type of the composition meta-operator for functions instance is:

```
> Mor y z -> Mor x y -> Mor x z
```

We could have written this type differently, for example:

```
> Mor (y -> z) (Mor (x -> y) (x -> z))
```

but this would only lead to confusion. In subsection 2.4 we will, much in the same spirit, introduce a type synonym `Prod` for (,) when dealing with products[4].

2.3 Opposite Categories

```
> type OpM mor x y = mor y x in idOpM,compOpM, ...
```

```
> idOpM :: Category mor => OpM mor x x
> idOpM = id
```

---

[4]We will not use (,) as a meta-notation. Meta-functions using (,) can be converted to meta-functions using (->).

```
> compOpM :: Category mor
>              => OpM mor y z -> OpM mor x y -> OpM mor x z
> g 'compOpM' f = f . g

> instance Category mor => Category (OpM mor) where
>    id = idOpM
>    (.) = compOpM
```

With every Category instance corresponds an opposite Category instance. The introduction of opposite categories reduces the number of classes of the prelude considerably: instead of introducing opposite classes over and over again, we simply make use of existing classes, instantiated with opposite categories. The OpM mor x y resticted type synonym has a very long list of access-functions: every time we introduce a new class instance which somehow has to deal with opposite categories, we need another access-function.

2.4 Product Categories

```
> class Category mor => FinalCategory mor where
>    final :: mor x ()
>
> class FinalCategory mor => ProdCategory mor prod where
>    exl :: mor (prod x y) x
>    exr :: mor (prod x y) y
>    (<*>) :: mor z x -> mor z y -> mor z (prod x y)
>    (>*<) :: mor u x -> mor v y -> mor (prod u v) (prod x y)

>    f >*< g = f . exl <*> g . exr
```

In subsection 2.2 we have dealt with the basic properties of the function space constructor and we have generalised these properties to Category instances. We now deal with the basic properties of the combination of the function space constructor (->), with the product space constructor (,) which can be used to define compound data, and generalise these properties to ProdCategory instances. Two binary constructors mor and prod (standing for product) are a ProdCategory instance if appropriate extraction morphisms exl and exr and an appropriate meta-operator (<*>) on morphisms are defined. We have also added a meta-operator (>*<) to the ProdCategory class together with a default definition of it in terms of other members of the class. This gives us the possiblity to override the default definition by a more efficient one whenever we define a particular ProdCategory instance. Notice that we have limited the FinalCategory instances to those for which the final object is the type (). The standard ProdCategory instance is:

```
> type Prod = (,)

> instance FinalCategory Mor where
>    final = \_ -> ()

> instance ProdCategory Mor Prod where
>    exl = \(x,_) -> x
>    exr = \(_,y) -> y
>    f <*> g = \x -> (f x,g x)
>    f >*< g = \(x,y) -> (f x,g y)
```

One can now, for example, represent the commutativity property of products
as a meta-function:

```
> swap :: ProdCategory mor prod
>          => mor (prod x y) z -> mor (prod y x) z
> swap f = f . (exr <*> exl)
```

2.5   Sum Categories

```
> instance Category mor => InitialCategory mor where
>    initial :: String -> mor a x

> class InitialCategory mor => SumCategory mor sum where
>    inl :: mor x (sum x y)
>    inr :: mor y (sum x y)
>    (<+>) :: mor x z -> mor y z -> mor (sum x y) z
>    (>+<) :: mor x u -> mor y v -> mor (sum x y) (sum u v)

>    f >+< g = inl . f <+> inr . g

> instance InitialCategory Mor where
>    initial = error

> data Sum x y = L x | R y

> instance SumCategory Mor Sum where
>    inl = L
>    inr = R
>    f <+> g = \s -> case s of L x -> f x ; R y -> g y
>    f >+< g = \s -> case s of L x -> L (f x) ; R y -> R (g y)
```

We now deal with the basic properties of the combination of the function space
constructor (->) with the | construct, which can be used to define union data,
and generalise these properties to SumCategory instances. Two binary con-

structors mor and sum (standing for sum) are a SumCategory instance if appropriate injection morphisms inl and inr and an appropriate meta-operator (<+>) on morphisms are defined. We have limited the InitialCategory instances to those for which the initial object is the polymorphic type a. We have also added an extra String argument to the initial meta-function. This argument is useful for generating error messages.

2.6   Function Categories

```
> class Category mor => FunCategory mor fun where
>    before :: mor x y -> mor (fun y z) (fun x z)
>    flip :: mor x (fun y z) -> mor y (fun x z)
>    bnd :: mor x (fun (fun x y) y)

>    bnd = flip id
```

We now deal with the basic properties of the combination of the function space constructor (->) with itself (the function space constructor (->) can also be used to define function-like data) and generalise these properties to FunCategory instances. Two binary constructors mor and fun (standing for function) are a FunCategory instance if appropriate meta-functions before and flip are defined. For many instances mor and fun will be the same binary constructor. The meta-function before is a contravariant iternal function composition (notice that, in its signature, y and z are swapped). The meta-function flip is a FunCategory equivalent of the swap meta-function of subsection 2.4. One can define a bnd morphism in terms of flip. It is a FunCategory equivalent for function argument binding. The standard FunCategory instance is:

```
> type Fun = (->)

> instance FunCategory Mor Fun where
>    flip f = \x y -> f y x
>    f 'before' g = \x -> g (f x)
>    x 'bnd' f = f x
```

Categories with internal functions turn out to be the framework in which it is possible to deal with continuations.

2.7   Closed Categories

```
> class (ProdCategory mor prod, FunCategory mor fun)
>        => ClosedCategory mor prod fun where
>    curry :: mor (prod x y) z -> mor x (fun y z)
>    uncurry :: mor x (fun y z) -> mor (prod x y) z
```

42

```
>    eval :: mor (prod (fun x y) x) y

>    eval = uncurry id
```

In this subsection we combine the properties of subsection 2.4 and subsection 2.6. There is an important relationship between products and functions: a function from a type (x,y) to a type z is essentially the same as function from the type x to the type y -> z. We now generalise this property to ClosedCategory instances (using meta-functions curry and uncurry). One can define a morphism eval in terms of uncurry. It is a ClosedCategory equivalent for function application. The standard ClosedCategory instance is:

```
> instance ClosedCategory Mor Prod Fun where
>    curry f = \x y -> f (x,y)
>    uncurry f = \(x,y) -> f x y
>    eval (f,x) = f x
```

Closed categories turn out to be the framework in which it is possible to deal with state. Notice that it is possible to define the FunCategory members in terms of the ClosedCategory members:

```
> before g = curry (eval . (id >*< g))
> flip = curry . swap . uncurry
```

2.8   Recursion Categories

```
> class Category mor => RecCategory mor rec where
>   iso :: mor (f (rec f)) (rec f)
>   osi :: mor (rec f) (f (rec f))
```

In this subsection we deal with recursive data definitions and generalise them to RecCategory instances. A binary constructor mor and a unary constructor rec (standing for recursion) are a RecCategory instance if all objects rec f and f (rec f) are isomorphic (by means of isomorphisms iso and osi). The standard RecCategory instance is:

```
> data Rec f = Rec (f (Rec f))
```

```
> instance RecCategory Mor Rec where
>    iso x = Rec x
>    osi (Rec x) = x
```

The unary constructor rec is exactly what we need to define recursive types (i. e. nullary constructors) rec f. For dealing with recursive unary constructors, another class (with a binary constructor recR) is needed:

```
> class Category mor => RecRCategory mor recR where
>   isoR :: mor (f x (recR f x)) (recR f x)
>   osiR :: mor (recR f x) (f x (recR f x))
```

2.9 Remark

There is nothing magic about the meta-functions and morphisms we have introduced so far: they correspond to the very basic functions which can be found
in any other prelude. Instead of defining them as functions we have defined
them as class members. This gives us the possibility to use them for a variety
of class instances. We finish this overview of categories and special categories
by showing how to deal with subtypes.

```
> class SumCategory mor sum => SubTypeOf mor sup sub where
>    inj :: mor sub sup
>    prj :: mor sup sub

> msg = "don't know where to go to"

> instance SubTypeOf mor sup sub
>           => SubTypeOf mor (sum sup any) sub where
>    inj = inl . inj
>    prj = prj <+> initial msg
```

2.10 Functors

```
> class (Category mor, Category mor') => Functor mor mor' f where
>    fun :: mor x y -> mor' (f x) (f y)
```

In subsection 2.2 and the ones following it we have defined the Category class
and some of its specialisations. The next natural step consists of defining a
Functor class. A Functor instance is a unary constructor f for which an
appropriate meta-function fun on morphisms is defined.

2.10.1 Examples

A whole range of general Functor instances can be defined. Trying to define
those instances both as general and as simple as possible leads to type problems:
the Gofer type checker will soon complain because of overlapping instances.
There is an easy way out of this: one can introduce restricted type synonyms.
This makes the code a bit more complex but it also has its advantages: one
can introduce meaningful names. Here are some useful Functor instances:

```
> type Rd mor r x = mor r x in funRd, ...
```

```
> funRd :: Category mor
>           => mor y z -> Mor (Rd mor x y) (Rd mor x z)
> funRd g f = g . f

> instance Category mor => Functor mor Mor (Rd mor x) where
>    fun = funRd

> type Gn prod x y = prod x y in funGn, ...

> funGn :: ProdCategory mor prod
>           => mor y z -> mor (Gn prod x y) (Gn prod x z)
> funGn f = id >*< f

> instance ProdCategory mor prod
>           => Functor mor mor (Gn prod x) where
>    fun = funGn

> type Ch sum x y = sum x y in funCh, ...

> funCh :: SumCategory mor sum
>           => mor y z -> mor (Ch sum x y) (Ch sum x z)
> funCh f = id >+< f

> instance SumCategory mor sum
>           => Functor mor mor (Ch sum x) where
>    fun = funCh
```

The Rd mor r functor (standing for read-functor) can be used for programs which need to read data (e. g. from an environment). The Gn prod s functor (standing for generate-functor) can be used for programs which need to generate data (e. g. write trace information). The Ch sum x functor (standing for choice-functor) can be used for programs which, depending on some condition, choose a different way to proceed (e. g. for error handling).

```
> type OpP prod x y = prod y x in funOpP ...

> funOpP :: ProdCategory mor prod
>            => mor y z -> mor (OpP prod x y) (OpP prod x z)
> funOpP f = f >*< id

> instance ProdCategory mor prod
>           => Functor mor mor (OpP prod x) where
>    fun = funOpP

> type OpF fun a b = fun b a in funOpF1, funOpF2, ...
```

```
> funOpF1 :: FunCategory mor fun
>                 => OpM mor x y -> mor (OpF fun a x) (OpF fun a y)
> funOpF1 = before

> instance FunCategory mor fun
>                 => Functor (OpM mor) mor (OpF fun a) where
>    fun = funOpF1

> funOpF2 :: FunCategory mor fun
>                 => mor x y -> OpM mor (OpF fun a x) (OpF fun a y)
> funOpF2 = before

> instance FunCategory mor fun
>                 => Functor mor (OpM mor) (OpF fun a) where
>    fun = funOpF2
```

The OpP prod x functor is not really useful on its own (it is isomorphic to the Gn prod s functor). However, it turns out that flipping the constructor arguments of prod is exactly what we need to use this functor as a building block for defining a state monad. Similarly, the two OpF fun a functors are not really useful on their own. They can be used as building blocks in for defining a continuation monad.

2.10.2   Auxiliary Functions

The Gofer type checker complains from time to time when it is offered fun (possibly dealing with two underlying Category instances mor and mor'). On the other hand we often do not need the full generality of the Functor class: the underlying categories will, as in the examples above, somehow be related. Therefore we introduce some auxiliary meta-functions which provide the type checker with the extra type information it sometimes needs.

```
> endofun :: Functor mor mor f
>               => mor x y -> mor (f x) (f y)
> endofun = fun

> opfunL :: Functor (OpM mor) mor f
>               => OpM mor x y -> mor (f x) (f y)
> opfunL = fun

> opfunR :: Functor mor (OpM mor) f
>               => mor x y -> OpM mor (f x) (f y)
> opfunR = fun
```

2.11 Recursion

Many unary constructors, even the simplest ones, are of a recursive nature. Proving that recursive unary constructors are Functor instances (given appropriate recursive definitions for fun) usually proceeds by using structural induction on the specific structure of the constructor. In this section we will show how one can deal with recursion in a general way.

2.11.1 Recursive Morphisms

```
> class (RecCategory mor rec, Functor mor mor f)
>       => Banana mor f rec where
>    cata :: mor (f x) x -> mor (rec f) x
>    ana :: mor x (f x) -> mor x (rec f)

>    cata phi = phi . endofun (cata phi) . osi
>    ana psi = iso . endofun (ana psi) . psi
```

The aim of the Banana class is to offer its user the possibility to define a whole range of recursive morphisms for the recursive type rec f. The meta-function cata is used for morphisms *from* the recursive type rec f to any other type x. The meta-function ana is used for morphisms from a type x *to* the recursive type rec f. The name Banana comes from the Squiggol community. The Squiggol syntax for cata phi is the Greek letter ϕ between banana brackets.

The Banana class can be used to define recursive morphisms from and to a recursive type (i. e. nullary constructor) rec f. If our aim is to define recursive morphisms from and to a type which is constructed by a recursive unary constructor, then another class is needed:

```
> class Category mor => FunctorR mor mor' f where
>    funR :: mor y z -> mor' (f x y) (f x z)

> class (RecRCategory mor recR, FunctorR mor mor f)
>       => BananaR mor f recR where
>    cataR :: mor (f x y) y -> mor (recR f x) y
>    anaR :: mor y (f x y) -> mor y (recR f x)

>    cataR phiR = phiR . endofunR (cataR phiR) . osiR
>    anaR psiR = isoR . endofunR (anaR psiR) . psiR
```

2.11.2 Binary Trees Revisited

In this subsection we return to the binary tree example of subsection 1.5.1. The idea is to replace the constructors Mor, Sum, Prod and RecR by constructor variables mor, sum, prod and recR. Notice that our definition of trees does not use any data definitions at all.

```
> type T sum prod a x = sum a (prod x x) in leafT, nodeT,
>                                             funRT, funLT, revT

> type Tree sum prod = recR (T sum prod)

> leafT :: SumCategory mor sum => mor a (T sum prod a x)
> leafT = inl

> nodeT :: SumCategory mor sum => mor (prod x x) (T sum prod a x)
> nodeT = inr

> leaf :: (SumCategory mor sum, RecRCategory mor recR)
>         => mor a (Tree sum prod a)
> leaf = isoR . leafT

> node :: (SumCategory mor sum, RecRCategory mor recR)
>         => mor (prod (Tree sum prod a) (Tree sum prod a))
>               (Tree sum prod a)
> node = isoR . nodeT
```

This finishes the code for the constructors leaf and node. Our next goal is to define recursive morphisms on Tree sum prod a. Therefore we need a FunctorR instance.

```
> funRT :: (SumCategory mor sum, ProdCategory mor prod)
>         => mor x y -> mor (T sum prod a x) (T sum prod a y)
> funRT g = id >+< g >*< g

> instance (SumCategory mor sum, ProdCategory mor prod)
>         => FunctorR (T sum prod) where
>    funR = funRT

> revT :: (SumCategory mor sum, ProdCategory mor prod)
>         => mor (T sum prod a (Tree sum prod a))
>               (Tree sum prod a)
> revT = leaf <+> node . (exr <*> exl)

> rev :: (SumCategory mor sum, ProdCategory mor prod,
>         BananaR mor (T sum prod) recR)
>         => mor (Tree sum prod a) (Tree sum prod a)
> rev = cataR revT
```

The code of the morphisms and meta-functions is exactly the same as the code of the functions of subsection 1.5.1. The types of the morphisms and meta-functions are more general. They are also more verbose: the type qualifiers show the categorical framework which is needed to define them.

2.11.3 Recursive Functors

```
> class Category mor => FunctorL mor mor f where
>    funL :: mor x y -> mor (f x z) (f y z)

> instance (BananaR mor f recR, FunctorL mor mor f)
>          => Functor mor mor (recR f) where
>    fun f = cataR (isoR . endofunL f)
```

In subsection 2.11.1 we have showed that for defining recursive morphisms on recR f x the binary constructor f has to be a FunctorR instance. In this subsection we introduce a FunctorL class which is exactly what we need for turning recR f into a Functor instance. The meta-function endofunL is defined in a similar way as the meta-function endofun of subsection 2.10 for keeping the Gofer type checker happy. Here is the FunctorL instance code for trees:

```
> funLT :: (SumCategory mor sum, ProdCategory mor prod)
>          => mor a b -> mor (T sum prod a x) (T sum prod b x)
> funLT g = g >+< id >*< id

> instance (SumCategory mor sum, ProdCategory mor prod)
>          => FunctorL mor mor (T sum prod) where
>    funL = funLT
```

Notice that the definition of funLT is very simple. However, combined with cataR it becomes a very powerful meta-function

3 Conclusion

We have shown that many concepts from category theory which turn out to be useful for functional programming can be encoded in a natural way in Gofer by making use of its constructor classes. Many of the classes and class instances of the prelude are used (in a less general setting) successfully for writing modular interpreters (see, for example, [6]). Combining subtypes, catamorphisms and monad transformers makes it possible to write reusable building blocks for modular interpreters in Gofer. In subsection 2.10.1 we have presented some functors which were claimed to be useful as building blocks for defining the state and the continuation monad. We have not shown *how* this can be done. The functors can be seen as the left and right functor of an adjunction. For every Adjunction instance with opposite underlying categories OpM mor and mor one can define a composed Triple instance:

```
> instance Adjunction (OpM mor) mor l r => Triple mor (CompOp r l)

> type Cnt fun a = CompOp (OpF fun a) (OpF fun a)
```

The `Cnt` composed `Triple` instance can be defined for any `FunCategory` instance. For every `Adjunction` instance with equal underlying categories `mor` one can define a composed `Triple` instance:

```
> instance Adjunction mor mor l r => Triple mor (Comp r l)

> type St fun prod s = Comp (Rd fun s) (OpP prod s)
```

The `St` composed `Triple` instance which can be defined for any `ClosedCategory` instance.

References

[1] D.E. Rydeheard, R.M. Burstall, *Computational Category Theory*. Prentice Hall, 1988.

[2] L. Duponcheel, E. Meijer, *On the expressive power of constructor classes*. Research Report RUU, 1994 (to appear).

[3] P. Hudak, S. Peyton Jones, P.Wadler, *Report on the programming language Haskell, version 1.2*. ACM SIGPLAN Notices, Vol. 27(5), May 1992.

[4] M.P. Jones, *A system of constructor classes: overloading and implicit higher-order polymorphism*. Proceedings of the ACM conference on Functional Programming Languages and Computer Architecture, 1993.

[5] M.P. Jones, L. Duponcheel, *Composing monads*. Research Report YALEU/DCS/RR-1004, 1993.

[6] S. Liang, P. Hudak, M.P. Jones, *Monad transformers and modular interpreters*. Research Report, YALEU/DCS, 1994.

[7] G.L. Steele Jr., *Building interpreters by composing monads*. Proceedings of the ACM SIGPLAN-SIGACT symposium on Principles of Programming Languages, 1994.

[8] P. Wadler, *The essence of functional programming*. Proceedings of the ACM SIGPLAN-SIGACT symposium on Principles of Programming Languages, 1992.

[9] P. Wadler, S.P. Jones, *Imperative functional programming*. Proceedings of the ACM SIGPLAN-SIGACT symposium on Principles of Programming Languages, 1993.

Programming
Reactive Systems
in
Haskell

Sigbjørn Finne[*]

Department of Computing Science, University of Glasgow

sof@dcs.gla.ac.uk

Simon Peyton Jones

Department of Computing Science, University of Glasgow

simonpj@dcs.gla.ac.uk

Abstract

Certain classes of applications are naturally described as a network of cooperating components, where each component reacts to input as and when it becomes available. This paper builds on previous work on expressing I/O and state-based algorithms safely in a functional language, and presents a new way of expressing reactive systems in a functional language that does not violate vital semantic properties. The approach taken is a pragmatic one in that it integrates constructs for expressing reactive systems within existing framework for writing I/O bound, state-based programs functionally.

The original contributions of this paper are twofold; first, we show how the existing monadic IO model can be extended to cope with non-determinism, and secondly, we introduce primitives for evaluating I/O actions concurrently.

1 Introduction

A large class of applications are naturally described as a collection of components cooperating to solve some task. Examples include operating systems and graphical user interfaces where partitioning the system into a set of independently running processes or threads of control separates out the different concerns, making for more modular solutions. Writing such reactive systems in a non-strict, purely functional language like Haskell[9] is in its very nature problematical, as the concept of having a component reacting to stimuli from multiple sources cannot be described by a (deterministic) function. Indeed, the straightforward introduction of constructs for expressing such non-determinate behaviour does interfere with fundamental semantic properties of the language [6], disallowing the unrestricted use of equational reasoning.

This paper builds on previous work on expressing I/O and safe state encapsulation, and addresses the problem of how to write reactive systems such

---

[*]Supported by a Research Scholarship from the Royal Norwegian Research Council.

as graphical user interface applications or operating systems in a pure functional language. Specifically, support for concurrency and non-determinism is introduced. To make the distinction clear, we use the term *concurrency* to refer to the *explicit* use of separate threads of control to structure a program, and not the *implicit* use of multiple threads or processes to achieve potential performance gains (parallelism). Also, the main reason for introducing non-determinism into a functional setting is the wish to write reactive systems *within* a functional language, rather than a wish to express non-deterministic algorithms.

The original contributions of this paper are:

- *Composable reactive systems.* The approach presented to the expression of reactive systems improves upon existing ways of writing reactive systems such as graphical user interface applications in that it is compositional and concurrent.

  We present our approach through a motivating example in Section 2.

- *Referentially transparent non-determinism.* Non-deterministic operators are provided *without* breaking much valued reasoning properties of the underlying language. This is not only important from the viewpoint of still being able to apply reasoning techniques to functional programs, but also avoids any special treatment of non-deterministic operators during the considerable transformation a program goes through during compilation.

  Our approach to the controlled introduction of non-determinism is presented in Section 3, and we survey some existing approaches to non-determinism in purely functional languages in Section 5.

- *Concurrent actions.* We also introduce a primitive for concurrently executing I/O bound computations or *threads* (Section 2.4). This allows us to partition programs into a set of concurrently running threads, and is used to structure the way we write reactive systems (Section 4.3).

- *Incorporation of non-deterministic operators into I/O framework.* The approach to non-determinism is connected to the IO monad[18], providing a unified framework for constructing programs that engage in I/O and require non-determinism, but still staying within a purely functional setting. This allows the two kinds of programming to be mixed, and offers rich possibilities for extending primitive non-deterministic operators to capture mechanisms such as timeouts, remote procedure calls etc. (Section 4).

2 Motivation

This section introduces our approach to programming reactive systems, motivating it through the discussion of how to best express a simple reactive system.

2.1 Example

As a motivating example, consider a graphical user interface representing a two-way counter with a pair of push buttons and one output display. One button increments the value on the display by one, the other decrements it. The natural way of structuring this application is to partition it into three distinct components:

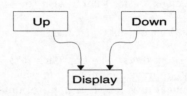

The components representing the buttons take care of giving them an appearance and appropriate interactive behaviour, while the output display keeps an updated view of the state of the counter. We depict the semantic feedback from the buttons via arcs feeding into the output display, a display that is *shared* between the two buttons.

How do we best translate this abstract view of the counter into a running program? We will leave that question open for the moment, but note that we somehow have to capture the fact that input from the buttons may arrive in any order at the display, and that the components may have to run independently from each other.

This example may appear overly trivial, but the problems it illustrates are found in more complex reactive systems such as an airline reservation system's central database or a resource manager in an operating system.

Before looking any further at how to express this application in a functional language, we will briefly review the approach taken to I/O and state-based computations in general.

2.2 IO Programming

The now-standard approach to structuring Haskell programs engaging in I/O is described at length elsewhere [18, 14], but to recap briefly:

- I/O operations side-effect the external world, and are represented by the abstract data type IO a. A value of type IO a represents an I/O performing *action* that when executed *may* perform side-effects on the external world, before returning a value of type a together with an updated world.

- Actions are composed with the sequencing combinator thenIO :: IO a -> (a -> IO b) -> IO b. m 'thenIO' val -> n constructs a new IO action, such that when it is performed, m is executed first, binding its result to val and returning an updated view of the outside world. The action n is then executed in this environment.

- The simplest possible I/O operation is returnIO, which just returns a value without affecting the external world: returnIO :: a -> IO a

In addition, I/O as implemented in the Glasgow Haskell compiler also provides a mechanism for calling C functions through the primitive action `ccall`. Because the only way of composing actions together is with the sequencing combinator `thenIO`, the access to the external world is single-threaded, and it can thus be updated safely in-place, allowing for an efficient compilation of I/O actions (see [18] for details). Informally, a program engaging in I/O may be represented as a thread of primitive actions, strung together with a series of `thenIO`s:

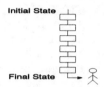

The primitive I/O actions, pictured here as boxes, are joined together in a chain, single-threading the state of the world. To force execution of an I/O bound program, there is a top level *demand* that forces evaluation by demanding the final state produced by the thread. We depict this above by an anthropomorphic character 'pulling' on the thread.

2.3 Explicit interleaving

The basic I/O model, as described in the previous section, for stringing together side-effecting I/O actions is similar to how programs in imperative languages are constructed. One possible way of implementing the two-way counter would be to borrow techniques used in imperative languages.

The conventional approach in such languages is to have a top level dispatcher that fetches events reporting user actions from the window system, and invokes a *callback* function to handle each event. The callback function is selected based on the contents of the event reported, and it makes the required changes to both interface and the state of the application. Using this approach, a set of predefined button and display widgets from a toolkit could be parameterised with appropriate callback functions to implement the two-way counter example. Unfortunately, the whole action-based, event loop paradigm has some serious flaws that does not fit well with functional languages:

- The callback functions deal not only with changes to the appearance of its components, but they also have the responsibility of updating the state of the application. This leads to the sharing of global application state between the different functions, resulting in monolithic, non-modular solutions. Global state could be emulated by threading application state through the different callback functions in addition to the I/O state, as done by Clean's Event I/O system[1].

- The application is centred around the dispatcher or event loop and to ensure adequate responsiveness to the interface, callbacks have to be coded with this in mind. Events have to be serviced every so often; this does not pose any problems for simple examples like a counter, but more complex applications have to be structured as a set of callback functions so that

54

the dispatcher will be visited at regular intervals. The fact that the application has a graphical user interface dictates the style of programming for the *whole* application, a most unfortunate situation.

Writing the two-way counter this way would certainly be possible, but the solution does not make use of the inherent features of a functional language such as abstraction and the ability to compose entities together with user-defined glue[10]. In the case of the two-way counter, we would very much like to be able to reuse it as part of a larger application, something that is hard to do using this paradigm *without* rewriting it first to fit its context. However, emulating the conventional approach does have the benefit of easily being able to plug into sophisticated toolkits that have been developed around this framework.

A clearer separation between the individual components of the counter can be achieved though by introducing more than one source of demand, each evaluating concurrently. Instead of having to take care of explicitly interleaving execution between the different components using a centralised dispatch mechanism, each component is now responsible for independently servicing input in the form of window system events or input from other components, as and when it becomes available. A response to some input might be to perform I/O operations to change the appearance of the component, e.g. highlighting the button when pressed, or output values to other components.

Fortunately, expressing concurrency in a functional language fits well into the I/O framework described in 2.2, and we introduce our approach to concurrency next.

2.4   Concurrent IO actions

IO actions can be executed concurrently using the forkIO operator:

```
forkIO :: IO a -> IO a
```

forkIO m dynamically creates a new demand which evaluates the IO action m concurrently to the thread that issued the forkIO action. The new thread executes in the same context as its creator, so thread creation does not involve any extensive copying of data into a separate address space. Using a plumbing diagram, forkIO can be represented as follows:

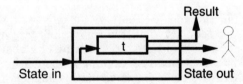

forkIO m splits the state thread into two strands, creating a new demand (the anthropoid) that pulls on the new strand independently of the thread that issued it. The original thread continues executing, but if it tries to inspect the result of m before it has been produced, the thread is blocked waiting until the producer thread has produced enough of the result for the blocked thread to continue.[1] Informally, a set of concurrent I/O threads can be depicted as follows:

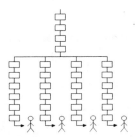

forkIO splits the state thread into two, and eagerly starts to demand the new strand. Is this 'unsafe', in the sense that is the state of the thread creator visible to the forked off action ? Yes; both threads have access to the 'whole' external world, so if they both choose to write to the same file, say, the resulting state of that file is dependent on the relative scheduling order of the threads. Should we outlaw such indeterminate interactions between the threads by enforcing that the state which they work on don't intersect, using the techniques developed in [14]? No, in most cases this would be overly restrictive, so we place instead a proof obligation on the programmer to ensure that potential interference between threads is benign and intended.[2]

Having got forkIO, a thread can now be created for each component in the two-way counter example. Each thread handles input events and, in the case of the buttons, outputs values on a stream to signal that it has been pressed. The resulting structure is now identical to the initial model we gave in Section 2.1, partitioned into a set of interacting components. But exactly how do components interact? We seem to need an operator that once invoked, is able to deliver the next input available from a set of sources. In the case of the output display, such a non-determinate operator is required to be able to service input from the window system and both buttons as values become available on their input streams.

Describe next our approach to incorporating non-determinism safely into the concurrent I/O framework just presented, conclude here by noticing that on the assumption of having an operator for *merging* input from several sources, the running example of a reactive system can be expressed naturally as a set of components communicating, achieving a separation of concerns not present in current ways of writing reactive systems such as graphical user interfaces.

3 Introducing non-determinism

Our idea is simple. We introduce non-deterministic choice through the following primitives:

---

[1]The mechanism for implicitly blocking threads is just the technique used in parallel functional languages for blocking processes trying to read values that are currently being evaluated.

[2]We also assume that the changes individual threads make to the outside world occur atomically, an assumption that does not hold in general. We return to this issue of atomicity briefly in Section 6.

```
chooseIO :: (_Data a, _Data b)
         => a -> b -> IO Bool
mergeIO :: _Data a
         => [a] -> [a] -> IO [a]
```

chooseIO val_a val_b is an action that when executed may perform some
IO before returning a boolean indicating which of its two arguments it selected
together with an updated view of the world. Its operational behaviour is equal
to that of amb[15], in that:

```
chooseIO  ⊥    val  =>  False
chooseIO  val  ⊥    =>  True
chooseIO  ⊥    ⊥    =>  ⊥
```

where val $\neq$ ⊥. chooseIO diverges if and only if both of its arguments diverge.

mergeIO performs a time-based merging of streams, making elements from
the input streams available on the output stream when (and if) they appear.
The merge is lazy, elements are produced on the result stream on demand.

3.1 Discussion

Introducing non-determinism into a functional language is problematic [6], so
why are chooseIO and mergeIO not harmful? The 'trick' here is to attach the
non-deterministic operators to the IO monad, so that the choice is made based
on the pair of values it is passed *and* the state of the world. Hence, there is
no reason to expect two identical calls to chooseIO to pick the same value
each time, since the state of the outside world may well be different when the
next choice is made. This is similar to an oracular approach [4], appearing
to consult the outside world to decide what choice to make. Since we are
threading the state of the world through a program, recording the choices made
is not necessary, as we can guarantee that actions such as chooseIO are not
accidentally copied. Thus, a choice will only be made once, so any recording is
superfluous.

The operators preserve referential transparency for the same reasons as
side-effecting programs expressed in an I/O framework do, i.e., the ordering of
evaluation is made explicit through threading of state, and only the result value
of an action can be shared, not the side-effecting action itself. This prevents
indeterminate operations from inadvertently being copied, so chooseIO implements *call-time* choice[6], referentially transparent view of non-determinism[19].
Although similar to *oracles* (Section 5), it avoids having to record choices in
pseudo-data to catch the cases where a non-deterministic expression is accidentally copied during compilation, say. Making the 'oracle' part of the outside
world also avoids the problem of explicitly handling a supply of oracles in your
program.

Requiring the non-deterministic operators to be attached to the I/O monad
might seem restricting, but this coupling is of practical importance to us, as
the main use non-determinism is to express reactive systems such as graphical,
I/O bound, user interface applications functionally. Hence, using an operator
like mergeIO, we can now formulate the two-way counter of Section 2.1 as a set
of concurrent I/O threads interacting via streams of values.

However, preserving a property like referential transparency for the overall
program does not imply that it is suddenly easy to reason about! The program

is still non-deterministic, and has thus a more complex semantics. But, the linking of non-deterministic choice and the IO monad does have its advantages:

- The choice is separated from its use, making it possible to isolate the non-deterministic parts of a program. Hence, standard reasoning techniques can be applied to the determinate parts.

- Relatively low syntactic burden. There is no danger of the programmer accidentally performing 'plumbing' errors, as the IO monad ensures that a choice is only performed once. This an improvement over the oracle approach (Section 5), where the programmer has to explicitly thread a supply of oracles through the program.

- The choice is pure. This differs from the set-based approach of [11, 22] where the formulation of merge requires the non-deterministic selection between computations that contained a mix of code directly relevant to the selection and code to set up further merging. Because of this mixture, providing an efficient implementation is hard. chooseIO avoids this by simply selecting between the two arguments it is passed, leaving it instead up to the context to interpret the boolean it returns.

- A single framework for writing programs that engage in I/O and depend on non-determinism to perform correctly. Previous monadic formulations of non-determinism (Section 5) did not consider how to combine it with state-based monads such as IO.

- Applying the Glasgow Haskell threads extensions technique of using type classes to discriminate against 'non-seqable' expressions, we avoid the problem of handling a choose between partial applications. One practical application of this is that it avoids having to handle the non-deterministic choice between I/O actions:

```
flarp = chooseIO (writeFile fname1 data1)
                 (writeFile fname2 data2)
```

The flarp action tries to write to two files, picking the first to complete as its result. If we were to allow a choice between I/O actions, the file operation that 'lost' would now have to be undone. Mechanisms for keeping track of all the changes made by the 'losing' branch are tricky to implement, let alone expensive, so we forbid choice between I/O actions by enforcing membership of the _Data type class on arguments to mergeIO and chooseIO.

Membership in the _Data type class is taken care of by the compiler, automatically making all non-function values members, avoiding programmer inserted instances to the _Data class for every data type defined.

Having presented the non-deterministic primitives, we will now look at examples of how they can be used together with forkIO.

4   Examples

4.1   Merging streams

Although we introduced `mergeIO` as a primitive in the previous section, it can be formulated in terms of `chooseIO`:

```
mergeIO :: _Data a => [a] -> [a] -> IO [a]
mergeIO ls rs
 = chooseIO ls rs 'thenIO' \ flg ->
   let
     (as,bs) = if flg then
                   (ls,rs)
               else
                   (rs,ls)
   in
     case as of
         []     -> returnIO bs
         (x:xs) -> mergeIO xs bs 'thenIO' \ vs ->
                   returnIO (x:vs)
```

`mergeIO` combines two streams of values into one by repeatedly calling `chooseIO` with the stream pair as arguments. The above version of `mergeIO` correctly merges the streams, but it is too inefficient to be the basis for programming reactive systems:

- A call to `chooseIO` result in the concurrent evaluation of the pair of arguments passed in until either of them has been evaluated to WHNF. The computation that 'lost' the choice has to either be undone or allowed to run until completion. If we perform the potentially complex and costly operation of undoing the evaluation of the argument, any further merging is delayed as we cannot proceed until we have restored the previous state of that argument. Allowing the computation to run until completion is also inefficent in the case of `mergeIO`, because subsequent calls to `chooseIO` will create new computations that tries to evaluate the very same value. Although this inefficiency can be worked around, the simplicity of the initial solution is lost, so we choose to provide `mergeIO` as a primitive instead.

- In some cases it is convenient to allow the merge to work ahead of the demand on the merged stream. In the implementation given above, when an element on the result stream is demanded, `chooseIO` will invoked and two concurrent computations will be created to produce the next element on the merged stream. This is inefficient in that the thread creation overheads are incurred for every element demanded. Implementing buffering or avoiding the repeated creation of threads to work on the merged streams is difficult to do in terms of `chooseIO`, which is another why choose to provide `mergeIO` as a primitive.

4.2 Timeout

Assuming that we have forkIO of Section 2.4 available, here is how a timeout mechanism can be built:

```
sleeper :: Int -> IO ()

timeoutIO :: _Data a => Int -> a -> IO Bool
timeoutIO period val
 = forkIO (sleeper period) 'thenIO' \ unit ->
   chooseIO val unit
```

Timeout is implemented by simply 'listening' to whichever completes first, the passing of the time period or the argument val. forkIO (sleeper ival) creates a thread that goes to sleep for period microseconds before returning () to signal the passing of that time period.[3]

This example shows that even though chooseIO explicitly forbids choice between IO actions, it is relatively straightforward to create own abstractions on top of the basic choice that selects between *results* of IO actions. It is the responsibility of the programmer to ensure that any side-effects performed by a failed IO action are satisfactorily undone.

4.3 Reactive systems

The example of a two-way counter given in Section 2.1, could be written using mergeIO and forkIO as follows:[4]

```
button ::  (Int->Int) -> IO [(Int->Int)]

display ::  Int -> [(Int->Int)] -> IO ()
display state (op:ops)
  =
   let
    state' = op state
   in
    ...update output window..
    display state' ops


counter ::  IO ()
counter
  = forkIO (button (+1)) 'thenIO'  ups ->
    forkIO (button (-1)) 'thenIO'  downs ->
    mergeIO ups downs 'thenIO'  mls ->
    display 0 mls
```

---

[3]sleeper is implemented by making a ccall to the underlying OS' sleep system call, and depends on having non-blocking I/O calls.

[4]This example is only intended to demonstrate how different components are joined up together, and does not reflect how we would like the user to write a graphical user interface application.

The `display` component takes care of the output display window and is passed the merged stream of commands from both buttons. It is simply a stream processor, translating commands into I/O actions that update the output window. The non-deterministic merging of the streams form the buttons is done *externally* to the `display` component. Albeit a small example, but it demonstrates that by separating the different components into separate threads of control, and providing a mechanism for selecting non-determinstically from a number of sources, a much more modular way of expressing reactive systems such as graphical user interface applications is possible. For example, the counter could now be reused as part of other applications *without* having to rewrite it to fit its context. We are currently working on a more general framework for expressing user interfaces using these techniques.

5 Related Work

Several proposals for expressing non-determinism in a functional language have been suggested, we survey some of them here.

One of the simplest ways of introducing non-determinism is with the `amb` operator[15]:

```
amb :: a -> a -> a
```

`amb x y` is locally bottom-avoiding, in that it non-deterministically chooses between `x` or `y` using to the following equations:

```
amb  ⊥  v  =  v
amb  v  ⊥  =  v
amb  ⊥  ⊥  =  ⊥
```

Its operational interpretation is that it evaluates both arguments concurrently until either of them reduces to WHNF. Clearly, `amb` is not a function and its introduction into a lazy functional language destroys important reasoning properties, as substitutivity of expressions is lost [19], the archetypal example of this being:

```
double x = x + x
```

The expression `double (amb 2 1)` is not equal to the instantiated right hand side `(amb 2 1) + (amb 2 1)`, as what was originally one choice has now become two.[5]

`merge`, the stream based version of `amb`, takes a pair of potentially infinite lists and merges them into one, based on the order in which the elements on the streams become available (*fair* merge). Using this operator as a primitive [8, 12] have shown how a variety of functional operating systems can be expressed in a functional framework.

In [4, 2], the potentially non-referentially transparent features of `amb` and Henderson's `merge` are avoided through the introduction of a new data structure, *oracles*. In addition to a pair of values, the `choose` operator[6] is also given

---

[5]In a lazy language, the expression representing x is shared between the right hand side occurrences of x, so the above situation will not be a problem. However, situations exist where it is beneficial to break this sharing.

[6]Operationally equivalent to `amb`.

an oracle, an external source which it consults in order to make the 'correct' choice. Internally, an oracle can take on three values, either it indicates what argument choice should select (first or second), or it is marked as being 'undecided'. When `choose` is evaluated, the oracle is consulted, and if it is in an undecided state it is free to select non-deterministically which value to choose, as long the decision made is recorded in the oracle afterwards. Side-effecting of the oracle is safe, as there is no way of seeing different decisions from the same oracle.[7] In the case of the `double` function in the previous section:

```
double (choose o 2 1) = (choose o 2 1) + (choose o 2 1)
```

the first `choose` that is evaluated will record its choice in the oracle, leaving the other `choose` to follow that decision, implementing a singular semantics[6].

Oracles carry the overhead of having to record choices even though each choice is ideally performed only once and programs uding oracles have to explicitly plumb a supply of them through the progrsm, unnecessarily cluttering the program and introducing the possibility of accidental plumbing errors.

The authors of the Fudgets system[5] for writing graphical user interfaces in Haskell, have proposed the adoption of oracles to handle non-determinism when implementing concurrent user interfaces.

An alternative approach to non-determinism is to move it outside the functional language completely. The conventional approach here is to rely on the run-time system provide the actual non-determinism, as exemplified by Stoye[20], Perry [17] and Cupitt[7]. To use Stoye's approach to writing functional operating systems as an example, individual processes are deterministic, modelled as stream processors mapping process requests to resulting responses. Each process is connected up to a global *sorting office*, which merges the output of all the processes, and routes individual messages to the right recipient.[8] The sorting office acts as a global merge, and is implemented as part of the run-time system.

Apart from the obvious restriction on typing of messages in Stoye's approach, which has been solved recently for *static* process networks by [23], all of these approaches rely on having a non-functional run-time system to take care of the 'dirty' bits. Non-deterministic programs have to be modelled as a single collection of processes, each of which is (potentially) a communicating partner with any other.

Related to our main interest in using non-determinism to express user interfaces, this approach is being used by [16] to construct concurrent interactive applications.

The `amb` operator can be turned into a function, by changing its definition just slightly:

```
amb ::  a -> a -> {a}
```

Instead of returning either of its two arguments, the set of possible values `amb` can produce is returned. This idea of representing non-deterministic computations by the sets of values they can denote is used in [11], where a collection of set operators for constructing and composing non-deterministic computations

---

[7]Assuming, of course, that oracle access is mutually exclusive.

[8]Process addressing is done using a simple numeric scheme.

are given. Referential transparency is retained, as none of the operators provided, inspect or select particular elements contained in a (non-deterministic) set. Non-deterministic choice simply becomes set union:

∪ :: {a} -> {a} -> {a}

The set of possible results from a pair of non-deterministic computations is just their combined sum. Computations are composed together using set map:

* :: (a -> b) -> {a} -> {b}

When two non-deterministic computations are composed, it is necessary to 'flatten' the resulting set of sets:[9]

∪ :: {{a}} -> {a}

The actual implementation of these sets is done by picking a representative element non-deterministically from the set, which is safe as no operators that inspect individual elements of the sets are provided. As a result, the map operator * is implemented as just function application on the representative element, while ∪ non-deterministically selects one of two representative elements.

In [21, 22], the set-based approach is given a monadic formulation, resulting in a less cumbersome and more familiar notation. Here is how merging could be expressed:[10]

```
data L a
unitL  :: a -> L a
bindL  :: L a -> (a -> L b) -> L b
unionL :: L a -> L a -> L a

merge :: [a] -> [a] -> L [a]
merge ls rs
 = (( ls 'seq' unitL (ls,rs)) 'unionL'
    ( rs 'seq' unitL (rs,ls))) 'bindL' \ (as,bs) ->
   case as of
        []      -> unitL bs
        (x:xs)  -> merge xs bs 'bindL' \ ms ->
                   unitL (x:ms)
```

A value of type (L a) represents a computation that when evaluated may perform some non-determinate actions before returning a value of type a. Non-determinate computations are composed using bindL, which has the advantage of automatically giving a handle on values of non-deterministic computations, avoiding the use of the ∪ operator in [11]. unionL selects non-deterministically between two non-determinate computations.

6   Conclusions and Further work

We have presented an approach to writing reactive systems such as graphical user interface applications functionally, where the existing framework for

---

[9]See [11] for explanations as to why such a flattening operator is required.

[10]seq :: _Data a => a -> b -> b, seq evaulates its first argument to weak head normal form(WHNF), before returning the second.

describing I/O bound programs was extended to handle concurrency and non-determinism. These ideas have been implemented on top of the Glasgow Haskell compiler and is currently being used to construct a general framework for creating composable user interfaces in Haskell.

In the previous sections we did not consider the consequences of having concurrency and mutable variables, as introduced in [13]. Briefly, issues of atomicity have to be dealt with here to ensure that mutable variables being shared between threads are accessed exclusively. We are currently experimenting with an approach where mutable variables can have additional synchronisation semantics, in the style of Id's M-structures[3]. Other features being experimented with is the incorporation of mechanisms to handle the other side of synchronisation in concurrent programming, conditional synchronisation. Indeed, having mechanisms for handling both mutual exclusion and conditional synchronisation, an efficient implementation of `mergeIO` can be provided in Haskell, but, sadly, details are outside the scope of this paper.

Acknowledgements

This work was done in the context of the Glasgow Haskell compiler team, and we wish to particularly thank the valiant efforts of Will Partain and Jim Mattson, especially Jim's implementation of the concurrent threads extensions to ghc and his speedy responses to numerous questions. Thanks also to the referees for their helpful comments on an earlier version of this paper.

References

[1] Peter Achten and Rinus Pasmeijer. Towards Distributed Interactive Programs in the Functional Programming Language Clean. In *Implementation of Functional Programming Languages Workshop*, University of East-Anglia, Norwich, September 1994.

[2] Lennart Augustsson. Functional non-deterministic programming -or- How to make your own oracle. Technical Report ??, Chalmers University of Technology, March 1989.

[3] Paul S. Barth, Rishiyur S. Nikhil, and Arvind. Non-strict, Functional Language with State. In J. Hughes, editor, *Proceedings of the 5th ACM Conference on Functional Programming Languages and Computer Architecture*, volume 523 of *Lecture Notes in Computer Science*, pages 538–568. Springer Verlag, August 1991.

[4] F. W. Burton. Nondeterminism with Referential Transparency in Functional Programming Languages. *Computer Journal*, 31(3):243–247, June 1988.

[5] Magnus Carlsson and Thomas Hallgren. FUDGETS – A Graphical User Interface in a Lazy Functional Language. In *ACM Conference on Functional Programming Languages and Computer Architecture*, pages 321 – 330. ACM Press, 1993.

[6] William Clinger. Nondeterministic Call by Need is Neither Lazy Nor by Name. In *Proceedings of the ACM Conference on Lisp and Functional Programming*, pages 226–234, 1982.

[7] John Cupitt. *The Design and Implementation of an Operating System in a Functional Language*. PhD thesis, Department of Computer Science, University of Kent at Canterbury, August 1992.

[8] Peter Henderson. Purely Functional Operating Systems. In J. Darlington, P. Henderson, and D.A. Turner, editors, *Functional Programming and its Applications*, pages 177–192. Cambridge University Press, 1982.

[9] Paul Hudak et al. Report on the Programming Language Haskell Version 1.2. *ACM SIGPLAN Notices*, 27(5), May 1992.

[10] John Hughes. Why Functional Programming Matters. *Computer Journal*, 32(2):98–107, April 1989.

[11] John Hughes and John O'Donnell. Expressing and Reasoning About Nondeterministic Functional Programs. In Kei Davis and John Hughes, editors, *Proceedings of the Glasgow Functional Workshop*, pages 308–328, 1989.

[12] Simon B. Jones and A. F. Sinclair. Functional Programming and Operating Systems. *Computer Journal*, 32(2):162–174, April 1989.

[13] John Launchbury and Simon L. Peyton Jones. Lazy Functional State Threads. In *Proceedings of the ACM Conference on Programming Language Design and Implementation*, June 1994.

[14] John Launchbury and Simon L Peyton Jones. State in Haskell. *Lisp and Symbolic Computation*, 1994. to appear.

[15] John McCarthy. A basic mathematical theory of computation. In P. Braffort and D. Hirschberg, editors, *Computer Programming and Formal Systems*, pages 33–70. North-Holland, Amsterdam, 1963.

[16] Rob Noble and Colin Runciman. Concurrent Process Extensions to Gofer. unpublished, September 1994.

[17] Nigel Perry. Towards a Concurrent Object/Process Oriented Functional Language. In *Proceedings of the 15th Australian Compture Science Conference*, 1992.

[18] Simon L. Peyton Jones and Philip Wadler. Imperative Functional Programming. In *ACM Conference on the Principles of Programming Languages*, pages 71 – 84. ACM Press, January 1993.

[19] Harald Sondergaard and Peter Sestoft. Referential Transparency, Definiteness and Unfoldability. *Acta Informatica*, 27:505–517, 1990.

[20] William Stoye. Message-Based Functional Operating Systems. *Science of Computer Programming*, 6:291–311, 1986.

[21] Philip Wadler. Comprehending Monads. In *Proceedings of the ACM SIG-PLAN '90 Principles of Programming Languages Conference*. ACM Press, June 1990.

[22] Philip Wadler. The essence of functional programming. In *Proceedings of the ACM SIGPLAN 19th Annual Symposium on Principles of Programming Languages*, January 1992. Invited talk.

[23] Malcolm Wallace and Colin Runciman. Type-checked message-passing between functional processes. In John O'Donnell and Kevin Hammond, editors, *Glasgow Functional Programming Group Workshop*, Ayr, September 1994. Springer Verlag.

Techniques for Simplifying the Visualization of Graph Reduction *

Sandra P. Foubister

Institute for Computer Based Learning, Heriot-Watt University,
Riccarton, Edinburgh EH14 4AS, UK

Colin Runciman

Department of Computer Science, University of York,
Heslington, York YO1 5DD, UK

Abstract

Space and time problems still occasionally dog the functional programmer, despite increasingly efficient implementations and the recent spate of useful profiling tools. There is a need for a model of program reduction that relates directly to the user's code and has a simple graphical representation. Naïve graph reduction provides this. We address the problems of displaying a series of program graphs which may be long, and the elements of which may be large and complex. We offer a scheme for compacting an individual display by creating a quotient graph through defining equivalence classes, and a similar scheme for reducing the number of graphs to show. A metalanguage to allow the user to define compaction rules gives the model flexibility. A prototype system exists in a Haskell implementation.

1 Motivation

People are often unable to predict the behaviour of a lazy functional program. Although the order of reduction is deterministic in a given sequential implementation, it is not intuitively obvious. Freeing the programmer from procedural concerns also removes the possibility of reading a computational procedure directly from a source program. Even with statistics, or diagrammatic summaries, as provided by profiling [2, 8, 9], the programmer may not gain understanding of what is going on in sufficient detail to be able to control it.

One solution would be to make all details of the reduction open to inspection. Two problems arise: the level at which to do this and, whatever level is used, the overwhelming amount of information that would be provided. There is also a need to be able to relate the data to the source code. To portray the reduction in terms of the combinators to which it may be translated is inadequate and potentially confusing.

Graph reduction by template instantiation is "The simplest possible implementation of a functional language" [7]. It fulfils the need to relate observations of the evaluation process to the source code. A visual presentation of graph reduction at this level would amount to an animation of its usual text book presentation [1], with possibilities

---

*This work was supported by a SERC grant to the first author and is described further in her D.Phil. thesis [3].

[1] See for example pp 33–34 in [7]

of focusing in on interesting looking regions, skipping over unwanted details of the reduction, and even stepping backwards. A proposal that is similar in spirit to this one is to be found in Jon Taylor's work [11]. Facilities for the user to focus on areas of interest in the reduction process are also found in Kamin's Centaur [4], Lieberman's Zstep [5] and Nilsson and Fritzon's "algorithm debugger" [6].

Having chosen a level of presentation we are left with the other problem — of too much to show. Apart from the simplest examples, the program graph cannot be displayed in its entirety on the screen: the display would be too complex. One source of complexity is the crossing of arcs in a display, another is its potential size. Furthermore there will be a large number of graphs to show, so there is a need to compact the *series* of graphs, as well as each displayed element.

We propose solutions to all of these problems, and a metalanguage to enable users to define their own filters over displays and over sequences of reduction steps.

Section 2 describes a simple functional language and illustrative reduction rules. Section 3 discusses the problems of displaying the reduction as a series of graphs and Section 4 proposes some solutions. Section 5 discusses the use of quotient rules for creating simplified displays, and presents a metalanguage for the definition of such rules. Section 6 concludes.

2 A simple functional language

A graphical stepping interpreter for a minimal functional language is used as a vehicle to illustrate possible displays of graph reduction. The language is called h, the interpreter: hint. The h language is mostly a subset of Haskell. It is similar to the Haskell *Core language*. Differences include:

No local definitions Function definitions are only allowed at the top level so that there is a "function name" to which they may be related for display purposes. There are no local definitions of any sort. To get round this the user writes auxiliary global definitions and effectively programs at a lifted, "supercombinator", level.

No static type checking There is no static type checking. There are built in types corresponding to Int, Bool and Char, and, for convenience, also List, Pair and Error. Programmers may use their own constructors, identified by an initial capital letter, but only in a saturated form as their arity is not explicitly declared. The justification of the lack of static type checking is that this does not radically alter the graph reduction process, yet allows the interpreter to be quicker and simpler than it might otherwise be.

No variables for arguments in patterns As in core Haskell there is no pattern matching in h of the implicit kind: recognising argument patterns to choose which equation in the definition of a function to apply. Instead h expresses pattern matching at an intermediate level with a *case expression* which maps constructors either to a constant, or to a function with the same arity as the constructor. This allows pattern matching to be displayed in a manner that is consistent with the rest of the reduction, and ensures that the display is not complicated by a need to include argument variables. Section 5.1 has an illustration of the use of the pattern matching case statement in the definition of `primes`.

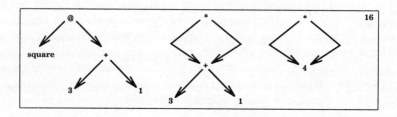

Figure 1: The reduction of `square (3 + 1)`

3 Problems in displaying the reduction

The idea is to display the program graph at each stage in the reduction, *i.e.* after each change engendered by a rewrite rule, or at less frequent intervals on request. Figure 1 shows the four stages in the reduction of the expression `square 3 + 1`. In addition to the question of how to lay out the graph, three problems arise:

The potential *complexity* **of the graphs** There is no guarantee that the program graph will be planar – indeed, the features of a lazy language: sharing, recursion, and "knot tying" in general, make planarity unlikely; so the display of the graph may be complicated by crossing of arcs, or by potentially long and unwieldy arcs if maximal planarity is attempted. A proposed solution to this is the creation of *graph-trees*.

The potential *size* **of the graphs** The program graph is a detailed and low-level structure. It will be very large in all but trivial examples. Two solutions are proposed for this: one is to use browsing, with a miniature version of the graph as a map; the other is to compact the graph by regarding certain connected patches of graph each to be *one* cluster in a graph of clusters. But the purpose of the display is to give *insight* to the user as to what is going on. There is no point finding a neat way of compacting the graph to display if it does not still convey the information that the user requires. We refer to this as *spatial filtering*.

The potential *number* **of graphs to show** The problem of there being too many reduction steps may be resolved by regarding the sequence of program graphs itself as a graph. (If alternative reduction paths were allowed, for example in a system that offered a "strict" option, it might be more than a linear sequence.) A similar scheme to the filtering of individual program graphs may be used to compact this graph of graphs, collapsing a whole chain of steps into one. We refer to this as *temporal filtering*.

4 Proposed solutions

4.1 Overcoming complexity: Graph-trees

One way of simplifying the display is to avoid any crossing of arcs. Rather than trying to display every arc in the graph, display a spanning tree enhanced with *display leaves* to represent arcs that would otherwise not be shown. Display leaves are labeled with a reference to the vertex to which they represent an arc. The problem of *graph* display is now limited to that of *tree* display. The special kind of tree being displayed is referred to as a *graph-tree* (Figure 2). The shared + node is now represented by its *instantiation* (on the right) labeled with a display reference: **0**, and by a display leaf (on the left) labeled *only* with the display reference.

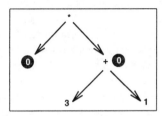

Figure 2: square (3 + 1) as a graph-tree

This might seem a rather drastic solution. In this example we already had planarity, and there will be non-planar graphs where planarity might be achieved much more simply, without the need to convert the graph into a tree. With the use of graph-trees there is also a danger of replacing the problem of deciphering a display complicated by crossing of arcs by the problem of disentangling *display references*: in order to identify a display leaf one has to find its instantiation by matching some visual label.

However the graph-tree:

- offers a simple and consistent technique;

- proves convenient when it comes to browsing and compacting the display;

- may be a useful intermediate representation from which to derive a cyclic yet still planar graph: joining display leaves to the vertex to which they refer, so long as this does not involve crossing an existing arc. The dual technique only breaks an arc if it crosses another — but lacks the advantage of intermediate representation as a tree which is more conveniently subjected to filtering.

4.2 Overcoming the problem of size I: Browsing

The problem of size, compounded by the addition of display leaves, may be simply resolved in two ways: by reducing the scale of the display, or by only showing part of it. But these both introduce further difficulties. Reducing the scale makes the labels harder, or impossible, to read; and showing only part of the display may cause the viewer to become disoriented in relation to the graph as a whole.

However the two solutions may be effectively combined by showing a *minigraph*, scaled to fit exactly into a small window, and using this as a map for browsing in the main display area, as advocated by Beard and Walker [1]. This has the advantage that all the structure is available to scrutiny if required, yet patterns within this, possibly hidden by the complexity of the full scale graph, may be revealed in the minigraph.

4.3   Overcoming the problem of size II: Filtering

In order to reduce the number of vertices in the graph to be displayed, without violating the meaning of the original graph, a quotient graph may be displayed instead. A cluster of vertices with their interconnecting arcs becomes **one** vertex in the quotient. This vertex inherits all the arcs from the vertices it incorporates that connect with the rest of the graph. The value of the new vertex is the piece of graph that it represents. The condensed sections retain their structure, which may be reconstituted on the basis of a mouse click. But the displayed label for the cluster may reflect any aspect of the part of the graph that it symbolises. This technique of condensing the graph is referred to as *spatial filtering*. It is a generalisation of a conventional technique: when graph reduction is presented, *Apply* nodes in the illustrative figures are frequently omited, as shown in Figure 3. This is equivalent to condensing a chain of Apply nodes, together with the function with which they are directly or indirectly associated. In the figure, dashed lines indicate arcs that will be collapsed.

In this case the label for the cluster of nodes is the function name, but the label needs to be specified independently from the clustering rule. It might, for example, include the size of the cluster that it represents.

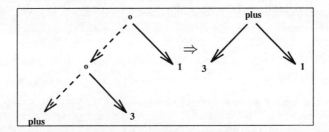

Figure 3: The effect of the NOAPPLY filter

4.4   Overcoming the problem of "Too many graphs to show"

The sequence of graphs may also be filtered so as only to show stages of interest. Defining the temporal filter in terms of adjacent graphs that may be regarded as equivalent rather than in terms of the properties of graphs of interest achieves a satisfying consistency: the user need only think in terms of compaction rules in both cases. This is

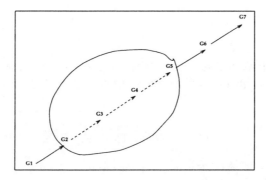

Figure 4: Collapsing a graph-chain: temporal filtering

illustrated in Figure 4 where, again, arcs to be collapsed are indicated by broken lines. G1, G2 etc. represent graphs in a reduction sequence. Usually the required display will be of the first graph or the last in the collapsed series.

The proposal is that the requisite quotient graphs be obtained in both spatial and temporal filtering by the definition of equivalence rules which determine whether two nodes are part of the same cluster, or two graphs part of the same series.

5 Defining the compaction

Both spatial and temporal filters require a compaction rule and a labeling function in their definition. The spatial filter comprises a quotient rule which determines whether two graph tree nodes are part of the same equivalence class, *i.e.* part of the same vertex in the clustered graph, and a labeling function which extracts information from the cluster tree at each vertex and formats this into a string label. The temporal filter analogously needs an equivalence rule to decide whether adjacent graphs are to be "collapsed" together, and a function which both selects a graph to display from the collapsed series, and may also collect information from the series of graphs to show with it, as a caption.

A bank of suitable rules and functions could be built into the system, possibly with facilities for composing them to give more flexibility. Ideally, however, the user would have the power to write his or her own filters in a *metalanguage* for expressing filtering rules. Such a metalanguage is being incorporated into the prototype, called whiff — for writing **h** interpreter **f**ilter **f**unctions.

For the system to be completely flexible and the user to have access to every aspect of the reduction process, the implementation of reduction and of filtering could be so closely tied that the user becomes an implementor. The ideal filtering provision lies between the two extremes of offering a choice of primitive filters and effectively exposing the implementation. What is needed is a simplified model of the interpreter that is consistent with the actual implementation.

5.1 Spatial filters

Spatial compaction rules

A spatial compaction rule determines whether two adjacent nodes are part of the same cluster, so that the arc between them will be "collapsed" in the clustered graph-tree.

```
type SpCompact = Node → Node → Bool
```

To express the rule, whiff offers primitives by which to refer to properties of a node. For example whiff has its own view of *nodekind* which does not mirror the datatypes in the implementation. The user may wish to express: "Is it a value?", "Is it an integer?", "Is it 12?". In whiff these become: is Val, is Int, and itis 12. Other attributes of a node reflect the information gathered by the interpreter during the reduction. In the prototype this includes: producer — the name of the function the application of which caused the node to be created; and step — the step number of its creation, thus indirectly, by reference to the current step number, also its age.

However the condition under which two nodes are to be part of the same cluster may involve their context in the display. For example a rule may only apply to nodes that are not descendants of the node currently being reduced. There is, then, a need for "family relationship" functions that transfer a whiff function to the relevant other node(s): *e.g.* parent — the display parent; anydescs — at least one descendant; child i — the child node at position i. As an example: parent (is Apply) is True if the display parent is an Apply node. The parent function can return any appropriate whiff value, and these may be combined using h functions and primitives in the definition of filters.

The availability of the parent function suggests that the spatial compaction rule may be defined solely in terms of a condition on the child node: if reference to the display parent is needed, the parent function may be used. The spatial compaction rule becomes a predicate which determines whether a node is coalesced with its parent:

```
type SpCompact = Node → Bool
```

A simple example of a spatial compaction rule is the NOAPPLY filter, illustrated in Figure 3, which may be defined at the hint interface as:

```
NOAPPLY = parent (is Apply) && ownpos == 0
```

Labeling the clustered graph tree

The compaction rule does not determine the appearance of the compacted graph. For this a labeling scheme is needed. Each vertex in the compacted graph represents a graph tree. A labeling function determines how the graph tree at each vertex is presented in the display. There may be alternative labeling functions for the same compaction rule.

As with the spatial filters, labeling functions might be provided as primitive for the user to choose and perhaps concatenate the output of several. An example would be "the leftmost node of the cluster tree", for use with the NOAPPLY filter. Other options could include a representation of the cluster tree as an expression, its size (number of raw graph tree nodes), the age of its root node in reduction steps, *etc.*. But here again it is preferable to have a consistent scheme, and to offer flexibility to users to define their own labels. The prototype system uses a folding function over the cluster tree, for which the user has to provide:

unit: a function to apply to leaves of type: `Node → info`

join: a function to apply at inner nodes of type: `Node → [info] → info`. The `[info]` is from the graph tree nodes below.

display: a function of type `info → String`, which controls the final formatting of the cluster label

The first two functions have the node in question as an implicit argument that may be accessed by `whiff` primitives; the display function also has appropriate primitives available, though its argument may also be explicitly referred to for manipulation by h functions. For example, to label application clusters created by the `NOAPPLY` filter with the function names, the unit function is: `u = show`, which shows a representation of the node, the join function: `j = head`, and the formatting function: `d = id`. The treefold arguments are associated using "keywords" u, j and d thus:

`NASHOW = u show j head d id`

The compaction rule and labeling function, which are defined separately and may be changed separately, may also be associated to create a named spatial filter thus:

`NA = (NOAPPLY,NASHOW)`

Examples of spatial filtering

To illustrate the definition, composition and visual effect of spatial filtering we take a step in the computation of the series of prime numbers using the sieve of Erastothenes. It is the one where the second number, 3, is just about to be output. Figure 5 gives the h definition of `primes`.

```
primes = sieve (from 2)
sieve pl = case pl of
              (p:l) -> sieve'
sieve' p l = p : sieve (pfilter p l)
pfilter p xl = case xl of
                 (x:l) -> pfilter' p
pfilter' p x l = if (x 'mod' p) == 0
                 then pfilter p l
                 else (x:pfilter p l)
from n = n : from (n + 1)
```

Figure 5: An h definition of `primes` using the sieve of Eratosthenes

Figure 6 shows the raw graph tree, and the effect of applying the `NOAPPLY` filter to this. The labeling function has been modified to include marking the node currently being reduced with ⁓, and representing display leaves as display references, here an integer between curly brackets. The {0} represents 3 in each case.

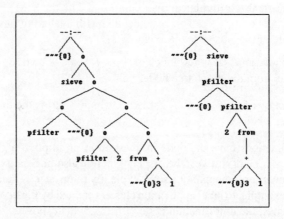

Figure 6: The raw graph and the effect of the NOAPPLY filter

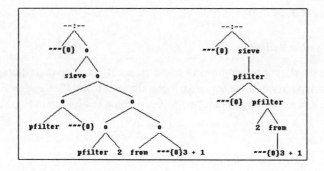

Figure 7: The ARITH filter, then this composed with the NOAPPLY filter

Figure 7 illustrates a slightly different view of the graph tree, using a spatial filter that collapses tree sections that represent arithmetic expressions. In this case it is labeled by the expression that it represents, using an "infix" function defined in h. The whiff definition of the compaction function, ARI is as follows:

```
ARI = parent AR
AR = is Mathop && alldescs (is Int || AR)
```

The labeling function shows leaf nodes unless they are display leaves, clustered sections are represented by infix expressions, and each vertex is also marked as appropriate with a display reference (sref) and whether it is the current focus of the reduction (sfocus).

```
ASHOW = u show j JAR d DAR
```

```
JAR lss = infix show lss
DAR ct = sfocus ++ sref ++ id ct
```

The spatial filter associates the compaction with the labeling: `ARITH = (ARI,ASHOW)`

Figure 7 also shows this arithmetical filter composed with the NOAPPLY filter: `NOAPAR = NOAPPLY || ARI`. This is associated with a labeling function that needs to take the nature of the cluster into account:

```
SCOMP = u show j JCOMP d DAR
JCOMP lss = if is Mathop && alldescs (is Int ||AR)
                then infix show lss else head lss
```

5.2 Temporal filters

The compacting and labeling elements of temporal filters have been combined in the prototype: the user is only able to define *checkpoints* which determine the graphs to show, and there is no extra "caption" information. Intermediate steps in the reduction are implicitly compacted. Checkpoints are displayed under the current spatial filter. Both the checkpointing function and the spatial filter, or either of its elements, may be changed at a checkpoint. Amongst other things this enables the user to see different views of a stage in the computation without the need to recompute.

Defining checkpoints

As the most likely graphs to be shown in a compacted series would be the first and/or the last, the checkpointing `whiff` primitives all exist in two forms to allow the user to choose which one as appropriate. For example the graph just before or just after any function application may be seen using definitions such as:
`CHECKBEFORE = isfun` or `CHECKAFTER = wasfun`, and to see both:
`CHECKBOTH = isfun || wasfun` To see graphs just before the application of a *particular* function, or set of functions one may use a definition such as:
`TARGETS = isin ["fname1","fname2", etc]`
The type of a checkpointing function is: `ReductionState → Bool`. Ideally all aspects of the reduction state would be accessible to the user *via* such primitives, including cumulative information such as the "function meter" that keeps track of the number of applications of each function,

The step illustrated in Figures 6 and 7 might have been defined as:
`FIGSTEP = hasout`: the step has some output, or even `FIGSTEP = outis "3"` indicating "show the graph when a 3 is about to be output". If the *next* graph had been wanted, the `hadout` and `outwas` primitives could have been used instead. A safeguard is needed to allow for a checkpoint never being reached in a non-terminating computation. This can be established by making use of a `gstep` primitive which returns the step number of the graph.

Other conditions on the overall state may also be of interest, such as the presence of particular application chains, but this would necessitate capabilities that the prototype system does not yet offer.

6 Future work

Browsing

A version of the prototype includes spatial browsing: clicking on the stub of an arc leading off the display brings the node to which it leads to the root of the display. For large displays it will probably be essential to include facilities such as this in order to explore the graph. The temporal equivalent of this is the capacity to "step" backwards and forwards in the reduction, to allow investigation of the *reduction-history space* [10].

Scaling up to full Haskell

Scaling the system up to include full Haskell would involve three main elements: type checking; local definitions; and conventional pattern matching. The first is well researched and would complicate the implementation, but should not be problematic. Local definitions are really needed: for example *circular* programs cannot be investigated using the current hint, yet their very circularity would make this of interest. Name clashes could be overcome, even allowing for anonymous definitions. The pattern matching should be displayed, as illustrated in hint in examples where Case expressions cascade, each "waiting" for the resolution of the next one. This may result in an unexpectedly large graph. The problem will be the translation of Haskell pattern matching to one that may be meaningfully displayed without overly complicating the display with pattern variables.

Marrying heap profiling and graph display

Experience with heap profiling suggests that there are occasions when the user would like to have more detailed information as to "what is going on". The ability to look at graphs with the aid of various filters may give the insight that at present is lacking. If both were available with the same system techniques could be developed for moving from one to the other.

The labeling of filtered graphs

Work is also needed on the *labeling* of filtered graphs. In the prototype labels are strings. It may be that this is too restrictive, and that a more useful system would make use of features such as: labels of varying depth, diagrammatic labeling, miniature graphs and the use of colour.

Filtering graphs rather than graph-trees

It would be interesting to develop a scheme of filtering graphs directly, without the intermediate representation as a graph-tree. The definition of the compaction rules there is complicated by a node having potentially more than one parent node. The display of the graph introduces the problem that graph-trees avoid: the crossing of arcs, but conversely it avoids the problems of graph-trees: the need for display references and the increased number of nodes to display.

The ideas of compacting a graph by equivalence rules, and providing a metalanguage for display rules, have potential for teaching and debugging, as well as for the investigation of time/space problems. Despite confirming the intractable nature of some of the problems, such as graph layout, use of the prototype also suggests that such a system would be worth developing further.

References

[1] David V. Beard and John Q. Walker II. Navigational techniques to improve the display of large two-dimensional spaces. *Behaviour and Information Technology*, 9(6):451–466, 1990.

[2] Chris Clack, Stuart Clayman, and David Parott. Lexical Profiling: Theory and Practice. Technical report, University College London, 1993 (to appear in the *Journal of Functional Programming*).

[3] Sandra P. Foubister. *Graphical application and visualization of lazy functional computation*. D.Phil thesis, University of York, 1995 (forthcoming).

[4] Samuel Kamin. A debugging environment for functional programming in Centaur. Technical Report 1265, INRIA - Sophia Antipolis, 1990.

[5] H. Lieberman. Steps Toward Better Debugging Tools for Lisp. In *ACM Symposium on LISP and Functional Programming*, pages 247–255, 1984.

[6] H. Nilsson and P. Fritzson. Algorithmic Debugging of Lazy Functional Languages. In M. Bruynooghe and M. Wirsing, editors, *Programming Language Implementation and Logic Programming*, pages 385–389, Leuven, Belgium, 1992. Springer Verlag.

[7] Simon Peyton Jones and David Lester. *Implementing functional languages: a tutorial*. Prentice Hall, 1992.

[8] Colin Runciman and David Wakeling. Heap profiling of lazy functional programs. *Journal of Functional Programming*, 3(2), 1993.

[9] Patrick M. Sansom. *Execution profiling for non-strict functional languages*. Ph.D. thesis, University of Glasgow, 1994.

[10] Robin A. Snyder. Lazy Debugging of Functional Programs. *New Generation Computing*, 8:139–161, 1990.

[11] J. Taylor. A System For Representing The Evaluation of Lazy Functions. Technical report, Department of Computer Science, Queen Mary and Westfield College, 1991.

A Tutorial on Co-induction and Functional Programming

Andrew D. Gordon*

University of Cambridge Computer Laboratory,
New Museums Site, Cambridge CB2 3QG, United Kingdom.
adg@cl.cam.ac.uk

Abstract

Co-induction is an important tool for reasoning about unbounded structures. This tutorial explains the foundations of co-induction, and shows how it justifies intuitive arguments about lazy streams, of central importance to lazy functional programmers. We explain from first principles a theory based on a new formulation of bisimilarity for functional programs, which coincides exactly with Morris-style contextual equivalence. We show how to prove properties of lazy streams by co-induction and derive Bird and Wadler's Take Lemma, a well-known proof technique for lazy streams.

The aim of this paper is to explain why co-inductive definitions and proofs by co-induction are useful to functional programmers.

Co-induction is dual to induction. To say a set is **inductively defined** just means it is the least solution of a certain form of inequation. For instance, the set of natural numbers $\mathbb{N}$ is the least solution (ordered by set inclusion, $\subseteq$) of the inequation

$$\{0\} \cup \{S(x) \mid x \in X\} \subseteq X. \tag{1}$$

The corresponding **induction principle** just says that if some other set satisfies the inequation, then it contains the inductively defined set. To prove a property of all numbers, let X be the set of numbers with that property and show that X satisfies inequation (1). If so then $\mathbb{N} \subseteq X$, since $\mathbb{N}$ is the least such set. This is simply mathematical induction.

Dually, a set is **co-inductively defined** if it is the greatest solution of a certain form of inequation. For instance, suppose that $\rightsquigarrow$ is the reduction relation in a functional language. The set of divergent programs, $\uparrow$, is the greatest solution of the inequation

$$X \subseteq \{a \mid \exists b(a \rightsquigarrow b \;\&\; b \in X)\}. \tag{2}$$

The corresponding **co-induction principle** is just that if some other set satisfies the inequation, then the co-inductively defined set contains it. For instance,

---

*Royal Society University Research Fellow.

suppose that program Ω reduces to itself, that is, $\Omega \leadsto \Omega$. To see that Ω is contained in $\uparrow$, consider set $X = \{\Omega\}$. Since X satisfies inequation (2), $X \subseteq \uparrow$, as $\uparrow$ is the greatest such set. Hence Ω is a member of $\uparrow$.

Bisimilarity is an equality based on operational behaviour. This paper seeks to explain why bisimilarity is an important co-inductive definition for functional programmers. Bisimilarity was introduced into computer science by Park (1981) and developed by Milner in his theory of CCS (1989). Bisimilarity in CCS is based on labelled transitions. A transition $a \xrightarrow{\alpha} b$ means that program (process) a can perform an observable action α to become successor program b. Any program gives rise to a (possibly infinite) **derivation tree**, whose nodes are programs and whose arcs are transitions, labelled by actions. Two programs are bisimilar if they root the same derivation trees, when one ignores the syntactic structure at the nodes. Bisimilarity is a way to compare behaviour, represented by actions, whilst discarding syntactic structure.

Contextual equivalence (Morris 1968) is widely accepted as the natural notion of operational equivalence for PCF-like languages (Milner 1977; Plotkin 1977). Two programs are contextually equivalent if, whenever they are each inserted into a hole in a larger program of integer type, the resulting programs either both converge or both diverge. The main technical novelty of this paper is to show how to define a labelled transition system for PCF-like languages (for instance, Miranda and Haskell) such that bisimilarity—operationally-defined behavioural equivalence—coincides with Morris' contextual equivalence. By virtue of this characterisation of contextual equivalence we can prove properties of functional programs using co-induction. We intend in a series of examples to show how co-induction formally captures and justifies intuitive operational arguments.

We begin in Section 1 by showing how induction and co-induction derive, dually, from the Tarski-Knaster fixpoint theorem. Section 2 introduces the small call-by-name functional language, essentially PCF extended with pairing and streams, that is the vehicle for the paper. We make two conventional definitions of divergence and contextual equivalence. In Section 3 we make a co-inductive definition of divergence, prove it equals the conventional one, and give an example of a co-inductive proof. The heart of the paper is Section 4 in which we introduce bisimilarity and prove it coincides with contextual equivalence. We give examples of co-inductive proofs and state a collection of useful equational properties. We derive the Take Lemma of Bird and Wadler (1988) by co-induction. Section 5 explains why bisimilarity is a precongruence, that is, preserved by arbitrary contexts, using Howe's method (1989). We summarise the paper in Section 6 and discuss related work.

This paper is intended to introduce the basic ideas of bisimilarity and co-induction from first principles. It should be possible to apply the theory developed in Section 4 without working through the details of Section 5, the hardest of the paper. In a companion paper (Gordon 1994a) we develop further co-inductive tools for functional programs. For more examples of bisimulation proofs see Milner (1989) or Gordon (1994b), for instance.

Here are our mathematical conventions. As usual we regard a **relation** $\mathcal{R}$ on a set X to be a subset of $X \times X$. If $\mathcal{R}$ is a relation then we write $x \,\mathcal{R}\, y$ to mean $(x, y) \in \mathcal{R}$. If $\mathcal{R}$ and $\mathcal{R}'$ are both relations on X then we write $\mathcal{R}\mathcal{R}'$ for their **relational composition**, that is, the relation such that $x\mathcal{R}\mathcal{R}'y$ iff there is z such that $x \,\mathcal{R}\, z$ and $z \,\mathcal{R}'\, y$. If $\mathcal{R}$ is a relation then $\mathcal{R}^{\mathrm{op}}$ is its **opposite**, the relation such that $x \,\mathcal{R}^{\mathrm{op}}\, y$ iff $y \,\mathcal{R}\, x$. If $\mathcal{R}$ is a relation, we write $\mathcal{R}^+$ for its transitive closure, and $\mathcal{R}^*$ for its reflexive and transitive closure.

1   A Tutorial on Induction and Co-induction

Let U be some universal set and $F : \wp(U) \to \wp(U)$ be a monotone function (that is, $F(X) \subseteq F(Y)$ whenever $X \subseteq Y$). Induction and co-induction are dual proof principles that derive from the definition of a set to be the least or greatest solution, respectively, of equations of the form $X = F(X)$.

First some definitions. A set $X \subseteq U$ is F-**closed** iff $F(X) \subseteq X$. Dually, a set $X \subseteq U$ is F-**dense** iff $X \subseteq F(X)$. A **fixpoint** of F is a solution of the equation $X = F(X)$. Let $\mu X. F(X)$ and $\nu X. F(X)$ be the following subsets of U.

$$\mu X. F(X) \stackrel{\text{def}}{=} \bigcap \{X \mid F(X) \subseteq X\}$$
$$\nu X. F(X) \stackrel{\text{def}}{=} \bigcup \{X \mid X \subseteq F(X)\}$$

Lemma 1

(1) $\mu X. F(X)$ *is the least F-closed set.*

(2) $\nu X. F(X)$ *is the greatest F-dense set.*

Proof   We prove (2); (1) follows by a dual argument. Since $\nu X. F(X)$ contains every F-dense set by construction, we need only show that it is itself F-dense, for which the following lemma suffices.

If every X_i is F-dense, so is the union $\bigcup_i X_i$.

Since $X_i \subseteq F(X_i)$ for every i, $\bigcup_i X_i \subseteq \bigcup_i F(X_i)$. Since F is monotone, $F(X_i) \subseteq F(\bigcup_i X_i)$ for each i. Therefore $\bigcup_i F(X_i) \subseteq F(\bigcup_i X_i)$, and so we have $\bigcup_i X_i \subseteq F(\bigcup_i X_i)$ by transitivity, that is, $\bigcup_i X_i$ is F-dense.   ∎

Theorem 1 (Tarski-Knaster)

(1) $\mu X. F(X)$ *is the least fixpoint of F.*

(2) $\nu X. F(X)$ *is the greatest fixpoint of F.*

Proof   Again we prove (2) alone; (1) follows by a dual argument. Let $\nu = \nu X. F(X)$. We have $\nu \subseteq F(\nu)$ by Lemma 1. So $F(\nu) \subseteq F(F(\nu))$ by monotonicity of F. But then $F(\nu)$ is F-dense, and therefore $F(\nu) \subseteq \nu$. Combining the inequalities we have $\nu = F(\nu)$; it is the greatest fixpoint because any other is F-dense, and hence contained in ν.   ∎

We say that $\mu X. F(X)$, the least solution of $X = F(X)$, is the set **inductively defined** by F, and dually, that $\nu X. F(X)$, the greatest solution of $X = F(X)$, is the set **co-inductively defined** by F. We obtain two dual proof principles associated with these definitions.

> **Induction:** $\mu X. F(X) \subseteq X$ if X is F-closed.
> **Co-induction:** $X \subseteq \nu X. F(X)$ if X is F-dense.

Let us revisit the example of mathematical induction, mentioned in the introduce. Suppose there is an element $0 \in U$ and an injective function $S : U \to U$. If we define a monotone function $F : \wp(U) \to \wp(U)$ by

$$F(X) \stackrel{\text{def}}{=} \{0\} \cup \{S(x) \mid x \in X\}$$

and set $\mathbb{N} \stackrel{\text{def}}{=} \mu X. F(X)$, the associated principle of induction is that $\mathbb{N} \subseteq X$ if $F(X) \subseteq X$, which is to say that

$$\mathbb{N} \subseteq X \text{ if both } 0 \in X \text{ and } S(x) \in X \text{ whenever } x \in X.$$

In other words, mathematical induction is a special case of this general framework. Winskel (1993) shows in detail how structural induction and rule induction, proof principles familiar to computer scientists, are induction principles obtained from particular kinds of inductive definition. As for examples of co-induction, Sections 3 and 4 are devoted to co-inductive definitions of program divergence and equivalence respectively. Aczel (1977) is the standard reference on inductive definitions. Davey and Priestley (1990) give a more recent account of fixpoint theory, including the Tarski-Knaster theorem.

2   A Small Functional Language

In this section we introduce a small call-by-name functional language. It is PCF extended with pairing and streams, a core fragment of a lazy language like Miranda or Haskell. We define its syntax, a type assignment relation, a 'one-step' reduction relation, $\rightsquigarrow$, and a 'big-step' evaluation relation, $\Downarrow$.

Let x and y range over a countable set of **variables**. The **types**, A, B, and **expressions**, e, are given by the following grammars.

$$A, B ::= \text{Int} \mid \text{Bool} \mid A \to A \mid (A, A) \mid [A]$$
$$e ::= x \mid e\,e \mid \lambda x{:}A.\,e \mid \text{if } e \text{ then } e \text{ else } e \mid k^A \mid \Omega^A \mid \delta^A$$

where k ranges over a finite collection of **builtin constants**, Ω is the **divergent constant** and δ ranges over a finite collection of **user-defined constants**. We assume these include map, iterate, take and filter; we give informal definitions below. The builtin constants are listed below. We say that k^A is

admissable if $k{:}A$ is an instance of one of the following schemas.

$$\underline{tt}, \underline{f\!f} : \texttt{Bool} \qquad\qquad \underline{i} : \texttt{Int}$$
$$\texttt{succ}, \texttt{pred} : \texttt{Int} \to \texttt{Int} \qquad \texttt{zero} : \texttt{Int} \to \texttt{Bool}$$
$$\texttt{fst} : (A, B) \to A \qquad\qquad \texttt{snd} : (A, B) \to B$$
$$\texttt{Pair} : A \to B \to (A, B) \quad \texttt{Nil} : [A]$$
$$\texttt{Cons} : A \to [A] \to [A] \qquad \texttt{scase} : B \to (A \to [A] \to B) \to [A] \to B$$

For each user-defined constant δ we assume given a definition $\delta{:}A \stackrel{\text{def}}{=} e_\delta$. In effect these are definitions by mutual recursion, as each body e_δ can contain occurrences of any constant; hence there is no need for an explicit $\texttt{fix}$ operator. We identify expressions up to alpha-conversion; that is, renaming of bound variables. We write $e[e'/x]$ for the substitution of expression e' for each variable x free in expression e. A **context**, $\mathcal{C}$, is an expression with one or more **holes**. A hole is written as $[\,]$ and we write $\mathcal{C}[e]$ for the outcome of filling each hole in $\mathcal{C}$ with the expression e.

The **type assignment** relation

$$\Gamma \vdash e : A \qquad \text{where } \Gamma \text{ is } x_1{:}A_1, \dots, x_n{:}A_n,$$

is given inductively by rules of simply typed λ-calculus plus

$$\frac{k^A \text{ admissable}}{\Gamma \vdash k^A : A} \qquad \frac{}{\Gamma \vdash \Omega^A : A} \qquad \frac{\delta{:}A \stackrel{\text{def}}{=} e}{\Gamma \vdash \delta : A}$$

$$\frac{\Gamma \vdash e_1 : \texttt{Bool} \qquad \Gamma \vdash e_2 : A \qquad \Gamma \vdash e_3 : A}{\Gamma \vdash \texttt{if } e_1 \texttt{ then } e_2 \texttt{ else } e_3 : A}$$

We assume that $\varnothing \vdash e_\delta : A$ is derivable whenever $\delta{:}A \stackrel{\text{def}}{=} e_\delta$ is a definition of a user-defined constant. Type assignment is unique in the sense that whenever $\Gamma \vdash e : A$ and $\Gamma \vdash e : B$, then $A = B$.

Given the type assignment relation, we can construct the following universal sets and relations.

$$Prog(A) \stackrel{\text{def}}{=} \{e \mid \varnothing \vdash e : A\} \qquad\qquad \text{(programs of type } A)$$
$$a, b \in Prog \stackrel{\text{def}}{=} \textstyle\bigcup_A Prog(A) \qquad\qquad \text{(programs of any type)}$$
$$Rel(A) \stackrel{\text{def}}{=} \{(a, b) \mid \{a, b\} \subseteq Prog(A)\} \quad \text{(total relation on } A \text{ programs)}$$
$$\mathcal{R}, \mathcal{S} \subseteq Rel \stackrel{\text{def}}{=} \textstyle\bigcup_A Rel(A) \qquad\qquad \text{(total relation on programs)}$$

The operational semantics is a one-step reduction relation, $\leadsto \subseteq Rel$. It is inductively defined by the axiom schemes

$$(\lambda x . e)a \leadsto e[a/x] \qquad\qquad \delta_i \leadsto e_i \quad \text{if } \delta_i \stackrel{\text{def}}{=} e_i$$
$$\Omega \leadsto \Omega \qquad \texttt{if } \underline{\ell} \texttt{ then } a_{tt} \texttt{ else } a_{f\!f} \leadsto a_\ell \quad \ell \in \{tt, f\!f\}$$
$$\texttt{succ } \underline{i} \leadsto \underline{i+1} \qquad\qquad \texttt{pred } \underline{i+1} \leadsto \underline{i}$$
$$\texttt{zero } \underline{0} \leadsto \underline{tt} \qquad\qquad \texttt{zero } \underline{i} \leadsto \underline{f\!f} \quad \text{if } i \neq 0$$
$$\texttt{fst } (\texttt{Pair } a\,b) \leadsto a \qquad\qquad \texttt{snd } (\texttt{Pair } a\,b) \leadsto b$$
$$\texttt{scase } f\,b\,\texttt{Nil} \leadsto b \qquad \texttt{scase } f\,b\,(\texttt{Cons } a\,as) \leadsto f\,a\,as$$

together with the scheme of structural rules

$$\frac{a \rightsquigarrow b}{\mathcal{E}[a] \rightsquigarrow \mathcal{E}[b]}$$

where $\mathcal{E}$ is an **experiment** (a kind of atomic **evaluation context** (Felleisen and Friedman 1986)), a context generated by the grammar

$$\mathcal{E} ::= [\,]\,a \mid \text{succ}\,[\,] \mid \text{pred}\,[\,] \mid \text{zero}\,[\,] \mid \text{if}\,[\,]\,\text{then}\,a\,\text{else}\,b$$
$$\mid \quad \text{fst}\,[\,] \mid \text{snd}\,[\,] \mid \text{scase}\,a\,b\,[\,].$$

In other words the single structural rule above abbreviates eight different rules, one for each kind of experiment. Together they specify a deterministic, call-by-name evaluation strategy. Now we can make the usual definitions of evaluation, convergence and divergence.

$$a \rightsquigarrow \stackrel{\text{def}}{=} \exists b(a \rightsquigarrow b) \qquad \text{'p reduces'}$$
$$a \Downarrow b \stackrel{\text{def}}{=} a \rightsquigarrow^* b \,\&\, \neg(b \rightsquigarrow) \qquad \text{'a evaluates to b'}$$
$$a\Downarrow \stackrel{\text{def}}{=} \exists b(a \Downarrow b) \qquad \text{'a converges'}$$
$$a\Uparrow \stackrel{\text{def}}{=} \text{whenever } a \rightsquigarrow^* b, \text{ then } b \rightsquigarrow \quad \text{'a diverges'}$$

By expanding the definition we can easily check that $\Downarrow$ and $\Uparrow$ are complementary, that is, $a\Uparrow$ iff $\neg a\Downarrow$. We can characterise the answers returned by the evaluation relation, $\Downarrow$, as follows. Let an $\rightsquigarrow$ **normal program** be a program a such that $\neg(a \rightsquigarrow)$. Let a **value**, u or v, be a program generated by the grammar

$$v ::= \lambda x.\, e \mid k \mid k_2\, a \mid k_2\, a\, b \text{ where } k_2 \in \{\text{Pair}, \text{Cons}, \text{scase}\}.$$

Lemma 2 *A program is a value iff it is $\rightsquigarrow$ normal.*

Proof By inspection, each value is clearly $\rightsquigarrow$ normal. For the other direction, one can easily prove by structural induction on a, that a is a value if it is $\rightsquigarrow$ normal. ∎

Two programs are contextually equivalent if they can be freely interchanged for one another in a larger program, without changing its observable behaviour. This is a form of Morris' "extensional equivalence" (Morris 1968). Here is the formal definition of **contextual equivalence**, $\simeq \subseteq Rel$. Recall that $\mathcal{C}$ stands for contexts.

$$a \sqsubseteq b \text{ iff } \text{whenever } (\mathcal{C}[a], \mathcal{C}[b]) \in Rel(\text{Int}), \text{ that } \mathcal{C}[a]\Downarrow \text{ implies } \mathcal{C}[b]\Downarrow.$$
$$a \simeq b \text{ iff } a \sqsubseteq b \text{ and } b \sqsubseteq a.$$

We have formalised 'observable behaviour' as termination at integer type. The relation is unchanged if we specify that $\mathcal{C}[a]$ and $\mathcal{C}[b]$ should both evaluate to the same integer. Contextual equivalence does not discriminate on grounds of termination at function or pair type. For instance, we will be able to prove that $\Omega^{A \to B} \simeq \lambda x{:}A.\, \Omega^B$. The two would be distinguished in a call-by-value setting, since one diverges and the other converges, but in our call-by-name setting no context of integer type can tell them apart.

We have introduced the syntax and operational semantics of a small functional language. Our definitions of divergence and contextual equivalence are natural and intuitive, but do not lend themselves to proof. In the next two sections we develop co-inductive characterisations of both divergence and contextual equivalence. Hence we obtain a theory admitting proofs of program properties by co-induction.

3 A Co-inductive Definition of Divergence

We can characterise divergence co-inductively in terms of unbounded reduction. Let $\mathcal{D} : \wp(Prog) \to \wp(Prog)$ and $\uparrow \subseteq Prog$ be

$$\mathcal{D}(X) \stackrel{\text{def}}{=} \{a \mid \exists b(a \leadsto b \;\&\; b \in X)\}$$
$$\uparrow \stackrel{\text{def}}{=} \nu X. \mathcal{D}(X)$$

We can easily see that $\mathcal{D}$ is monotone. Hence by its co-inductive definition we have:

$\uparrow$ is the greatest $\mathcal{D}$-dense set and $\uparrow = \mathcal{D}(\uparrow)$.

Hughes and Moran (1993) give an alternative, 'big-step', co-inductive formulation of divergence.

As a simple example we can show that $\Omega\uparrow$. Let $X_\Omega \stackrel{\text{def}}{=} \{\Omega\}$. X_Ω is $\mathcal{D}$-dense, that is, $X_\Omega \subseteq \mathcal{D}(X_\Omega)$, because $\Omega \leadsto \Omega$ and $\Omega \in X_\Omega$. So $X_\Omega \subseteq \uparrow$ by co-induction, and therefore $\Omega\uparrow$.

We have an obligation to show that this co-inductive definition matches the earlier one, that $a\Uparrow$ iff whenever $a \leadsto^* b$, then $b \leadsto$.

Theorem 2 $\Uparrow = \uparrow$.

Proof $(\uparrow \subseteq \Uparrow)$. Suppose that $a\uparrow$. We must show whenever $a \leadsto^* b$, that $b \leadsto$. If $a\uparrow$, then $a \in \mathcal{D}(\uparrow)$ so there is an a' with $a \leadsto a'$ and $a'\uparrow$. Furthermore since reduction is deterministic, a' is unique. Hence, whenever $a\uparrow$ and $a \leadsto^* b$ it must be that $b\uparrow$. Therefore $b \leadsto$.

$(\Uparrow \subseteq \uparrow)$. By co-induction it suffices to prove that set $\Uparrow$ is $\mathcal{D}$-dense. Suppose that $a\Uparrow$. Since $a \leadsto^* a$, we have $a \leadsto$, that is, $a \leadsto b$ for some b. But whenever $b \leadsto^* b'$ it must be that $a \leadsto^* b'$ too, and in fact $b' \leadsto$ since $a\Uparrow$. Hence $b\Uparrow$ too, $a \in \mathcal{D}(\Uparrow)$ and $\Uparrow$ is $\mathcal{D}$-dense. ∎

4 A Co-inductive Definition of Equivalence

We begin with a **labelled transition system** that characterises the immediate observations one can make of a program. It is defined in terms of the one-step operational semantics, and in some sense characterises the interface between the language's interpreter and the outside world. It is a a family of relations $(\stackrel{\alpha}{\longrightarrow} \subseteq Prog \times Prog \mid \alpha \in Act)$, indexed by the set Act of **actions**. If we let Lit, the set of **literals**, indexed by ℓ, be $\{tt, ff\} \cup \{\ldots, -2, -1, 0, 1, 2, \ldots\}$, the actions are given as follows.

$$\alpha, \beta \in Act \overset{\text{def}}{=} Lit \cup \{@a \mid a \in Prog\} \cup \{\texttt{fst}, \texttt{snd}, \texttt{Nil}, \texttt{hd}, \texttt{tl}\}$$

We partition the set of types into active and passive types. The intention is that we can directly observe termination of programs of active type, but not those of passive type. Let a type be **active** iff it has the form $\texttt{Bool}$, $\texttt{Int}$ or $[A]$. Let a type be **passive** iff it has the form $A \to B$ or $\texttt{Pair}\, A\, B$. Arbitrarily we define $\mathbf{0} \overset{\text{def}}{=} \Omega^{\texttt{Int}}$. Given these definitions, the labelled transition system may be defined inductively as follows.

$$\ell \overset{\ell}{\longrightarrow} \mathbf{0} \qquad \texttt{Nil} \overset{\texttt{Nil}}{\longrightarrow} \mathbf{0} \qquad \texttt{Cons}\, a\, b \overset{\texttt{hd}}{\longrightarrow} a \qquad \texttt{Cons}\, a\, b \overset{\texttt{tl}}{\longrightarrow} b$$

$$\frac{a\, b \in Prog}{a \overset{@b}{\longrightarrow} a\, b} \qquad \frac{a \in Prog((A,B))}{a \overset{\texttt{fst}}{\longrightarrow} \texttt{fst}\, a} \qquad \frac{a \in Prog((A,B))}{a \overset{\texttt{snd}}{\longrightarrow} \texttt{snd}\, a}$$

$$\frac{a \rightsquigarrow a'' \qquad a'' \overset{\alpha}{\longrightarrow} a'}{a \overset{\alpha}{\longrightarrow} a'} \quad \left\{ \begin{array}{l} a \in Prog(A) \\ A \text{ active} \end{array} \right.$$

The **derivation tree** of a program a is the potentially infinite tree whose nodes are programs, whose arcs are labelled transitions, and which is rooted at a. For instance, the trees of the constant Ω^A are empty if A is active. In particular, the tree of $\mathbf{0}$ is empty. We use $\mathbf{0}$ in defining the transition system to indicate that after observing the value of a literal there is nothing more to observe. Following Milner (1989), we wish to regard two programs as behaviourally equivalent iff their derivation trees are isomorphic when we ignore the syntactic structure of the programs labelling the nodes. We formalise this idea by requiring our behavioural equivalence to be a relation $\sim \,\subseteq Rel$ that satisfies property $(*)$: whenever $(a,b) \in Rel$, $a \sim b$ iff

(1) Whenever $a \overset{\alpha}{\longrightarrow} a'$ there is b' with $b \overset{\alpha}{\longrightarrow} b'$ and $a' \sim b'$;

(2) Whenever $b \overset{\alpha}{\longrightarrow} b'$ there is a' with $a \overset{\alpha}{\longrightarrow} a'$ and $a' \sim b'$.

In fact there are many such relations; the empty set is one. We are after the largest or most generous such relation. We can define it co-inductively as follows. First define two functions $[-], \langle - \rangle : \wp(Rel) \to \wp(Rel)$ by

$$[S] \overset{\text{def}}{=} \{(a,b) \mid \text{whenever } a \overset{\alpha}{\longrightarrow} a' \text{ there is } b' \text{ with } b \overset{\alpha}{\longrightarrow} b' \text{ and } a'\, S\, b'\}$$
$$\langle S \rangle \overset{\text{def}}{=} [S] \cap [S^{\text{op}}]^{\text{op}}$$

where $S \subseteq Rel$. By examining element-wise expansions of these definitions, it is not hard to check that a relation satisfies property $(*)$ iff it is a fixpoint of function $\langle - \rangle$. One can easily check that both functions $[-]$ and $\langle - \rangle$ are monotone. Hence what we seek, the greatest relation to satisfy $(*)$, does exist, and equals $\nu S.\langle S \rangle$, the greatest fixpoint of $\langle - \rangle$. We make the following standard definitions (Milner 1989).

- **Bisimilarity**, $\sim \,\subseteq Rel$, is $\nu S.\langle S \rangle$.

- A **bisimulation** is an $\langle - \rangle$-dense relation.

Bisimilarity is the greatest bisimulation and $\sim = \langle\sim\rangle$. Again by expanding the definitions we can see that relation $S \subseteq Rel$ is a bisimulation iff $a\,S\,b$ implies

- Whenever $a \xrightarrow{\alpha} a'$ there is b' with $b \xrightarrow{\alpha} b'$ and $a'\,S\,b'$;
- Whenever $b \xrightarrow{\alpha} b'$ there is a' with $a \xrightarrow{\alpha} a'$ and $a'\,S\,b'$.

An asymmetric version of bisimilarity is of interest too.

- **Similarity**, $\precsim \subseteq Rel$, is $\nu S.\,[S]$.
- A **simulation** is an $[-]$-dense relation.

We can easily establish the following basic facts.

Lemma 3

(1) $\precsim$ *is a preorder and* $\sim$ *an equivalence relation.*

(2) $\sim\, = \,\precsim \cap \precsim^{\mathrm{op}}$.

(3) *Both* $\rightsquigarrow\, \subseteq\, \sim$ *and* $\Downarrow\, \subseteq\, \sim$.

Proof These are easily proved by co-induction. We omit the details. Parts (2) and (3) depend on the determinacy of $\rightsquigarrow$. Part (1) corresponds to Proposition 4.2 of Milner (1989). ∎

4.1 A co-inductive proof about lazy streams

To motivate study of bisimilarity, let us see how straightforward it is to use co-induction to establish that two lazy streams are bisimilar. Suppose map and iterate are a couple of builtin constants specified by the following equations.

```
map f Nil = Nil
map f (Cons x xs) = Cons (f x) (map f xs)
iterate f x = Cons x (iterate f (f x))
```

These could easily be turned into formal definitions of two user-defined constants, but we omit the details. Pattern matching on streams would be accomplished using scase. Intuitively the streams

$$\text{iterate}\,f\,(f\,x) \quad\text{and}\quad \text{map}\,f\,(\text{iterate}\,f\,x)$$

are equal, because they both consist of the sequence

$$f\,x,\quad f\,(f\,x),\quad f\,(f\,(f\,x)),\quad f\,(f\,(f\,(f\,x))),\quad \ldots$$

We cannot directly prove this equality by induction, because there is no argument to induct on. Instead we can easily prove it by co-induction, via the following lemma.

Lemma 4 *If* $S \subseteq Rel$ *is*

$$\{(\text{iterate}\,f\,(f\,x), \text{map}\,f\,(\text{iterate}\,f\,x)) \mid$$
$$\exists A(x \in Prog(A)\ \&\ f \in Prog(A \to A))\}$$

then $(S \cup \sim) \subseteq \langle S \cup \sim \rangle$.

Proof   It suffices to show that $S \subseteq \langle S \cup \sim \rangle$ and $\sim \subseteq \langle S \cup \sim \rangle$. The latter is obvious, as $\sim = \langle \sim \rangle$. To show $S \subseteq \langle S \cup \sim \rangle$ we must consider arbitrary a and b such that $a \, S \, b$, and establish that each transition $a \xrightarrow{\alpha} a'$ is matched by a transition $b \xrightarrow{\alpha} b'$, such that either $a' \, S \, b'$ or $a' \sim b'$, and vice versa. Suppose then that a is iterate $f \, (f \, x)$, and b is map f (iterate $f \, x$). We can calculate the following reductions.

$$a \rightsquigarrow^{+} \text{Cons} \, (f \, x) \, (\text{iterate} \, f \, (f \, (f \, x)))$$
$$b \rightsquigarrow^{+} \text{Cons} \, (f \, x) \, (\text{map} \, f \, (\text{iterate} \, f \, (f \, x)))$$

Whenever $a \rightsquigarrow^{*} a'$ we can check that $a \xrightarrow{\alpha} a''$ iff $a' \xrightarrow{\alpha} a''$. Using the reductions above we can enumerate all the transitions of a and b.

$$a \xrightarrow{\text{hd}} f \, x \tag{1}$$

$$a \xrightarrow{\text{tl}} \text{iterate} \, f \, (f \, (f \, x)) \tag{2}$$

$$b \xrightarrow{\text{hd}} f \, x \tag{3}$$

$$b \xrightarrow{\text{tl}} \text{map} \, f \, (\text{iterate} \, f \, (f \, x)) \tag{4}$$

Now it is plain that $(a, b) \in \langle S \cup \sim \rangle$. Transition (1) is matched by (3), and vice versa, with $f \, x \sim f \, x$ (since $\sim$ is reflexive). Transition (2) is matched by (4), and vice versa, with iterate $f \, (f \, (f \, x)) \, S$ map f (iterate $f \, (f \, x)$). ∎

Since $S \cup \sim$ is $\langle - \rangle$-dense, it follows that $(S \cup \sim) \subseteq \sim$. A corollary then is that

$$\text{iterate} \, f \, (f \, x) \sim \text{map} \, f \, (\text{iterate} \, f \, x)$$

for any suitable f and x, what we set out to show.

4.2   Operational Extensionality

We have an obligation to show that bisimilarity, $\sim$, equals contextual equivalence, $\simeq$. The key fact we need is the following, that bisimilarity is a precongruence.

Theorem 3 (Precongruence) *If $a \sim b$ then $C[a] \sim C[b]$ for any suitable context C. The same holds for similarity, $\lesssim$.*

The proof is non-trivial; we shall postpone it till Section 5.

Lemma 5 $\sqsubseteq \, = \, \lesssim$.

Proof   ($\lesssim \, \subseteq \, \sqsubseteq$) Suppose $a \lesssim b$, that $(C[a], C[b]) \in Rel(\text{Int})$ and that $C[a]\Downarrow$. By precongruence, $C[a] \lesssim C[b]$, so $C[b]\Downarrow$ too. Hence $a \sqsubseteq b$ as required.

($\sqsubseteq \, \subseteq \, \lesssim$) This follows if we can prove that contextual order $\sqsubseteq$ is a simulation. The details are not hard, and we omit them. For full details of a similar proof see Lemma 4.29 of Gordon (1994b), which was based on Theorem 3 of Howe (1989). ∎

Contextual equivalence and bisimilarity are the symmetrisations of contextual order and similarity, respectively. Hence a corollary, usually known as **operational extensionality** (Bloom 1988), is that bisimilarity equals contextual equivalence.

Theorem 4 (Operational Extensionality) $\simeq \; = \; \sim$.

4.3   A Theory of Bisimilarity

We have defined bisimilarity as a greatest fixpoint, shown it to be a co-inductive characterisation of contextual equivalence, and illustrated how it admits co-inductive proofs of lazy streams. In this section we shall note without proof various equational properties needed in a theory of functional programming. Proofs of similar properties, but for a different form of bisimilarity, can be found in Gordon (1994b). We noted already that $\rightsquigarrow \; \subseteq \; \sim$, which justifies a collection of beta laws. We can easily prove the following unrestricted eta laws by co-induction.

Proposition 1 (Eta) *If* $a \in Prog(A \rightarrow B)$, $a \sim \lambda x. a\,x$.

Proposition 2 (Surjective Pairing)
If $a \in Prog((A, B))$, $a \sim \texttt{Pair}\,(\texttt{fst}\,a)\,(\texttt{snd}\,a)$.

Furthermore we have an unrestricted principle of extensionality for functions.

Proposition 3 (Extensionality) *Suppose* $\{f, g\} \subseteq Prog(A \rightarrow B)$. *If* $f\,a \sim g\,a$ *for any* $a \in Prog(A)$, *then* $f \sim g$.

Here are two properties relating Ω and divergence.

Proposition 4 (Divergence)

(1) $\mathcal{E}[\Omega] \sim \Omega$ *for any experiment* $\mathcal{E}$.

(2) *If* $a\Uparrow$ *then* $a \sim \Omega$.

As promised, we can prove that $\lambda x{:}A.\,\Omega^B \simeq \Omega^{A \rightarrow B}$, in fact by proving $\lambda x{:}A.\,\Omega^B \sim \Omega^{A \rightarrow B}$. Consider any $a \in Prog(A)$. We have $(\lambda x{:}A.\,\Omega^B)\,a \sim \Omega^B$ by beta reduction and $\Omega^{A \rightarrow B}\,a \sim \Omega^B$ by part (1) of the last proposition. Hence $\lambda x{:}A.\,\Omega^B \sim \Omega^{A \rightarrow B}$ by extensionality. In fact, then, the converse of (2) is false, for $\lambda x{:}A.\,\Omega^B \sim \Omega^{A \rightarrow B}$ but $\lambda x{:}A.\,\Omega^B \Downarrow$.

We can easily prove the following adequacy result.

Proposition 5 (Adequacy) *If* $a \in Prog(A)$ *and* A *is active,* $a\Uparrow$ *iff* $a \sim \Omega$.

The condition that A be active is critical, because of our example $\lambda x{:}A.\,\Omega^B \sim \Omega^{A \rightarrow B}$, for instance.

Every convergent program equals a value, but the syntax of values includes partial applications of curried function constants. Instead we can characterise each of the types by the simpler grammar of **canonical programs**.

$$c ::= \ell \mid \lambda x.\,e \mid \texttt{Pair}\,a\,b \mid \texttt{Nil} \mid \texttt{Cons}\,a\,b.$$

Proposition 6 (Exhaustion) *For any program* $a \in Prog(A)$ *there is a canonical program* c *with* $a \sim c$ *iff either* a *converges or* A *is passive.*

The λ, Pair and Cons operations are injective in the following sense.

Proposition 7 (Canonical Freeness)

(1) *If $\lambda x{:}A.\,e \sim \lambda x{:}A.\,e'$ then $e[a/x] \sim e'[a/x]$ for any $a \in Prog(A)$.*

(2) *If* Pair $a_1\,a_2 \sim$ Pair $b_1\,b_2$ *then $a_1 \sim b_1$ and $a_2 \sim b_2$.*

(3) *If* Cons $a_1\,a_2 \sim$ Cons $b_1\,b_2$ *then $a_1 \sim b_1$ and $a_2 \sim b_2$.*

4.4 Bird and Wadler's Take Lemma

Our final example in this paper is to derive Bird and Wadler's Take Lemma (1988) to illustrate how a proof principle usually derived by domain-theoretic fixpoint induction follows also from co-induction.

We begin with the take function, which returns a finite approximation to an infinite list.

```
take 0 xs = Nil
take n Nil = Nil
take (n+1) (Cons x xs) = Cons x (take n xs)
```

Here is the key lemma.

Lemma 6 *Define $S \subseteq Rel$ by $a\,S\,b$ iff $\forall n \in \mathbb{N}$(take $\underline{n+1}\,a \sim$ take $\underline{n+1}\,b$).*

(1) *Whenever $a\,S\,b$ and $a \Downarrow$ Nil, $b \Downarrow$ Nil too.*

(2) *Whenever $a\,S\,b$ and $a \Downarrow$ Cons $a'\,a''$ there are b' and b'' with $b \Downarrow$ Cons $b'\,b''$, $a' \sim b'$ and $a''\,S\,b''$.*

(3) *$(S \cup \sim) \subseteq \langle S \cup \sim \rangle$.*

Proof   Recall that values of stream type take the form Nil or Cons $a\,b$. For any program, a, of stream type, either $a{\Uparrow}$ or there is a value v with $a \Downarrow v$. Hence for any stream a, either $a \sim \Omega$ (from $a{\Uparrow}$ by adequacy, Proposition 5) or $a \Downarrow$ Nil or $a \Downarrow$ Cons $a'\,a''$. Note also the following easily proved lemma about transitions of programs of active type, such as streams.

Whenever $a \in Prog(A)$ and A active, $a \xrightarrow{\alpha} b$ iff $\exists$value v $(a \Downarrow v \xrightarrow{\alpha} b)$.

(1) Using $a\,S\,b$ and $n = 0$ we have take $\underline{1}\,a \sim$ take $\underline{1}\,b$. Since $a \Downarrow$ Nil, we have $a \sim$ Nil, and in fact that Nil $\sim$ take $\underline{1}\,b$ by definition of take. We know that either $b \sim \Omega$, $b \Downarrow$ Nil or $b \Downarrow$ Cons $b'\,b''$. The first and third possibilities would contradict Nil $\sim$ take $\underline{1}\,b$, so it must be that $b \Downarrow$ Nil.

(2) We have

take $\underline{n+1}$ (Cons $a'\,a''$) $\sim$ take $\underline{n+1}\,b$.

With $n = 0$ we have

Cons a' Nil $\sim$ take $\underline{1}\,b$

which rules out the possibilities that $b \sim \Omega$ or $b \Downarrow \mathtt{Nil}$, so it must be that $b \Downarrow \mathtt{Cons}\ b'\ b''$. So we have

$$\mathtt{Cons}\ a'\ (\mathtt{take}\ \underline{n}\ a'') \sim \mathtt{Cons}\ b'\ (\mathtt{take}\ \underline{n}\ b'')$$

for any n, and hence $a' \sim b'$ and $a''\ \mathcal{S}\ b''$ by canonical freeness, Proposition 7.
(3) As before it suffices to prove that $\mathcal{S} \subseteq \langle \mathcal{S} \cup \sim \rangle$. Suppose that $a\ \mathcal{S}\ b$. For each transition $a \stackrel{\alpha}{\longrightarrow} a'$ we must exhibit b' satisfying $b \stackrel{\alpha}{\longrightarrow} b'$ and either $a'\ \mathcal{S}\ b'$ or $a' \sim b'$. Since a and b are streams, there are three possible actions α to consider.

(1) Action α is $\mathtt{Nil}$. Hence $a \Downarrow \mathtt{Nil}$ and a' is $\mathbf{0}$. By part (1), $b \Downarrow \mathtt{Nil}$ too. Hence $b \stackrel{\mathtt{Nil}}{\longrightarrow} \mathbf{0}$, and $\mathbf{0} \sim \mathbf{0}$ as required.

(2) Action α is $\mathtt{hd}$. Hence $a \Downarrow \mathtt{Cons}\ a'\ a''$. By part (2), there are b' and b'' with $b \Downarrow \mathtt{Cons}\ b'\ b''$, hence $b \stackrel{\mathtt{hd}}{\longrightarrow} b'$, and in fact $a' \sim b'$ by part (2).

(3) Action α is $\mathtt{tl}$. Hence $a \Downarrow \mathtt{Cons}\ a'\ a''$. By part (2), there are b' and b'' with $b \Downarrow \mathtt{Cons}\ b'\ b''$, hence $b \stackrel{\mathtt{tl}}{\longrightarrow} b''$, and in fact $a''\ \mathcal{S}\ b''$ by part (2).

This completes the proof of (3). ∎

The Take Lemma is a corollary of (3) by co-induction.

Theorem 5 (Take Lemma) *Suppose $a, b \in Prog([A])$.*
Then $a \sim b$ iff $\forall n \in \mathbb{N}(\mathtt{take}\ \underline{n+1}\ a \sim \mathtt{take}\ \underline{n+1}\ b)$.

See Bird and Wadler (1988) and Sander (1992), for instance, for examples of how the Take Lemma reduces a proof of equality of infinite streams to an induction over all their finite approximations.

Example equations such as

$$\mathtt{map}\ (f \circ g)\ as\ \sim\ \mathtt{map}\ f\ (\mathtt{map}\ g\ as)$$

(where o is function composition) in which the stream processing function preserves the size of its argument are easily proved using either co-induction or the Take Lemma. In either case we proceed by a simple case analysis of whether $as \Uparrow$, $as \Downarrow \mathtt{Nil}$ or $as \Downarrow \mathtt{Cons}\ a\ as'$. Suppose however that $\mathtt{filter}\ f$ is the stream processing function that returns a stream of all the elements a of its argument such that $f\ a \Downarrow \underline{tt}$. Intuitively the following equation should hold

$$\mathtt{filter}\ f\ (\mathtt{map}\ g\ as)\ \sim\ \mathtt{map}\ g\ (\mathtt{filter}\ (f \circ g)\ as)$$

but straightforward attacks on this problem using either the Take Lemma or co-induction in the style of Lemma 4 fail. The trouble is that the result stream may not have as many elements as the argument stream.

These proof attempts can be repaired by resorting to a more sophisticated analysis of as than above. Lack of space prevents their inclusion, but in this way we can obtain proofs of the equation using either the Take Lemma or a simple co-induction. Alternatively, by more refined forms of co-induction—developed elsewhere (Gordon 1994a)—we can prove such equations using a simple-minded case analysis of the behaviour of as. These proof principles need more effort to justify than the Take Lemma, but in problems like the `map/filter` equation are easier to use.

5 Proof that Bisimilarity is a Precongruence

In this section we make good our promise to show that bisimilarity and similarity are precongruences, Theorem 3. We need to extend relations such as bisimilarity to open expressions rather than simply programs. Let a **proved expression** be a triple (Γ, e, A) such that $\Gamma \vdash e : A$. If $\Gamma = x_1{:}A_1, \ldots, x_n{:}A_n$, a Γ-**closure** is a substitution $\cdot[\vec{a}/\vec{x}]$ where each $a_i \in Prog(A_i)$. Now if $\mathcal{R} \subseteq Rel$, let its **open extension**, $\mathcal{R}^\circ$, be the least relation between proved expressions such that

$$(\Gamma, e, A)\, \mathcal{R}^\circ\, (\Gamma, e', A) \text{ iff } e[\vec{a}/\vec{x}]\, \mathcal{R}\, e'[\vec{a}/\vec{x}] \text{ for any } \Gamma\text{-closure } [\vec{a}/\vec{x}].$$

For instance, relation Rel° holds between any two proved expressions (Γ, e, A) and (Γ', e', A') provided only that $\Gamma = \Gamma'$ and $A = A'$. As a matter of notation we shall write $\Gamma \vdash e\, \mathcal{R}\, e' : A$ to mean that $(\Gamma, e, A)\, \mathcal{R}\, (\Gamma, e', A)$ and, in fact, we shall often omit the type information.

We need the following notion, of compatible refinement, to characterise what it means for a relation on open expressions to be a precongruence. If $\mathcal{R} \subseteq Rel^\circ$, its **compatible refinement**, $\widehat{\mathcal{R}} \subseteq Rel^\circ$, is defined inductively by the following rules.

$$\Gamma \vdash e\, \widehat{\mathcal{R}}\, e \text{ if } e \in \{x, k, \Omega, \delta_j\}$$

$$\frac{\Gamma, x{:}A \vdash e\, \mathcal{R}\, e'}{\Gamma \vdash \lambda x{:}A.\, e\, \widehat{\mathcal{R}}\, \lambda x{:}A.\, e'} \qquad \frac{\Gamma \vdash e_1\, \mathcal{R}\, e_1' \qquad \Gamma \vdash e_2\, \mathcal{R}\, e_2'}{\Gamma \vdash e_1\, e_2\, \widehat{\mathcal{R}}\, e_1'\, e_2'}$$

$$\frac{\Gamma \vdash e_i\, \mathcal{R}\, e_i' \quad (i = 1, 2, 3)}{\Gamma \vdash \text{if } e_1 \text{ then } e_2 \text{ else } e_3\, \widehat{\mathcal{R}}\, \text{if } e_1' \text{ then } e_2' \text{ else } e_3'}$$

Define a relation $\mathcal{R} \subseteq Rel^\circ$ to be a **precongruence** iff it contains its own compatible refinement, that is, $\widehat{\mathcal{R}} \subseteq \mathcal{R}$. This definition is equivalent to saying that a relation is preserved by substitution into any context.

Lemma 7 *Assume that $\mathcal{R} \subseteq Rel^\circ$ is a preorder. $\mathcal{R}$ is a precongruence iff $\Gamma \vdash C[e]\, \mathcal{R}\, C[e']$ whenever $\Gamma \vdash e\, \mathcal{R}\, e'$ and C is a context.*

The proof of the 'only if' direction is by induction on the size of context C; the other direction is straightforward. Note that whenever a and b are programs of type A, that $a \sim b$ iff $(\varnothing, a, A) \sim^\circ (\varnothing, b, A)$, and similarly for similarity, $\precsim$. Hence given the Lemma 7, to prove Theorem 3 it will be enough to show that $\sim^\circ$ and $\precsim^\circ$ are precongruences, that is $\widehat{\sim^\circ} \subseteq \sim^\circ$ and $\widehat{\precsim^\circ} \subseteq \precsim^\circ$.

We shall use a general method established by Howe (1989). First we prove that the open extension of similarity is a precongruence. We define a second relation $\precsim^\bullet$, which by construction satisfies $\widehat{\precsim^\bullet} \subseteq \precsim^\bullet$ and $\precsim^\circ \subseteq \precsim^\bullet$. We prove by co-induction that $\precsim^\bullet \subseteq \precsim^\circ$. Hence $\precsim^\bullet$ and $\precsim^\circ$ are one and the same relation, and $\lesssim^\circ$ is a precongruence because $\lesssim^\bullet$ is.

Second we prove that the open extension of bisimilarity is a precongruence. Let $\gtrsim = \lesssim^{\mathrm{op}}$. Recall Lemma 3(2), that $\sim = \lesssim \cap \gtrsim$. Furthermore $\sim^\circ = \lesssim^\circ \cap \gtrsim^\circ$ follows by definition of open extension. We can easily prove another fact, that $\widehat{\mathcal{R} \cap \mathcal{S}} = \widehat{\mathcal{R}} \cap \widehat{\mathcal{S}}$ whenever $\mathcal{R}, \mathcal{S} \subseteq Rel^\circ$. We have

$$\widehat{\sim^\circ} = \widehat{(\lesssim^\circ \cap \gtrsim^\circ)} = \widehat{\lesssim^\circ} \cap \widehat{\gtrsim^\circ} \subseteq \lesssim^\circ \cap \gtrsim^\circ = \sim^\circ$$

which is to say that $\sim^\circ$ is a precongruence. Indeed, being an equivalence relation, it is a congruence.

We have only sketched the first part, that $\lesssim^\circ$ is a precongruence. We devote the remainder of this section to a more detailed account. Compatible refinment, $\widehat{}$, permits a concise inductive induction of Howe's relation $\lesssim^\bullet \subseteq Rel^\circ$ as $\mu S.\, \widehat{S} \lesssim^\circ$, which is to say that $\lesssim^\bullet$ is the least relation to satisfy the rule

$$\frac{\Gamma \vdash e \, \widehat{\lesssim^\bullet} \, e'' \qquad \Gamma \vdash e'' \lesssim^\circ e'}{\Gamma \vdash e \lesssim^\bullet e'}$$

Sands (1992) found the following neat presentation of some basic properties of $\lesssim^\bullet$ from Howe's paper.

Lemma 8 (Sands) $\lesssim^\bullet$ *is the least relation closed under the rules*

$$\frac{\Gamma \vdash e \lesssim^\circ e'}{\Gamma \vdash e \lesssim^\bullet e'} \qquad \frac{\Gamma \vdash e \, \widehat{\lesssim^\bullet} \, e'}{\Gamma \vdash e \lesssim^\bullet e'} \qquad \frac{\Gamma \vdash e \lesssim^\bullet e'' \qquad \Gamma \vdash e'' \lesssim^\circ e'}{\Gamma \vdash e \lesssim^\bullet e'}.$$

We claimed earlier that $\widehat{\lesssim^\bullet} \subseteq \lesssim^\bullet$ and $\lesssim^\circ \subseteq \lesssim^\bullet$; these follow from the lemma. The proof is routine, as is that of the following substitution lemma.

Lemma 9 *If* $\Gamma, x{:}B \vdash e_1 \lesssim^\bullet e_2$ *and* $\Gamma \vdash e_1' \lesssim^\bullet e_2' : B$ *then* $\Gamma \vdash e_1[e_1'/x] \lesssim^\bullet e_2[e_2'/x]$.

What remains of Howe's method is to prove that $\lesssim^\bullet \subseteq \lesssim^\circ$, which we do by co-induction. First note the following lemma—which is the crux of the proof— relating $\lesssim^\bullet$ and transition.

Lemma 10 *Let* $S \stackrel{\mathrm{def}}{=} \{(a,b) \mid \varnothing \vdash a \lesssim^\bullet b\}$.

(1) *Whenever* $a \, S \, b$ *and* $a \rightsquigarrow a'$ *then* $a' \, S \, b$.

(2) *Whenever* $a \, S \, b$ *and* $a \xrightarrow{\alpha} a'$ *there is* b' *with* $b \xrightarrow{\alpha} b'$ *and* $a' \, S \, b'$.

Proof The proofs are induction on the depth of inference of reduction $a \rightsquigarrow a'$ and transition $a \xrightarrow{\alpha} a'$ respectively. Details of similar proofs may be found in Howe (1989) and Gordon (1994b). ∎

By this lemma, S is a simulation, and hence $S \subseteq \lesssim$ by co-induction. Open extension is monotone, so $S^\circ \subseteq \lesssim^\circ$. Now $\lesssim^\bullet \subseteq S^\circ$ follows from the substitution lemma (Lemma 9) and the reflexivity of $\lesssim^\bullet$ (Lemma 8 and reflexivity of $\lesssim^\circ$). Hence we have $\lesssim^\bullet \subseteq \lesssim^\circ$. But the reverse inclusion follows from Lemma 8, so in fact $\lesssim^\bullet = \lesssim^\circ$ and hence $\lesssim^\circ$ is a precongruence.

6 Summary and Related Work

We explained the dual foundations of induction and co-induction. We defined notions of divergence and contextual equivalence for a small functional language, an extension of PCF. We gave co-inductive characterisations of both divergence and contextual equivalence, and illustrated their utility by a series of examples and properties. In particular we derived the 'Take Lemma' of Bird and Wadler (1988). We explained Howe's method for proving that bisimilarity, our co-inductive formulation of contextual equivalence, is a precongruence. We hope to have shown both by general principles and specific examples that there is an easy path leading from the reduction rules that define a functional language to a powerful theory of program equivalence based on co-induction.

Although our particular formulation is new, bisimilarity for functional languages is not. Often it is known as 'applicative bisimulation' and is based on a natural semantics style evaluation relation. The earliest reference I can find is to Abramsky's unpublished 1984 work on Martin-Löf's type theory, which eventually led to his study of lazy lambda-calculus[1] (Abramsky and Ong 1993). Other work includes papers by Howe (1989), Smith (1991), Sands (1992, 1994), Ong (1993), Pitts and Stark (1993), Ritter and Pitts (1994), Crole and Gordon (1994) and my book (1994b). The present formulation is the first to coincide with contextual equivalence for PCF-like languages. It amounts to a co-inductive generalisation of Milner's original term model for PCF (1977). Since it equals contextual equivalence it answers Turner's (1990, Preface) concern that Abramsky's applicative bisimulation makes more distinctions than are observable by well-typed program contexts.

Domain theory is one perspective on the foundations of lazy functional programming; this paper offers another. Any subject benefits from multiple perspectives. In this case the two are of about equal expressiveness. Domain theory is independent of syntax and operational semantics, and provides fixpoint induction for proving program properties. If we take care to distinguish denotations from texts of programs, the theory of bisimilarity set out in Section 4 can be paralleled by a theory based on a domain-theoretic denotational semantics. Winskel (1993), for instance, shows how to prove adequacy for a lazy language with recursive types (albeit one in which functions and pairs are active types). Pitts (1994) develops a co-induction principle from domain theory. On the other hand, Smith (1991) shows how operational methods based on a form of bisimilarity can support fixpoint induction. One advantage of the operational approach is that bisimilarity coincides exactly with contextual equivalence. The corresponding property of a denotational semantics—full abstraction—is notoriously hard to achieve (Ong 1994).

---

[1] The earliest presentation of lazy lambda-calculus appears to be Abramsky's thesis (1987, Chapter 6), in which he explains that the "main results of Chapter 6 were obtained in the setting of Martin-Löf's Domain Interpretation of his Type Theory, during and shortly after a visit to Chalmers in March 1984."

Acknowledgements

The idea of defining bisimilarity on a deterministic functional language via a labelled transition system arose in joint work with Roy Crole (1994). Martin Coen pointed out the map/filter example to me. I hold a Royal Society University Research Fellowship. This work has been partially supported by the CEC TYPES BRA, but was begun while I was a member of the Programming Methodology Group at Chalmers. I benefitted greatly from presenting a tutorial on this work to the Functional Programming group at Glasgow University. I am grateful to colleagues at the Ayr workshop, and at Chalmers and Cambridge, for many useful conversations.

References

Abramsky, S. (1987, October 5). **Domain Theory and the Logic of Observable Properties**. Ph. D. thesis, Queen Mary College, University of London.

Abramsky, S. and L. Ong (1993). Full abstraction in the lazy lambda calculus. **Information and Computation 105**, 159–267.

Aczel, P. (1977). An introduction to inductive definitions. In J. Barwise (Ed.), **Handbook of Mathematical Logic**, pp. 739–782. North-Holland.

Bird, R. and P. Wadler (1988). **Introduction to Functional Programming**. Prentice-Hall.

Bloom, B. (1988). Can LCF be topped? Flat lattice models of typed lambda calculus. In **Proceedings 3rd LICS**, pp. 282–295.

Crole, R. L. and A. D. Gordon (1994, September). A sound metalogical semantics for input/output effects. In **Computer Science Logic'94, Kazimierz, Poland**. Proceedings to appear in Springer LNCS.

Davey, B. A. and H. A. Priestley (1990). **Introduction to Lattices and Order**. Cambridge University Press.

Felleisen, M. and D. Friedman (1986). Control operators, the SECD-machine, and the λ-calculus. In **Formal Description of Programming Concepts III**, pp. 193–217. North-Holland.

Gordon, A. D. (1994a). Bisimilarity as a theory of functional programming. Submitted for publication.

Gordon, A. D. (1994b). **Functional Programming and Input/Output**. Cambridge University Press. Revision of 1992 PhD dissertation.

Howe, D. J. (1989). Equality in lazy computation systems. In **Proceedings 4th LICS**, pp. 198–203.

Hughes, J. and A. Moran (1993, June). Natural semantics for non-determinism. In **Proceedings of El Wintermöte**, pp. 211–222. Chalmers PMG. Available as Report 73.

Milner, R. (1977). Fully abstract models of typed lambda-calculi. **TCS 4**, 1–23.

Milner, R. (1989). **Communication and Concurrency**. Prentice-Hall.

Morris, J. H. (1968, December). **Lambda-Calculus Models of Programming Languages**. Ph. D. thesis, MIT.

Ong, C.-H. L. (1993, June). Non-determinism in a functional setting (extended abstract). In **Proceedings 8th LICS**, pp. 275–286.

Ong, C.-H. L. (1994, January). Correspondence between operational and denotational semantics: The full abstraction problem for PCF. Submitted to **Handbook of Logic in Computer Science** Volume 3, OUP 1994.

Park, D. (1981, March). Concurrency and automata on infinite sequences. In P. Deussen (Ed.), **Theoretical Computer Science: 5th GI-Conference**, Volume 104 of **Lecture Notes in Computer Science**, pp. 167–183. Springer-Verlag.

Pitts, A. and I. Stark (1993, June). On the observable properties of higher order functions that dynamically create local names (preliminary report). In **SIPL'93**, pp. 31–45.

Pitts, A. M. (1994). A co-induction principle for recursively defined domains. **TCS 124**, 195–219.

Plotkin, G. D. (1977). LCF considered as a programming language. **TCS 5**, 223–255.

Ritter, E. and A. M. Pitts (1994, September). A fully abstract translation between a λ-calculus with reference types and Standard ML. To appear in TLCA'95.

Sander, H. (1992). **A Logic of Functional Programs with an Application to Concurrency**. Ph. D. thesis, Chalmers PMG.

Sands, D. (1992). Operational theories of improvement in functional languages (extended abstract). In **Functional Programming, Glasgow 1991**, Workshops in Computing, pp. 298–311. Springer-Verlag.

Sands, D. (1994, May). Total correctness and improvement in the transformation of functional programs (1st draft). DIKU, University of Copenhagen.

Smith, S. F. (1991). From operational to denotational semantics. In **MFPS VII, Pittsburgh**, Volume 598 of **Lecture Notes in Computer Science**, pp. 54–76. Springer-Verlag.

Turner, D. (Ed.) (1990). **Research Topics in Functional Programming**. Addison-Wesley.

Winskel, G. (1993). **The Formal Semantics of Programming Languages**. MIT Press, Cambridge, Mass.

Unboxing using Specialisation

Cordelia Hall   Simon L. Peyton Jones

University of Glasgow   University of Glasgow

Patrick M. Sansom

University of Glasgow[*]

Abstract

In performance-critical parts of functional programs substantial performance improvements can be achieved by using *unboxed*, instead of boxed, data types. Unfortunately, polymorphic functions and data types cannot directly manipulate unboxed values, precisely because they do not conform to the standard boxed representation. Instead, specialised, monomorphic versions of these functions and data types, which manipulate the unboxed values, have to be created. This can be a very tiresome and error prone business, since specialising one function often requires the functions and data types it uses to be specialised as well.

In this paper we show how to automate these tiresome consequential changes, leaving the programmer to concentrate on where to introduce unboxed data types in the first place.

1 Introduction

Non-strict semantics certainly add to the expressive power of a language [8]. Sometimes the performance cost of this extra expressiveness is slight, but not always. It can happen that an inner loop of a program is made seriously less efficient by non-strictness. For example, consider the following fragment of a complex-number arithmetic package:

```
data Complex = Cpx Float Float

addCpx :: Complex -> Complex -> Complex
addCpx (Cpx r1 i1) (Cpx r2 i2) = Cpx (r1+r2) (i1+i2)
```

In a strict language, a complex number would be represented a pair of unboxed floating point numbers, and `addCpx` would actually perform the additions of the components. In a non-strict language such as Haskell [7], though, a complex number is a pair of pointers to possibly-unevaluated thunks. The function `addCpx` cannot actually force these thunks, since they might be bottom, but rather must build further thunks representing (`r1+r2`) and (`i1+i2`) respectively. If complex arithmetic is in the inner loop of the program, the performance penalty is quite substantial.

Let us suppose, then, that a profiler has focussed the programmer's attention on this arithmetic package. What can be done to make it more efficient?

---

[*]Authors' address: Dept of Computing Science, University of Glasgow, Glasgow G12 8QQ, Scotland. E-mail: {cvh,simonpj,sansom}@dcs.glasgow.ac.uk.

Peyton Jones & Launchbury [16] suggested that unboxed data types could be made "first class citizens", and that the programmer be allowed to declare data types involving them, thus:

```
data Complex = Cpx Float# Float#
```

Here, `Float#` is the type of unboxed floating-point numbers. (An immediate consequence is that the components of a complex number must be evaluated before the complex number itself is constructed, so that the representation is stricter than before.) Modifications of this kind can have a dramatic impact on the performance of some programs.

There is a catch, though. Suppose we wanted to transform a list of complex numbers to a list of their imaginary components. We might try to write:

```
imags :: [Complex] -> [Float#]
imags cs = [im | Cpx re im <- cs]
```

Unfortunately, we cannot form a list of unboxed floating point numbers, because both the size and the pointer-hood of a `Float#` differs from that of a pointer. Instead, a new data type must be declared for lists of `Float#`:

```
data LFloat = NilF
            | ConsF Float# LFloat
```

Alas, none of the usual list-manipulating functions (`map`, `filter` etc) work over `LFloat`, so new versions of them have to be defined, and so it goes on.

In general, Peyton Jones & Launchbury [16] put forward the restriction that: *polymorphic functions (and data constructors) cannot be used at unboxed types*. We use the term "creeping monomorphism" to describe the sad necessity to declare new functions simply because of this restriction. The goal of this paper is to lift the restriction, by automating the production of new versions of existing functions and data constructors.

Even the humble + function in `addCpx` is an example. When the `Complex` data type is changed, type inference will find that `r1` and `r2` are of type `Float#`. Since + is an overloaded function, with type

```
(+) :: Num a => a -> a -> a
```

Peyton Jones & Launchbury would prohibit + from being applied to a value of type `Float#`. However, if the restriction is lifted, and `Float#` is made an instance of class `Num`, then the code for `addCpx` will compile without modification.

Our goal is to allow the programmer to use profiling information [19] to improve run-time performance by making minimal changes to data type declarations and type signatures. The system we describe in this paper propagates these changes throughout the program, compiling specialised versions of polymorphic functions and constructors where they are now used at unboxed types.

We begin by describing our Core language (Section 2). We then examine the use of polymorphic functions and data types in the presence of unboxed values (Section 3), formalising Peyton Jones & Launchbury's unboxing restriction, describing the process of specialisation which enables us to relax this restriction (Section 3.1), and presenting a partial evaluator which performs this specialisation (Section 3.2). In Section 4 we discuss the practical implications, before presenting some preliminary results (Section 5) and discussing related work (Section 6).

Expression	e	$::=$	x
		$\mid$	$\lambda x\!:\!\tau.e$
		$\mid$	$e\ x$
		$\mid$	let $x\!:\!\sigma = e_1$ in e_2
		$\mid$	$\Lambda\alpha.e$
		$\mid$	$e\ \{\tau\}$
		$\mid$	$C\ \{\tau_1 \cdots \tau_n\}\ x_1 \cdots x_a$
		$\mid$	case e of $\{C_j\ x_{j1}\!:\!\tau_{j1} \cdots x_{ja_j}\!:\!\tau_{ja_j}\ \text{->}\ e_j\}_{j=1}^m$
PolyType	σ	$::=$	$\forall\alpha.\sigma \mid \tau$
MonoType	τ	$::=$	$\pi \mid v$
BoxedType	π	$::=$	α
		$\mid$	$\tau_1 \to \tau_2$
		$\mid$	$\chi\ \tau_1 \cdots \tau_n$
UnboxedType	v	$::=$	int# $\mid$ float# $\mid$ char#
		$\mid$	χ# $\tau_1 \cdots \tau_n$

Figure 1: Core Language Syntax

2 The Core Language

Our source language is Haskell, but the language we discuss in this paper is the intermediate language used by our compiler, the Core language [15]. There are three reasons for studying this intermediate language. First, it allows us to focus on the essential aspects of the algorithm, without being distracted by Haskell's syntactic sugar. Second, Haskell's implicit overloading is translated into explicit function abstractions and applications so that no further special treatment of overloading is necessary. Third, the type abstractions and applications which are implicit in a Haskell program, are made explicit in the Core program. Thus, each polymorphic application which manipulates unboxed values can easily be identified by looking at the type arguments in the application. Our transformation identifies any applications involving unboxed types and replaces this with an appropriately specialised version of the function.

The syntax of the Core language is given in Figure 1. It is an explicitly typed second-order functional language with (recursive) let, (saturated) data constructors, algebraic case and explicit boxing. This language combines the higher-order explicit typing of Core-XML [11] with the explicit boxing and type structure of Peyton Jones & Launchbury [16].

In this language the argument of an application is always a simple variable. A non-atomic argument is handled by first binding it to a variable using a let-expression. This restriction reflects the fact that a non-atomic argument must be bound to a heap-allocated closure before the function is applied. In the case of a strict, unboxed value ($\sigma \in$ UnboxedType), the let-expression evaluates the bound expression and binds the result value before the function is applied.

A *type normalised* expression [6] is one that satisfies the following two conditions. 1) The type abstractions occur only as the bound expression of let-expressions; i.e. let $x:\sigma = \Lambda\alpha_1.\Lambda\alpha_2.\cdots\Lambda\alpha_n.e_1$ in e_2 which we will abbreviate with let $x:\sigma = \Lambda\alpha_1\cdots\alpha_n.e_1$ in e_2. 2) Type applications are only allowed for variables; i.e. $x\{\tau_1\}\cdots\{\tau_n\}$ which we will write $x\{\tau_1\cdots\tau_n\}$. Henceforth we will assume that all expressions are type normalised.

2.1 Data constructors

In this second-order language a data constructor must be (fully) applied to both the type arguments of the data type and the value arguments of the data object being constructed. For example, the standard list data type

$$\texttt{data List } \alpha = \texttt{Nil} \mid \texttt{Cons } \alpha \texttt{ (List } \alpha\texttt{)}$$

has two constructors, Nil and Cons. The implied constructor declarations might be expressed in the higher-order calculus as follows:

$$
\begin{aligned}
\texttt{Nil} \quad &: \quad \forall\alpha.\texttt{List } \alpha \\
&= \Lambda\alpha.[\texttt{Nil}] \\
\texttt{Cons} \quad &: \quad \forall\alpha.\alpha \to \texttt{List } \alpha \to \texttt{List } \alpha \\
&= \Lambda\alpha.\lambda v_1:\alpha.\lambda v_2:\texttt{List } \alpha.[\texttt{Cons } v_1\ v_2]
\end{aligned}
$$

where [ ] indicates actual construction of the data object. Even though the constructor Nil has an arity of zero the higher-order constructor still requires a type parameter to indicate what type it is being used at, e.g. Nil {Int}. In general, a data declaration has the form

$$\texttt{data } \chi\ \alpha_1\cdots\alpha_n = \texttt{C}_1\ \tau_{11}\cdots\tau_{1a_1} \mid \cdots \mid \texttt{C}_m\ \tau_{m1}\cdots\tau_{ma_m}$$

which gives rise to m higher-order constructors with the form

$$
\begin{aligned}
\texttt{C}_j \quad &: \quad \forall\alpha_1\cdots\alpha_n.\tau_{j1} \to \cdots \to \tau_{ja_j} \to \chi\ \alpha_1\cdots\alpha_n \\
&= \Lambda\alpha_1\cdots\alpha_n.\lambda v_{j1}:\tau_{j1}.\cdots.\lambda v_{ja_j}:\tau_{ja_j}.[\texttt{C}_j\ v_{j1}\cdots v_{ja_j}]
\end{aligned}
$$

where n is the number of type parameters of the data type and a_j is the arity of the data constructor. Since the number of type parameters is determined by the arity of the type constructor, χ, it is the same for all data constructors of that type.

2.2 Well-formed expressions

We call an expression e *well-formed* under type assumption Γ if we can derive the typing judgement $\Gamma \vdash e : \sigma$. The typing rules are quite standard [11] and are not given here (but see Section 3).

2.3 Notation

For notational convenience we abbreviate sequences such as $x_1\cdots x_n$ with $\overline{x}$, where $n = \texttt{length } \overline{x}$. This is extended to sequences of pairs which are abbreviated with paired sequences, e.g. $x_{j1}:\tau_{j1}\cdots x_{ja_j}:\tau_{ja_j}$ is abbreviated with $\overline{x_j}:\overline{\tau_j}$. We use $\equiv$ for syntactical identity of expressions.

3 Polymorphism and Unboxed Values

A pure polymorphic function is usually compiled by treating all polymorphic values in a uniform way. Typically all such values are required to be represented as a pointer to a heap allocated closure i.e. they must be boxed. For example, consider the permuting combinator C:

$$C \; f \; x \; y \; = \; f \; y \; x \qquad\qquad \text{(Haskell)}$$

$$C \; = \; \Lambda a \; b \; c.\lambda f : a \to b \to c.\lambda x : b.\lambda y : a.f \; y \; x \qquad\qquad \text{(Core)}$$

To generate the code for C we must know the representation of the polymorphic values, x and y, being manipulated.[1] By insisting that such polymorphic values are always boxed we can compile code which assumes that such values are always represented by a single pointer into the heap.

It follows that a polymorphic function can only be used at boxed types, since the representation of an unboxed type violates the assumption above. We impose a restriction in the typing rules for expressions which prevents a polymorphic function being applied to an unboxed type.[2]

$$\frac{\Gamma \vdash e : \forall \alpha.\sigma}{\Gamma \vdash e \; \{\tau\} : \sigma[\tau/\alpha]} \; \tau \notin \text{UnboxedType} \qquad\qquad (*)$$

A similar restriction is imposed in the typing rule for data constructors. This prohibits the construction of polymorphic data objects with unboxed components, e.g. `List Float#`.

These restrictions cause the "creeping monomorphism", described in Section 1, since the programmer must declare suitable monomorphic versions of any polymorphic functions and data types used at unboxed types. This can be exceedingly tedious and error prone.

To address this problem we propose to relax the unboxing restriction $(*)$, allowing the programmer unrestricted use of unboxed values. During the compilation we undertake automatically to generate the necessary monomorphic function versions: converting the unrestricted program into one which satisfies the unboxing restriction $(*)$. We can then generate code which directly manipulates the unboxed values since their type, and hence their representation, is known at compile time. For example, here is the monomorphic version of C which manipulates `Float#`s:

$$C' \; = \; \lambda f : \texttt{Float\#} \to \texttt{Float\#} \to \texttt{Float\#}.\lambda x : \texttt{Float\#}.\lambda y : \texttt{Float\#}.f \; y \; x$$

Since the code generator knows that x and y have type `Float#` it produces code which manipulates floating point numbers, instead of pointers. This is the only difference between the code produced for C and C'.

---

[1] The representation information that is typically required is the size of a value and the position of any heap pointers (so that all roots can be identified during garbage collection). When more sophisticated calling conventions are used, such as passing arguments in registers, the actual type may also affect the treatment of a value. For example a boxed value may be passed in a pointer register, an `Int#` in an integer register, and a `Float#` in a dedicated floating point register.

[2] This restriction is equivalent to "Restriction 1: loss of polymorphism" in Peyton Jones & Launchbury [16].

3.1 Specialisation

The transformation of program with unrestricted use of unboxed types into one which satisfies the unboxing restriction above is performed using a partial evaluator. The idea is to remove all type applications involving unboxed types by creating new versions of the functions being applied, specialised on the unboxed types. These specialised versions are created by partially evaluating the unboxed type applications.

Before launching into the definition of the partial evaluator itself, we give an overview of the algorithm. Each time a function (or constructor) is applied to a sequence of types, a new version of the function (or constructor), specialised on any unboxed types in the application, is created, unless such a version has already been created. For example, given the code[3]

```
append {Int#}
       xs (map {[Int#] Int#}
              (sum {Int#}) (append {[Int#]} yss zss)
```

a version of append, specialised at type Int#, is created. Given the definition of append:

$$\text{append} = \Lambda\alpha.\lambda\text{xs} : [\alpha].\lambda\text{ys} : [\alpha].e$$

the specialised version, append_Int#, is:

$$\begin{aligned}
\text{append\_Int\#} &= \text{append } \{\text{Int\#}\} \\
&= (\Lambda\alpha.\lambda\text{xs} : [\alpha].\lambda\text{ys} : [\alpha].e) \ \{\text{Int\#}\} \\
&= (\lambda\text{xs} : [\alpha].\lambda\text{ys} : [\alpha].e)[\text{Int\#}/\alpha] \\
&= \lambda\text{xs} : [\text{Int\#}].\lambda\text{ys} : [\text{Int\#}].e[\text{Int\#}/\alpha]
\end{aligned}$$

The name of the specialised version, append_Int#, is constructed by appending the specialising type(s) to the original name.

When a function is applied to a boxed type, there is no need to specialise on that type argument since the polymorphic version, which assumes a boxed type will suffice. Consequently, we make the specialisation polymorphic in any boxed type arguments. For example, the application of map is only specialised on the second type argument, Int#, since the first type argument, [Int#], is a boxed type.

$$\text{map} = \Lambda\alpha \ \beta.\lambda\text{f} : \alpha \to \beta.\lambda\text{xs} : [\alpha].e$$

$$\begin{aligned}
\text{map\_*\_Int\#} &= \Lambda\alpha_*.\text{map } \{\alpha_* \text{ Int\#}\} \\
&= \Lambda\alpha_*.(\Lambda\alpha \ \beta.\lambda\text{f} : \alpha \to \beta.\lambda\text{xs} : [\alpha].e) \ \{\alpha_* \text{ Int\#}\} \\
&= \Lambda\alpha_*.(\lambda\text{f} : \alpha \to \beta.\lambda\text{xs} : [\alpha].e)[\alpha_*/\alpha, \text{Int\#}/\beta] \\
&= \Lambda\alpha_*.\lambda\text{f} : \alpha_* \to \text{Int\#}.\lambda\text{xs} : [\alpha_*].e[\alpha_*/\alpha, \text{Int\#}/\beta]
\end{aligned}$$

A * is used to indicate a boxed type argument in which the specialised version remains polymorphic. This reduces the number of specialised versions created since all boxed type arguments will be treated as a * type when determining the specialisation required. For example, the application map {Bool Int#} would also use the specialised version map_*_Int#.

---

[3]For notational convenience we use the standard [ ] list notation, where $[\alpha] \equiv \text{List } \alpha$.

The applications can now be modified to use the specialised versions, with all unboxed types new removed from the application. The final version of the code for the example above is:

```
append_Int#
        xs (map_*_Int# {[Int#]}
                    sum_Int# (append_* {[Int#]} yss zss))
```

In summary the specialisation algorithm is:

while the unboxing restriction $(*)$ is not satisfied:
1. Find a type application, $f\{\overline{\tau}\}$, involving an unboxed type.
2. Create a suitably specialised version of f (if it does not already exist).
3. Use the specialised version at this application site, removing the unboxed types from the application.

Since all polymorphic values must be let-bound (see Figure 1), the definition of f, which has to be specialised, will always be visible in the enclosing scope.

Notice that the specialised versions must themselves be specialised since the substitution of the unboxed type over the body of the function may introduce further unboxed type applications. To ensure termination in the presence of recursive functions we rely on Hindley-Milner type inference having guaranteed that all recursive references occur at the same type; thus no new versions of a function will be created while specialising its body, since we must be creating the specialised version required.

3.2   The partial evaluator

The specialisation algorithm is efficiently implemented using a partial evaluator.

The partial evaluator, $\mathcal{T}$, takes an expression with unrestricted use of unboxed types, and two environments: one containing the polymorphic let-bindings and the other the specialised versions of those let-bindings which have been created so far. It returns a triple containing an equivalent expression which satisfies the unboxing restriction, a modified environment of specialised versions, and a set of specialised data types required.

$$\mathcal{T} :: \text{Exp} \rightarrow \text{BEnv} \rightarrow \text{SEnv} \rightarrow (\text{Exp, Senv, TSet})$$

$$\rho \in \text{BEnv} :: \text{Name} \rightarrow (\text{Type, Exp})$$
$$\delta \in \text{SEnv} :: \text{Name} \rightarrow ((\text{Name, [Type]}) \rightarrow (\text{Type, Exp}))$$
$$\gamma \in \text{TSet} :: \{(\text{Name, [Type]})\}$$

The environments are partial maps with suitable domain and lookup functions. BEnv simply maps a variable name to its type and unrestricted expression. SEnv is a nested environment, mapping a variable name to an environment containing the specialised versions for that variable. The domain of this specialised environment is the variable name and the specialising types (a vector containing unboxed types and $*$s), which uniquely identifies the specialised version. We use a subscript notation $x_{\overline{v}}$ to refer to the specialised version. We also use the notation $\{\}$ for the empty environment and $\rho[x \rightarrow v]$ to extend (or modify) an environment ρ with the mapping $x \rightarrow v$.

$$\mathcal{T} [\![\mathbf{x}]\!]\ \rho\ \delta\ =\ ([\![\mathbf{x}]\!], \delta, \{\}) \tag{1}$$

$$\mathcal{T} [\![\lambda\ \mathbf{x}{:}\tau.\mathbf{e}]\!]\ \rho\ \delta \tag{2}$$
$$=\ \text{let}\quad (\mathbf{e}', \delta^1, \gamma^1)\ =\ \mathcal{T}\ \mathbf{e}\ \rho\ \delta$$
$$\text{in}\quad ([\![\lambda\ \mathbf{x}{:}\tau.\mathbf{e}']\!],\ \delta^1,\ \gamma^1)$$

$$\mathcal{T} [\![\mathbf{e}\ \mathbf{x}]\!]\ \rho\ \delta \tag{3}$$
$$=\ \text{let}\quad (\mathbf{e}', \delta^1, \gamma^1)\ =\ \mathcal{T}\ \mathbf{e}\ \rho\ \delta$$
$$\text{in}\quad ([\![\mathbf{e}'\ \mathbf{x}]\!],\ \delta^1,\ \gamma^1)$$

$$\mathcal{T} [\![\mathbf{let}\ \mathbf{x}{:}\sigma = \mathbf{e_1}\ \mathbf{in}\ \mathbf{e_2}]\!]\ \rho\ \delta\ \mid\ \mathbf{e_1} \not\equiv \Lambda\overline{\alpha}.\mathbf{e},\ \ \sigma \in \text{MonoType} \tag{4}$$
$$=\ \text{let}\quad (\mathbf{e_1'}, \delta^1, \gamma^1)\ =\ \mathcal{T}\ \mathbf{e_1}\ \rho\ \delta$$
$$(\mathbf{e_2'}, \delta^2, \gamma^2)\ =\ \mathcal{T}\ \mathbf{e_2}\ \rho\ \delta^1$$
$$\text{in}\quad ([\![\mathbf{let}\ \mathbf{x}{:}\sigma = \mathbf{e_1'}\ \mathbf{in}\ \mathbf{e_2'}]\!],\ \delta^2,\ \gamma^1 \cup \gamma^2)$$

$$\mathcal{T} [\![\mathbf{let}\ \mathbf{x}{:}\sigma = \mathbf{e_\Lambda}\ \mathbf{in}\ \mathbf{e}]\!]\ \rho\ \delta\ \mid\ \mathbf{e_\Lambda} \equiv \Lambda\overline{\alpha}.\mathbf{e},\ \ \sigma \in \text{PolyType} \tag{5}$$
$$=\ \text{let}\quad (\mathbf{e}', \delta^1, \gamma^1)\ =\ \mathcal{T}\ \mathbf{e}\ \rho[\mathbf{x} \to (\sigma, \mathbf{e_\Lambda})]\ \delta[\mathbf{x} \to \{\}]$$
$$\text{in}\quad ([\![\mathbf{let}\ (\delta^1\ \mathbf{x})\ \mathbf{in}\ \mathbf{e}']\!],\ \delta^1[\mathbf{x} \to \bot],\ \gamma^1)$$

$$\mathcal{T} [\![\mathbf{x}\ \{\overline{\tau}\}]\!]\ \rho\ \delta \tag{6}$$
$$=\ \text{let}\quad (\overline{v}, \overline{\pi})\quad =\quad \text{spectys}\ \overline{\tau}$$
$$\text{in}$$
$$\text{case}\ \mathbf{x}_{\overline{v}} \in \text{dom}\ (\delta\ \mathbf{x})\ \text{of}$$
$$\text{True}\quad \to\quad ([\![\mathbf{x}_{\overline{v}}\ \{\overline{\pi}\}]\!],\ \delta,\ \{\})$$
$$\text{False}\quad \to\quad \text{let}\quad (\delta^1, \gamma^1)\ =\quad \text{specfn}\ \mathbf{x}\ \overline{v}\ \rho\ \delta$$
$$\text{in}\quad ([\![\mathbf{x}_{\overline{v}}\ \{\overline{\pi}\}]\!],\ \delta^1,\ \gamma^1)$$

$$\mathcal{T} [\![\mathbf{C}\ \{\overline{\tau}\}\ \overline{\mathbf{x}}]\!]\ \rho\ \delta \tag{7}$$
$$=\ \text{let}\quad (\overline{v}, \overline{\pi})\quad =\quad \text{spectys}\ \overline{\tau}$$
$$\chi\quad =\quad \Gamma\ \mathbf{C}$$
$$\text{in}\quad ([\![\mathbf{C}_{\overline{v}}\ \{\overline{\pi}\}\ \overline{\mathbf{x}}]\!],\ \delta,\ \{\chi_{\overline{v}}\})$$

$$\mathcal{T} [\![\mathbf{case}\ \mathbf{e}\ \mathbf{of}\ \{\mathbf{C_j}\ \overline{\mathbf{x_j}}{:}\overline{\tau_j} \to \mathbf{e_j}\}_{j=1}^{m}]\!]\ \rho\ \delta \tag{8}$$
$$=\ \text{let}\quad (\mathbf{e}', \delta^0, \gamma^0)\ =\ \mathcal{T}\ \mathbf{e}\ \rho\ \delta$$
$$(\mathbf{e_1'}, \delta^1, \gamma^1)\ =\ \mathcal{T}\ \mathbf{e_1}\ \rho\ \delta^0$$
$$\cdots$$
$$(\mathbf{e_n'}, \delta^m, \gamma^m)\ =\ \mathcal{T}\ \mathbf{e_n}\ \rho\ \delta^{m-1}$$
$$\text{in}\quad ([\![\mathbf{case}\ \mathbf{e}'\ \mathbf{of}\ \{\mathbf{C_j}\ \overline{\mathbf{x_j}}{:}\overline{\tau_j} \to \mathbf{e_j'}\}_{j=1}^{m}]\!],\ \delta^m, \gamma^0 \cup \cdots \cup \gamma^m)$$

Figure 2: The partial evaluator $\mathcal{T}$

```
spectys τ̄
    =   let  v̄  =  [v | τ ← τ̄, v = if τ ∈ BoxedType then * else τ]
             π̄  =  [τ | τ ← τ̄, τ ∈ BoxedType]
        in  (v̄, π̄)


specfn x v̄ ρ δ
    =   let  (∀ᾱ.τ, Λᾱ.e)  =  ρ x
             n              =  length ᾱ

             e′             =  e [(if vᵢ ≢ * then vᵢ else αᵢ)/αᵢ]ⁿᵢ₌₁
             (e″, δ¹, γ¹)   =  𝒯 e′ ρ δ′
             δ′             =  δ[x → (δ x)[x_v̄ → (σ, e_Λ)]]

             ᾱ_*            =  [αᵢ | i ← [1..n], vᵢ ≡ *]
             e_Λ            =  Λᾱ_*.e″

             τ′             =  τ [(if vᵢ ≢ * then vᵢ else αᵢ)/αᵢ]ⁿᵢ₌₁
             σ              =  ∀ᾱ_*.τ′
        in  (δ¹, γ¹)
```

$$\text{spectys } \overline{\tau}$$
$$= \text{ let } \quad \overline{v} = [v \mid \tau \leftarrow \overline{\tau}, \; v = \text{if } \tau \in \text{BoxedType then } * \text{ else } \tau]$$
$$\overline{\pi} = [\tau \mid \tau \leftarrow \overline{\tau}, \; \tau \in \text{BoxedType}]$$
$$\text{in } \quad (\overline{v}, \overline{\pi})$$

$$\text{specfn } \mathbf{x} \; \overline{v} \; \rho \; \delta$$
$$= \text{ let } \quad (\forall \overline{\alpha}.\tau, \Lambda \overline{\alpha}.\mathbf{e}) = \rho \; \mathbf{x}$$
$$n = \text{length } \overline{\alpha}$$
$$\mathbf{e}' = \mathbf{e}\, [(\text{if } v_i \not\equiv * \text{ then } v_i \text{ else } \alpha_i)/\alpha_i]_{i=1}^{n}$$
$$(\mathbf{e}'', \delta^1, \gamma^1) = \mathcal{T} \, \mathbf{e}' \, \rho \, \delta'$$
$$\delta' = \delta[\mathbf{x} \to (\delta \; \mathbf{x})[\mathbf{x}_{\overline{v}} \to (\sigma, \mathbf{e}_\Lambda)]]$$
$$\overline{\alpha_*} = [\alpha_i \mid i \leftarrow [1..n], \; v_i \equiv *]$$
$$\mathbf{e}_\Lambda = \Lambda \overline{\alpha_*}.\mathbf{e}''$$
$$\tau' = \tau \, [(\text{if } v_i \not\equiv * \text{ then } v_i \text{ else } \alpha_i)/\alpha_i]_{i=1}^{n}$$
$$\sigma = \forall \overline{\alpha_*}.\tau'$$
$$\text{in } \quad (\delta^1, \gamma^1)$$

Figure 3: Specialisation functions

TSet is the set of specialised data types required by the expression. The partial evaluator does not explicitly specify the data type transformation — it just collects the data types required. These are subsequently given to the code generator which creates the required constructor functions directly from the data type specifications.

The partial evaluator is defined in Figure 2. The equations for simple variables (1), λ-abstraction (2), application (3), monomorphic **let**-binding (4), and **case** (8) are quite straightforward.

For a polymorphic **let**-binding (equation 5) **let** $\mathbf{x}:\sigma = \mathbf{e}_\Lambda$ **in** $\mathbf{e}$ the body $\mathbf{e}$ is evaluated using the following environments: ρ extended with the binding for $\mathbf{x}$; and δ extended with an empty set of specialised bindings for $\mathbf{x}$. (We assume that all bound variables have unique names.) The set of specialised bindings for $\mathbf{x}$, returned in the modified specialisation environment δ^1, are then **let**-bound and returned. For simplicity, we assume that the target form of the core language allows the set of specialised bindings to be bound in a single **let**.

A polymorphic application (equation 6) is replaced with an application of an appropriately specialised version of the binding. The auxiliary function **spectys** (Figure 3) determines:

$\overline{v}$: the unboxed types on which the binding must be specialised. A $*$ type indicates that the specialised version is still polymorphic in that type parameter.

$\overline{\pi}$: the boxed types the specialised version remains polymorphic in. These correspond to the $*$ types in $\overline{v}$.

The specialised version $\mathbf{x}_{\overline{v}}$ is then applied to the remaining boxed type arguments $\overline{\pi}$ and returned. The auxiliary function `specfn` (Figure 3) is used to extend the environment δ with a newly created specialisation (if it does already contain it). The original binding is extracted from ρ and the specialising types substituted for the corresponding type variable. (The usual alpha substitution to avoid capture is assumed.) The partial evaluator is then applied to the specialised body, e', in an environment, δ', extended with the specialisation being created. This ensures termination in the presence of recursion since recursive references will assume that the required specialisation already exists (see Section 3.1).

Finally, a constructor application (equation 7) is replaced with an application of an appropriately specialised version of the constructor and returned with a specification of the specialised data type required. The global environment Γ maps constructors to their data type.

4   Practical Considerations

The specialiser described above interacts with a number of other language features including: overloading, and separate module compilation. We address these issues and discuss the process of introducing unboxing below.

4.1   Overloaded functions

In Haskell many primitive functions, such as comparison and addition, are overloaded. This allows these operations to be applied to a number of different types. For example, addition belongs to the class `Num`

```
class Num a where
   (+) :: a -> a -> a
   ...
```

which has instances for types such as `Int`, `Integer`, `Float` and `Complex`. Each of these instances provides a definition of the function which is called when it is used at that type. For example:

```
instance Num Int where
   (+) x y = plusInt x y
   ...
```

Since an overloaded function can now be applied to an unboxed type (it was prohibited by the unboxing restriction (*) before), it makes sense to introduce new instances declarations for these unboxed types. For example:

```
instance Num Int# where
   (+) x y = plusInt# x y
   ...
```

This allows us to manipulate unboxed values in the same way as we manipulate their boxed counterparts, greatly reducing the code modifications required when introducing unboxing. It also overloads the literals, allowing us to write 1 instead of 1#, where an `Int#` is required.

4.2 Character I/O

In Haskell I/O is often a major performance bottleneck. One reason for this is that the I/O operations read and write strings i.e. [Char]. Given the ability to manipulate unboxed values directly, it would be nice to extend the I/O system to provide the ability to read and write strings containing unboxed characters i.e. [Char#], as well. One approach would be to introduce a parallel set of I/O operations, such as appendChan#, which read and write [Char#]. This would give the programmer the ability to choose unboxed I/O if desired.

Unfortunately these unboxed I/O operations must be used explicitly (since they require the # in the name). We are currently exploring an alternative approach which overloads the original I/O operations, enabling them to output lists of Char or lists of Char#.

4.3 Separate module compilation

In a language with separate module compilation type information flows from the defining module to the importing module. However, specialisation requires information about the use of a function to flow from the importing module back to the defining module. For example, consider the module structure:

```
module Tree (Tree(..), maptree) where
data Tree k a = Leaf k a | Branch k (Tree a) (Tree a)
maptree :: (a->b) -> Tree k a -> Tree k b
maptree f t = ...

module Use where
import Tree (Tree, maptree)
unbox_inttree :: Tree Int# Int -> Tree Int# Int#
unbox_inttree inttree = maptree int_to_int# inttree
```

In this example, module Use requires the maptree_*_Int#_Int# version of the imported function maptree. However, since Use imports Tree, Tree must be compiled before Use. When we compile Tree there is no requirement to create the maptree_*_Int#_Int# version of maptree since we have no information about module Use. When we subsequently compile Use we are faced with the problem that the required version of maptree has not been created.

One simple solution is to place this responsibility on the programmer: requiring them to request any specialised versions, which are not automatically generated, using pragmas. For example:

```
{-# SPECIALISE maptree :: (Int->Int#) -> Tree Int# Int
                                      -> Tree Int# Int# #-}
```

The SPECIALISE pragma is converted to the corresponding second-order type application: maptree {Int Int# Int#}. This is then processed by the partial evaluator and the specialised versions maptree_*_Int#_Int# produced. The specialised versions of the Tree data type: Tree_Int#_* and Tree_Int#_Int#, will also be created.

The existence of all specialised versions created is recorded in the module's interface. If any specialised versions required by an importing module are not in the interface an error message is generated and the programmer has to add the appropriate specialise pragma to the declaring module and recompile. Unfortunately, the amount of programmer intervention and recompilation required is very unsatisfactory. To reduce these overheads, we plan to develop a scheme which automatically propagates the SPECIALISE pragmas back to the appropriate source modules and only recompiles once.

4.4 Introducing unboxing

In a lazy language, the programmer has to be careful when introducing unboxing, since an unboxed value is also strict. It is only safe to introduce unboxing where the implied strictness does not cause the program to bottom. This is normally not a problem, since the programmer is usually aware of the strictness implications.

We suggest that the programmer ensure that any intended unboxing is made explicit by introducing data type declarations with unboxed components or explicit type signatures for unboxing polymorphic data types. For example, the intention to unbox the list of prime numbers could be specified using the type signature:

```
primes :: [Int#]
```

After introducing this unboxing signature type errors may occur where the unboxed data structure is created and used.[4] In modifying the code to correct these type errors the programmer has to introduce explicit unboxing/boxing coercions at the "boundaries" of the unboxed values. We believe this is a "good thing", since the programmer is forced to identify these boundaries and consider the strictness implications. If the unboxing does cause the program to bottom the boundaries can be moved or the unboxing modifications abandoned.

It remains to be seen what the practical overheads of introducing this form of explicit unboxing are. However, we believe that when performance is an issue, and resources are allocated to improving it[5], it is essential that the programmer has access to language features, such as this, which enable them to optimise the execution.

5 Preliminary Results

We have not yet completed the implementation of the specialiser. However, we do have some preliminary results for programs in which we have introduced some unboxing and performed the necessary specialisation by hand. These are summarised in Figure 4. The Unbox column reports the modifications required to introduce the unboxing while the Boundary column reports the modifications required to coerce data at the boundaries of the unboxing (see Section 4.4). The Specialise and Overload columns report the modifications which we expect to be automated (either by specialisation or as a result of extending the class operations to the unboxed types). The small number of changes required to introduce the unboxing is very encouraging.

---

[4]These boundary type errors will not occur where the unboxed values are created/used by overloaded functions which have instances for the unboxed type (see Section 4.1).

[5]We would also avocate that such improvements are carefully directed at the actual hotspots identified by an execution profiler [18].

Program	Brief Description	Unboxing Modifications
clausify	converts logical formula to their clausal form [17,18]	unbox the character symbols
life	list based implementation of Conway's Life algorithm [2]	unbox the integers used in the board representation
pseudoknot	floating point intensive molecular biology application [5]	unbox all integers and floating point numbers

Program	#lines code	#lines modified/added				Speedup
		Unbox	Boundary	Specialise	Overload	
clausify	112	1	3	25	3	1.25x
life	75	1	1	42	9	1.06x
pseudoknot	3146	3	1	10	2366^6	4.42x

Figure 4: Preliminary results

6   Related Work

Other treatments of polymorphism in the presence of unboxed values fall into two categories. The first automatically introduces coercions which box/unbox values when they are passed to/from a polymorphic function [6,10,13,20]. The costs of creating and manipulating boxed values is only incurred when polymorphic code is used. This has the unfortunate consequence that it penalises the performance of polymorphic code, since unboxing is not possible.

The second approach compiles each polymorphic function in such a way that it can manipulate unboxed values. This is done by passing enough additional information at runtime to describe the representation of the values being manipulated [4,14]. This scheme also penalises the performance of polymorphic code since it must interpret the representation information. It has the unfortunate property that the performance penalty is paid even when the code is manipulating boxed values.

In contrast, our scheme generates specialised versions of polymorphic functions and data types which directly manipulate unboxed values. The performance of polymorphic code is not penalised since the polymorphism is removed precisely where it would impose a performance penalty. It also enables arbitrary data types to contain unboxed components. Traded off against this is the resulting code expansion and the difficulties associated with separate module compilation.

In a strict language, such as ML, both boxed and unboxed values have the same semantics. Consequently, the approaches to unboxing in strict languages focus on *automatically* unboxing values, because doing so is always possible when the type is known at compile time [4,6,10,14,20]. In a non-strict language, such as Haskell, unboxed values can only be introduced if we can be sure that the implied strictness will not change the behaviour of the program. Rather than relying on the often poor results of a strictness analyser, we ask the programmer to indicate where the unboxing is to be introduced. A similar

---

[6]The large number of modifications for pseudoknot were due to the amount of literal data (about 70% of the program) which had to by unboxed by added #s.

approach is taken by Nocker & Smetsers [13]. They require the programmer to introduce explicit strictness annotations which they then use to safely unboxed values.

The use of partial evaluation to produce specialised code is not new. Hall [3] uses partial evaluation of special type arguments to create specialised versions which produce and consume an optimised list representation, while both Augustsson [1] and Jones [9] use partial evaluation to eliminate the overheads of overloading: creating versions which are specialised on their dictionary arguments.[7] Jones [9] also proposes an overloaded implementation of data types which cause the specialisation of overloading to specialises the data types as well. Unfortunately this requires a more powerful system of type classes.

7 Future Work

Our immediate goal is to complete the implementation of the specialiser, and develop a scheme for automatically propagating information about the required specialisations back to the declaring module. This should enable us to experiment with the unboxing of large programs by examining the practicalities of introducing the unboxing and the performance improvements which result.

We also plan to experiment with monomorphisation in general. By modifying the definition of spectys (Figure 3) the partial evaluator can be directed to introduce an arbitrary degree of monomorphisation. For example, if we define spectys $\bar{\tau} = (\bar{\tau}, [\ ])$ we get a completely monomorphic program. Our intention is to explore the practical benefits of optimisations which require monomorphic code to produce good results.

Bibliography

[1] L Augustsson, "Implementing Haskell overloading," *Functional Programming Languages and Computer Architecture*, Copenhagen, Denmark, June 1993, 65–73.

[2] M Gardner, "Wheels, Life and Other Mathematical Amusements," W.H. Freeman and Company, New York, 1993.

[3] CV Hall, "Using Hindley-Milner type inference to optimise list representation," *ACM Conference on Lisp and Functional Programming*, Orlando, Florida, June 1994.

[4] R Harper & G Morrisett, "Compiling Polymorphism Using Intensional Type Analysis," Technical Report CMU-CS-94-185, School of Computer Science, Carnegie Mellon University, Sept 1994.

[5] PH Hartel et al., "Pseudoknot: a float-intensive benchmark for functional compilers," in *Proc Sixth International Workshop on the Implementation of Functional Languages, Norwich*, JRW Glauert, ed., University of East Anglia, Norwich, Sept 1994.

---

[7]Within our compiler we also use our partial evaluator to eliminate overloading by specialising on all overloaded type arguments, in addition to any unboxed type arguments. Care must be taken to ensure that the dictionary argument(s), introduced by the translation into the Core language, are also eliminated.

[6] F Henglein & J Jorgensen, "Formally optimal boxing," in *21st ACM Symposium on Principles of Programming Languages*, ACM, Portland, Oregon, Jan 1994, 213–226.

[7] P Hudak, SL Peyton Jones, PL Wadler, Arvind, B Boutel, J Fairbairn, J Fasel, M Guzman, K Hammond, J Hughes, T Johnsson, R Kieburtz, RS Nikhil, W Partain & J Peterson, "Report on the functional programming language Haskell, Version 1.2," *ACM SIGPLAN Notices* 27(5), May 1992.

[8] John Hughes, "Why functional programming matters," *The Computer Journal* 32(2), April 1989.

[9] MP Jones, "Partial evaluation for dictionary-free overloading," Research Report YALE/DCS/RR-959, Dept of Computer Science, Yale University, April 1993.

[10] X Leroy, "Unboxed objects and polymorphic typing," *19th ACM Symposium on Principles of Programming Languages*, Albuquerque, New Mexico, Jan 1992, 177–188.

[11] JC Mitchell & R Harper, "On the type structure of Standard ML," *ACM Transactions on Programming Languages and Systems* 15(2), April 1993, 211–252.

[12] R Morrison, A Dearle, RCH Conner & AL Brown, "An ad-hoc approach to the implementation of polymorphism," *ACM Transactions on Programming Languages and Systems* 13(3), July 1991, 342–371.

[13] E Nocker & S Smetsers, "Partially strict non-recursive data types," *Journal of Functional Programming* 3(2), April 1993, 191–217.

[14] A Ohori & T Takamizawa, "A polymorphic unboxed calculus and efficient compilation of ML," Research Institute for Mathematical Sciences, Kyoto University, Japan, 1994.

[15] SL Peyton Jones, CV Hall, K Hammond, WD Partain & PL Wadler, "The Glasgow Haskell compiler: a technical overview," *Joint Framework for Information Technology (JFIT) Technical Conference Digest*, Keele, March 1993, 249–257.

[16] SL Peyton Jones & J Launchbury, "Unboxed values as first class citizens," *Functional Programming Languages and Computer Architecture*, Cambridge, Massachusetts, Sept 1991.

[17] C Runciman & D Wakeling, "Heap profiling of lazy functional programs," *Journal of Functional Programming* 3(2), April 1993, 217–245.

[18] PM Sansom, "Execution profiling for non-strict functional languages," PhD thesis, Research Report FP-1994-09, Dept of Computing Science, University of Glasgow, Sept 1994.

[19] PM Sansom & SL Peyton Jones, "Time and space profiling for non-strict, higher-order functional languages," *22nd ACM Symposium on Principles of Programming Languages*, San Francisco, California, Jan 1995.

[20] PJ Thiemann, "Unboxed values and polymorphic typing revisited," in *Proc Sixth International Workshop on the Implementation of Functional Languages, Norwich*, JRW Glauert, ed., University of East Anglia, Norwich, Sept 1994.

Improving Granularity in Parallel Functional Programs: A Graphical Winnowing System for Haskell

Kevin Hammond*   Hans Wolfgang Loidl†

Dept. of Computing Science, University of Glasgow, Glasgow, U.K.

E-mail: {kh,hwloidl}@dcs.gla.ac.uk

Andrew Partridge

Dept. of Computer Science, University of Tasmania, Australia.

E-mail: A.S.Partridge@cs.utas.edu.au

Abstract

To take advantage of distributed-memory parallel machines it is essential to have good control of task granularity. This paper describes a fairly accurate parallel simulator for Haskell, based on the Glasgow compiler, and complementary tools for visualising task granularities. Together these tools allow us to study the effects of various annotations on task granularity on a variety of simulated parallel architectures. They also provide a more precise tool for the study of parallel execution than has previously been available for Haskell programs.

These tools have already confirmed granularity results previously obtained for our novel GRIP architecture, demonstrated a close correlation between thread execution times and total heap allocations, and revealed that conservative granularity analysis may well be too conservative.

Winnow (v.):   To treat (as grain) by exposure to a current of air so that waste matter is eliminated.

1   Introduction

Our aim is to produce fast, cost-effective implementations of lazy functional languages. One way to improve speed is to introduce parallelism, and pure functional languages offer long-term hope for good speedups on many processors without much programmer effort.

We have already successfully shown that good absolute speedups can be achieved on a machine which has a limited number of processors and a relatively small interprocessor communications latency, the novel GRIP multiprocessor [8]. This is comparatively straightforward, because such machines can

---

*Supported by a SOED Research Fellowship from the Royal Society of Edinburgh and the UK EPSRC Parade project.

†Supported by a Kurt-Gödel scholarship (GZ 558.012/38-IV/5a/93) of the Austrian Ministry of Science and Research and by a KIP scholarship of the government of Upper Austria.

take advantage of quite fine grains of parallelism. However, as the number of processors in the machine is increased, architectural constraints tend to force an increase in interprocessor communication latency. This means that to achieve acceptable speedups, it is necessary to break the program into appropriately-sized grains for parallel execution.

In his thesis, Goldberg explored the idea of "optimal" grains of parallelism through the use of serial combinators [4]. Unfortunately, this level of granularity proved far from optimal for the Alfalfa implementation [5] on the distributed-memory Intel iPSC, despite showing promising performance for the Buckwheat implementation on the shared-memory Encore Multimax. Although other authors have returned to this issue (e.g. [14]) there has been very little systematic research on the granularity displayed by real programs and the mechanisms which are necessary to control that granularity in a general framework. Partly this is due to the lack of realistic monitoring tools which can be used to obtain information about a program's granularity. One approach for dealing with that problem is to compile and run a program with monitoring code inserted. The statistics information gained by that test run is then fed back into the compiler for producing optimised parallel code ([17]).

In this paper we describe a tool for investigating task granularity, and propose annotations which will enable us to exploit granularity information in a parallel environment. As a first step, we are simply investigating the mechanisms which should be used to control granularity. Since we do not know what information an automated system might need to use, we have currently annotated the programs by hand. However, it is our intention that the annotations will eventually be inserted by a *static granularity analysis*, so as to provide automated control of parallel programs.

The structure of this paper is as follows. Section 2 describes the design of a fairly realistic parallel machine simulator, based on the Glasgow Haskell compiler. Section 3 presents a set of annotations we intend to use to improve parallel performance through optimising grain size. Section 4 describes the tool we have built for visualising thread granularities and related information. Section 5 gives some early simulation results obtained using the simulator and visualisation tool. Finally, Section 6 concludes.

2 Granularity simulation

To help decide what information a granularity analysis should produce, we need to know how annotations can be used to control granularity in practice, and how granularity information can be used to determine where to insert these annotations with best effect[1].

Before committing serious effort to designing a granularity analysis, it is therefore highly desirable to experiment with the effects of using various annotations in a variety of programs running on a range of architectures. To this end, we have built a simulator for distributed-memory machines running Haskell with annotations to control task scheduling.

In a recent paper Runciman and Wakeling describe an idealised simulator for parallel machines [15]. This simulator is similar to previous work (e.g. [1], [14])

---

[1] For some reason, the opposite approach has generally been taken with strictness analysis, but luckily most strictness information is useful, at least to identify potentially parallel tasks!

in adding pseudo-parallel traces to an otherwise sequential run, but has the advantage of producing a graphical profile of the simulated processor activity in terms of blocked, runnable and running tasks. While such a tool is potentially highly useful in identifying programs which are insufficiently parallel (the FLARE project produced several such examples [16]), it has a number of deficiencies which make it an unreliable predictor of real parallel performance:

- each supercombinator reduction takes an identical amount of time;

- communication costs are not accounted for;

- task creation costs are not considered; and

- the scheduling algorithm is highly unrealistic.

Typically these inaccuracies will lead to an overstatement of the degree of parallelism in a program, but we cannot honestly state that the figure derived is a strict upper bound on parallelism.

A more detailed simulator than the one built by Runciman and Wakeling, tunable to suit different classes of architecture, but based on the same ideas, would seem to be ideal for monitoring granularity effects.

2.1 Threads

Our simulator is built around the threaded interpreter which Mattson has developed for work on concurrency in a sequential setting. In Mattson's threaded interpreter, there is a single thread pool which is scheduled in a round-robin fashion. There is also a single pool of sparks, which represent potential parallel work, and which are turned into threads as required (if sparked expressions are already in WHNF then the sparks are discarded without ever becoming threads). Threads context-switch after a pre-defined time interval when they reach a suitably safe point in the computation. This is normally at the next heap allocation, where the thread must be prepared to transfer control to the garbage collector, and thus where registers and heap pointers are in a known state. By setting the timeout to zero, a context-switch can be forced at each heap allocation. Finne exploits this effect in his work on concurrency and non-determinism [3].

To adapt Mattson's threaded interpreter for parallel simulation, we introduce *multiple* thread and spark pools, one of each per processor that is being simulated. Context-switches are forced at the end of every basic block, so that each simulated processor is scheduled as frequently as possible. The scheduling algorithm is changed from round-robin to an *unfair* scheduler, so that each processor executes the same thread for as long as possible (typically until it communicates). In the future we plan to investigate different scheduling strategies.

The overall structure of the parallel simulator is shown in Figure 1. In the parallel simulation each thread has a *statistics buffer* attached to its thread state object (TSO). This records:

- a label identifying the spark which created the thread;

- when the thread started;

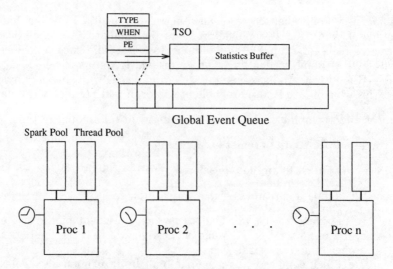

Figure 1: Overall structure of the simulator

- whether the thread was produced by an exportable spark;
- whether the thread was migrated from another processor;
- how many exportable/non-exportable sparks the thread has generated;
- how many heap allocations have been performed;
- how many basic blocks the thread has executed;
- how long overall the thread has been blocked;
- if it is currently blocked, when it became blocked; and
- how much time has been spent reading remote data.

When a thread terminates, the contents of this buffer and the time it terminated are dumped to a trace file.

2.2 Global events

We introduce a global event queue, whose entries are: <TYPE, WHEN, PE, TSO>. WHEN gives the time at which the event should occur. PE identifies the processor on which the event should occur. TSO is an optional pointer to a *thread state object* which identifies a thread on PE when this is relevant to the event.

The possible event types in the TYPE field are:

CONTINUE:	Continue running a thread
START:	Convert a spark into a new thread
RESUME:	Resume a previously blocked thread
FISH:	Search for work
MOVESPARK:	Move a spark to a new processor
MOVETHREAD:	Move (migrate) a thread to a new processor

The events in the queue are ordered by time (the WHEN field). Each processor has its own local clock, which is used to timestamp events which occur on that processor. Events involving multiple processors are timestamped by combining the clocks of the participating processors. This helps avoid large differences in local clock times.

2.3 Running threads

At each context switch, a CONTINUE event for the current thread is added to the event queue. We then create new threads from the spark pool of each idle processor as START events at CREATE-TIME steps in the future.

When a thread terminates, the processor chooses a runnable thread, if it has one, from its local thread pool, and posts a CONTINUE event. If there are no runnable threads but its spark pool is not empty, it starts a new thread, posting a START event. Otherwise it is idle, so it posts a FISH event.

A FISH event simulates the action of an idle processor looking for work. If any processor has excess work, then this is stolen by the idle processor by generating a MOVESPARK or MOVETHREAD event at STEAL-TIME in the future. Sparks are stolen in preference to threads, and have a lower steal time reflecting their smaller size. Although many implementations ignore thread migration on the grounds that it is costly and difficult to implement, experiments on GRIP have shown that it is essential for good parallel performance of coarse-grained applications [9].

2.4 Blocking and resumption

If a thread demands the value of a node which another thread is evaluating, and which therefore has been turned into a "black hole", then it *blocks* and a blocking queue is created. When a node that has a blocking queue is updated, a RESUME event is scheduled at RESUME-TIME in the future for each <PE,TSO> which is in the blocking queue. When a RESUME event occurs, the corresponding TSO is added to the queue of executable threads on PE.

2.5 Measuring costs

Heap allocations

Each time a heap allocation occurs, the number of words allocated is added to the appropriate part of the statistics buffer. This provides an accurate count of the number of words allocated by each thread, which can be directly compared with results previously obtained on GRIP [7].

Time

Each basic block is analysed to produce a count of the number of operations in each of five categories: arithmetic/register operations, loads, stores, branches, and floating-point operations. These counts are passed to the simulator each time the basic block is executed. Using these categories rather than an exact measure is much simpler (determining the exact runtime without running a program is a black art for many modern architectures) and allows the operations to be weighted appropriately for different architectures such as the MC68020 used in GRIP or the SPARC used in the ICL Goldrush.

Shared data

Each object has a fixed-size bitmask attached, which shows which processors have a copy of that object. Newly created objects reside on the current processor. When a node is entered to retrieve its value, a check is made to see if there is a local copy. If not, the current thread becomes temporarily suspended and the object is copied to the current processor by setting a bit in the bitmask. Figure 2 shows the layout of closures in the global heap using this scheme.

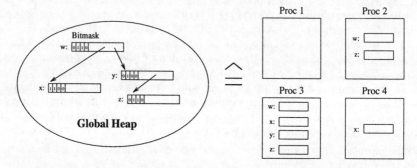

Figure 2: Space-efficient representation of globally shared closures

This technology has the advantage of avoiding duplicate copies in the simulator and eliminates the need to simulate the FETCHME closures etc. which are used in GRAPH for UMM [18]. It is, however, limited to simulating at most a fixed number of processors because of the use of a fixed-size bitmask. A 32- or 64-bit bitmask is easily provided, and should be capable of representing an interesting number of processors. If it becomes necessary to model large numbers of processors, the bitmask could easily be replaced by a linked-list of processor numbers.

Accuracy

Much of the esoterica needed for a real parallel machine has been abstracted away: fetching data, garbage collection costs, etc. However, we believe that enough of a real machine is being simulated that our results will be meaningful to an adequate extent.

We assume that each instruction of a given class takes a fixed number of clock cycles. While this is a reasonable abstraction for the initial version of the simulator, there may be some inaccuracy with instructions whose cost varies depending on cache effects. Given our experiences in [6], modelling caches in this simulator might be an interesting extension in the future. There may also be some inaccuracy where the cost of different instructions in the same class varies significantly. To overcome the latter problem, we have calibrated our results with real instruction traces as described in Section 5.

Garbage collection and other memory overheads are not modelled, but could easily be simulated on a per-processor basis by including appropriate costs after a certain number of heap allocations on each processor.

The simulator accurately models interprocessor communication latency for fetching data and migrating threads and sparks. However, we currently model only the GRAPH for GRIP style of incremental data-fetching [8]. This is potentially disastrous in a distributed-memory setting since it significantly increases the number of packets which must be sent when copying a large data structure between processors. In future, we plan to model the more sophisticated data-fetching models proposed for GRAPH for UMM [18], which are similar to those used by the Concurrent Clean implementation [11].

3 Granularity annotations

Our primary concern is executing functional programs on distributed memory machines, where access to data which is local to a processor is much cheaper than access to non-local data. On such machines the decisions of what data and work to distribute are both difficult and crucial. The purpose of the annotations described in this section is to assist the scheduler in achieving a good mapping of threads to processors. It is our intention that these annotations will eventually be inserted automatically by the compiler.

The annotations (really combinators) used on GRIP are par and seq, which have the following behaviour:

- par s e sparks a thread to evaluate s to WHNF. The sparking thread continues to evaluate and returns e. In order to ensure correct functional semantics, s must terminate whenever e does.

- seq x y evaluates x to WHNF, then evaluates and returns y as part of the same thread.

For the most part these two annotations will be all that is necessary to use the results of granularity analysis. We are considering a few additional annotations, which are similar to ones previously suggested in the literature (e.g. [2]).

- parGlobal name s e is identical to par except that it takes an extra integer name parameter, for use in identifying the spark location.

- parLocal name s e is identical to parGlobal except that the sparks it produces are local and cannot be exported to another processor.

- parAt name v s e is identical to parGlobal except that it evaluates s on the processor which owns v.

- copyable closures are ones which are cheap to compute but which give large results (for example, an expression such as [1..x]). To avoid space leaks and excess communication, only the unevaluated form of the expression is fetched.

4 Visualisation

We provide a set of graphical tools to help analyse the results of the simulation. Most of these tools give information about the *granularity* of threads. However, we also provide some tools for showing overall *activity* profiles.

The visualisation tool we have built especially for granularity analysis takes a trace file produced by a simulator run and produces graphical profiles of the number of threads by:

- granularity (pure execution time);

- amount of heap allocation (in words);

- number of local sparks created by the thread;

- number of global sparks created by the thread;

- total communication time; and

- percentage of the total runtime spent communicating.

Each profile can be specialised for threads created via `parLocal` or `parGlobal`. For the latter threads we can distinguish between those that have been exported and those that have been executed locally.

In addition, because each spark site can be named, each kind of profile can be generated individually for just those threads that are produced by a given spark site. This allows us to focus on the most interesting points of thread creation without being overwhelmed with irrelevant information.

The time, heap, and communications profiles can also be produced as cumulative graphs. These have the advantage that the appearance of the profile does not depend on arbitrarily-chosen categories. In addition, several cumulative graphs can be plotted on a single set of axes. This provides an easy way to compare the runtime behaviour of an algorithm while varying parameters such as the number of processors or the communication latency.

For showing the overall runtime behaviour of a parallel program with respect to its execution time, three kinds of activity profiles can also be produced:

- Overall activity. This profile shows the total number of running, runnable, migrating, sparked and blocked threads at each point in time. It is similar to, but more accurate than the activity profile produced by the Runciman/Wakeling simulator [15].

- Per-processor activity. This profile shows how many runnable and blocked threads each processor has at any point in time. It can optionally be overlaid with thread migration information.

- Per-thread activity. This profile shows the periods during which each thread is active, runnable or blocked.

These profiles deliver very important information about parallel algorithms. The detail provided by using each level of profile in turn allows a very efficient way of performance-debugging. This has already proved to be invaluable for parallelising a linear-equation solving algorithm.

In summary, the activity and especially the granularity profiles let us do the following:

- identify spark sites that generate threads which communicate too much;
- check that the most suitable sparks are being exported;
- check that `parLocal` and `parGlobal` are used appropriately;
- identify excessively large threads which may be split into smaller ones in order to improve parallelism;
- identify which threads and/or spark sites cause space problems;
- distinguish the behaviour of threads generated from different spark sites.

The following section shows how some of these profiles can be used to obtain interesting granularity results, and gives comparisons with previous results obtained from GRIP.

5 Results

This section gives some results obtained using our simulation tools. We have used three test programs: a simple functional ray-tracer *ray* described in [16], a word searching program *word*, also described in [16], and a divide-and-conquer factorial program *factorial*.

```
main inp = [AppendChan stdout (show (factorial 5000))]

factorial x = pf 1 x

pf x y | x < y     = parGlobal 1 f1 (seq f2 (f1+f2))
       | otherwise = x
                where m  = (x+y) 'div' 2
                      f1 = pf x m
                      f2 = pf (m+1) y
```

5.1 Accuracy of the Simulation

If we are to have any confidence in the results from our simulator, it is important to calibrate it carefully.

Time

Obviously the simulator cannot give perfect static costings in all cases (the cost of an update will depend on the number of objects which are updated, for example), but we hope that the simulator will be accurate to within a small margin of error.

We use the following weights for the cost classes, as a rough estimate of the corresponding costs on a SPARC (including cache effects): arithmetic/float 1 cycle; load/store 4 cycles; branches 2 cycles. These settings give the following simulated instruction counts which can be compared with those obtained from a dynamic instruction trace (we used Gordon Irlam's SPA trace package for the SPARC). The traced values include cache costs for a 64K direct-mapped cache as used on, e.g. a Sun SparcStation 2.

Program	Cycles (Simulated)	Cycles (Traced)	Error
factorial	1,450,659	1,497,400	-3%
ray	381,633,153	369,060,385	+3%

Heap Allocation

In a previous paper [7] we presented granularity profiles for several versions of *ray*, using the heap allocations performed by a thread to approximate its execution time. We used heap allocations rather than a timer because on a real machine such as GRIP, it is hard to measure small time differences without biasing the performance results. Previous research [10] has demonstrated a correspondence between program duration and the amount of heap allocated, so this is not an unreasonable choice, but anecdotal evidence suggests that modern compilers, such as the Glasgow Haskell compiler used for GRIP, might no longer exhibit the same behaviour.

Our own research does indeed suggest that allocation rates can vary significantly from one program to another. Table 1 gives rates for several programs from the noFib benchmark suite [13].

Benchmark	Time (s)	Allocation (MByte)	Allocation rate (MByte/s)
anna	1040.44	224	0.22
fulsom	83.59	496	6.40
ray	71.27	64	0.93
rsa	19.02	30	1.58
infer	6.12	10	1.64
parser	4.99	16	0.43
compress	4.09	12	3.00
pic	2.56	11	4.58
fluid	1.06	4.81	4.54
reptile	0.98	6.59	6.73
hpg	0.95	3.65	3.88
veritas	0.21	0.44	2.04
prolog	0.16	0.81	4.94

Table 1: Execution times and heap allocation rates for some noFib programs

However, for some simple parallel programs there is a strong correlation between execution time and heap allocation for different threads in the same program (Table 2). While this does not hold in general, it does validate the use of heap allocation as a measure of granularity for the programs studied in [7].

PEs	word	factorial	ray
2	0.998784	1.000000	0.999997
4	0.983595	0.999967	0.999934
8	0.978600	0.999992	0.999946
16	0.970150	0.999968	0.999961
32	0.968747	0.999914	0.999966

Table 2: Correlation between execution time and heap allocation

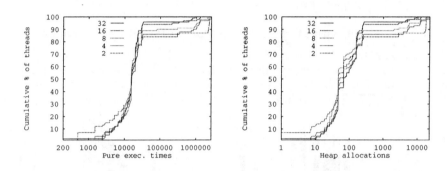

Figure 3: Cumulative time and heap profiles: Word Search, Simulator

5.2 Granularity

Figure 3 shows the simulated cumulative time and heap profiles for *word*. These graphs are plotted with a logarithmic time scale to enable the wide range of the data to fit. The correlation between the heap and time profiles is clearly visible. As with the GRIP results reported in [7], there is a strong family resemblance between profiles for varying numbers of processors, with the 2-processor case being the most dissimilar.

The cumulative profiles for *ray* also show remarkable visual correspondence between the results for different numbers of processors, and for runtime and heap (Figure 4).

Figure 5 compares the heap granularity profiles for the 16-processor cases for the simulator and GRIP. There are clear similarities between the two sets of profiles. The comparison for other numbers of processors is similar.

For *word*, both profiles show a clustering of small and medium sized threads (with many more medium than small threads), then a gap before the one or two sets of large threads. Significantly, the number of threads in the largest category is approximately the same in both cases. The simulator reports fewer heap allocations for the large threads than were observed on GRIP. This may be due to small differences in the compilers used in each case, or may be because the simulator is breaking some threads into smaller parts.

For *ray*, there are two principal clusters in each set of profiles, due to the way the program is parallelised: each thread in the cluster of small threads has the sole duty of walking down a list and sparking a thread to evaluate each

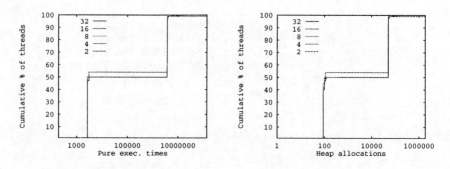

Figure 4: Cumulative time and heap profiles: Ray Tracer, Simulator

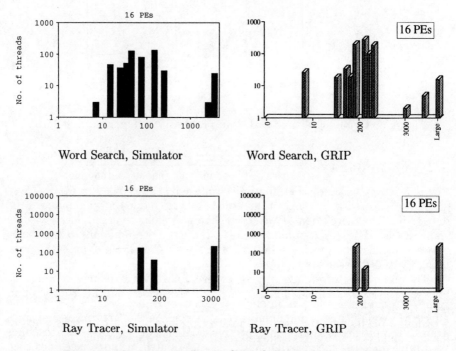

Word Search, Simulator   Word Search, GRIP

Ray Tracer, Simulator   Ray Tracer, GRIP

Figure 5: Granularity Profile [Heap]: Simulator v. GRIP

element of that list in parallel. The cluster of large threads is comprised of
those threads sparked by the small threads. Removing the small threads would
have a deleterious effect on performance, since this would result in almost no
parallelism being created. For the *ray* case, the correspondence between the
profiles obtained from the simulator and GRIP is almost exact. This is clear
confirmation that the simulation is a good model of real parallel performance.

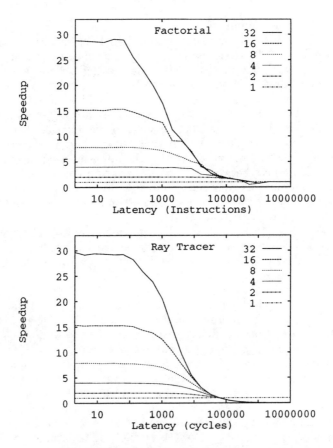

Figure 6: Speedup v. Latency

5.3 Latency

Although not a primary objective, the simulator has also given us an opportunity to study the effect of latency on execution times. Figure 6 shows the effects of varying latency and number of processors on the *factorial* and *ray* programs. To put these graphs in perspective, a latency of 5–10 cycles corresponds to a typical shared-memory machine, fast distributed-memory machines such as GRIP or the Meiko CS2 have latencies in the 100–500 cycle range, while typical distributed-memory machines such as the IBM SP2 have latencies of 1,000–5,000 cycles. Fully distributed machines connected over an ethernet LAN would typically have latencies of 25,000–100,000 cycles.

For the *factorial* program, for latencies below 200 instruction cycles, we see good speedups for all numbers of processors, dropping to a maximum of around 15 as the latency rises to 1,000 cycles. Interestingly, the speedup only drops below one (giving a parallel slowdown) when the latency rises above around 500,000 cycles. Beyond around 4,000,000 cycles the speedup returns to one, because the latency is too high to allow any significant distribution of work before the program terminates.

For the *ray* program, we observe chaotic behaviour with 32 processors for latencies below 2,000 cycles. There is also some evidence of a similar effect for *factorial* at low latency values. This is due to slight variations in scheduling causing small threads to be executed early, leaving only a few longer threads at the end of the run. This causes a processor load imbalance at the end of the run that would normally have been prevented by moving small threads.

Parallel slowdown cuts in somewhat earlier for *ray* than for *factorial*, at a latency of almost 100,000 cycles. Because of the longer running time of *ray*, the speedup does not return to one for the latencies used in the experiment. The other differences between the two programs are probably due to the fact that the shared data used by each ray tracer thread is significantly larger than for *factorial*. Hence communication costs are more important and the program is more sensitive to changes in latency.

We have also run *ray* with thread migration disabled. The result was poor speedups for low latencies, and, paradoxically, good speedups at intermediate latencies. This occurs because at low latencies when an early started thread becomes temporarily blocked, the processor is able to quickly acquire another thread to run. Without thread migration, when the temporarily-blocked thread resumes, both it and the newly-acquired thread are locked to the same processor, leading to a loss of parallelism. At intermediate latencies it takes longer to acquire a thread, so processors are not able to do so while another thread is temporarily blocked, and the problem does not occur.

The slowdown results are potentially significant for granularity analysis: Garcia et al. have built their granularity analysis for first-order logic programs on a conservative speedup assumption [12]. If the lower bound derived by their analysis for a given spark site is less than one then their system will not distribute work. Obviously, if this assumption is *too* conservative then much useful parallelism will be lost. However, if the results obtained for *factorial* and *ray* hold for a range of programs, then this suggests that we can safely ignore a derived lower bound for program complexity, and schedule sparks solely on the basis of a good upper bound. We should then avoid sparking threads altogether on machines with known high latencies. This approach is not only likely to yield greater parallelism than a conservative approach, but should also require less analysis since only one bound need be computed.

6   Conclusions

This paper has introduced an accurate and tunable simulator for a wide range of parallel machine architectures. Unlike most other simulators our objective is to discover information about the granularity of parallel threads. To assist this task, the simulator is provided with a powerful graphical visualisation tool, which helps isolate patterns of granularity.

We intend to use this simulator to explore annotations for granularity control with a view to producing automatic granularity analysis. In order to produce a high-quality analysis we need high-quality performance metrics for each thread that the program produces. Simple overall execution-time, or average thread length metrics are unlikely to locate problems with the placement of annotations. We have already obtained some detailed granularity results for

GRIP [7], but these earlier results are limited to allocation-based profiling, and do not allow us to explore latency-related issues. Since we plan to target our compiler for other parallel machines, it is important to obtain as broad a range of results as possible for particular annotations before investing significant implementation effort.

There is, of course, a danger that the design of the simulator may obscure real artefacts or introduce false ones. The only true performance measure is execution on a real machine. We have attempted to avoid these problems as far as possible by building our simulator on a state-of-the-art compiler, by modelling exactly the scheduling algorithm we propose to use for GRAPH for UMM, by careful modelling of significant events such as communication, and by comparing the results of the simulation with equivalent datapoints obtained from real hardware (both sequential and parallel).

The results shown in Section 5 confirm earlier results obtained from GRIP. There are clear similarities between granularity profiles for varying numbers of processors, though the profile for the 2 processor case bears the least family resemblance. The heap profiles from the simulator are very similar to those obtained for GRIP, which lends extra credence to the general accuracy of our simulation.

An important new result to arise from the simulation is that there is a close correlation between time and heap granularity profiles for the programs studied, even though there is no correlation between program length and the amount of heap allocated. We have also discovered some interesting interactions between latency and performance. Most significant for our work on granularity is the observation that for sensible latencies (i.e. those likely to be encountered in the real world), there is no parallel slowdown for the programs that we have studied. If confirmed, this result will help simplify the cost of static granularity analysis by eliminating the need for lower as well as upper-bound cost estimation.

References

[1] JM. Deschner. Simulating Multiprocessor Architectures for Compiled Graph-Reduction. In MK. Davis and RJM. Hughes (Eds), *Glasgow Workshop on Functional Programming*, pp. 225–237, Fraserburgh, Scotland, August 21–23, 1989. Springer.

[2] MCJD. van Eekelen, EGJMH. Nöcker, MJ. Plasmeijer, and JEW. Smetsers. Concurrent Clean. Technical Report 89–18, Univ. of Nijmegen, October 1989.

[3] S. Finne and SL. Peyton Jones. Supporting Concurrent State Threads. In *Glasgow Workshop on Functional Programming*, Ayr, Scotland, September 12–14, 1994. Springer.

[4] B. Goldberg. *Multiprocessor Execution of Functional Programs*. PhD thesis, Dept. of Computer Science, Yale University, April 1988.

[5] B. Goldberg and P. Hudak. Alfalfa: Distributed Graph Reduction on a Hypercube Multiprocessor. In *Workshop on Graph Reduction and Techniques*, LNCS 279, pp. 94–113. Springer, 1987.

[6] K. Hammond, GL. Burn, and DB. Howe. Spiking your Caches. In JT. O'Donnell and K. Hammond (Eds), *Glasgow Workshop on Functional Programming*, pp. 58–68, Ayr, Scotland, July 5–7, 1993. Springer.

[7] K. Hammond, JS. Mattson Jr., and SL. Peyton Jones. Automatic Spark Strategies and Granularity for a Parallel Functional Language Reducer. In B. Buchberger and J. Volkert (Eds), *CONPAR'94*, LNCS 854, pp. 521–532, Linz, Austria, September 6–8, 1994.

[8] K. Hammond and SL. Peyton Jones. Some Early Experiments on the GRIP Parallel Reducer. In MJ. Plasmeijer (Ed), *Second Intl. Workshop on the Parallel Implementation of Functional Languages*, Univ. of Nijmegen, The Netherlands, pp. 51–72, June 1990.

[9] K. Hammond and SL. Peyton Jones. Profiling Scheduling Strategies on the GRIP Multiprocessor. In H. Kuchen and R. Loogen (Eds), *Fourth Intl. Workshop on the Parallel Implementation of Functional Languages*, pp. 73 – 98, RWTH Aachen, Germany, September 1992.

[10] PH. Hartel and AH. Veen. Statistics on Graph Reduction of SASL Programs. *Software—Practice and Experience*, 18(3):239–253, March 1988.

[11] M. Kesseler. Reducing Graph Copying Costs – Time to Wrap it up. In H. Hong (Ed), *PASCO '94*, pp. 244–253, Linz, Austria, September 26–28, 1994. World Scientific.

[12] P. López Garcia, M. Hermenegildo, and SK. Debray. Towards Granularity Based Control of Parallelism in Logic Programs. In H. Hong (Ed), *PASCO'94*, pp. 133–144, Linz, Austria, September 26–28, 1994. World Scientific.

[13] W. Partain. The nofib Benchmark Suite of Haskell Programs. In J. Launchbury and P. Sansom (Eds), *Glasgow Workshop on Functional Programming*, pp. 195–202, Ayr, Scotland, July 6–8, 1992. Springer.

[14] P. Roe. *Parallel Programming using Functional Languages*. PhD thesis, Dept. of Computing Science, Univ. of Glasgow, February 1991.

[15] C. Runciman and D. Wakeling. Profiling Parallel Functional Computations (Without Parallel Machines). In JT. O'Donnell and K. Hammond (Eds), *Glasgow Workshop on Functional Programming*, pp. 236–251, Ayr, Scotland, July 5–7, 1993. Springer.

[16] C. Runciman and D. Wakeling (Eds). *Functional Languages Applied to Realistic Examplars: the FLARE Project*. UCL Press, 1994.

[17] J. Sargeant. Improving Compilation of Implicit Parallel Programs by Using Runtime Information. *Workshop on Compilation of Symbolic Langs. for Parallel Computers*, Argonne National Lab. Technical Report ANL–91/34, pp. 129–148, 1991.

[18] P. Trinder, K. Hammond, H-W. Loidl, JS. Mattson Jr., A. Partridge, and SL. Peyton Jones. GRAPHing the Future. In J. Glauert (Ed), *Sixth Intl. Workshop on the Implementation of Functional Languages*, Univ. of East Anglia, Norwich, U.K., September 7–9, 1994.

Fold-Unfold Transformations on State Monadic Interpreters

Thomas Johnsson

Department of Computer Science

Chalmers University of Technology

Göteborg, Sweden

Abstract

In this paper we advocate the use of fold-unfold transformations for mastering the complexity of abstract machines intended for real implementations. The idea is to express the abstract machine as an interpreter in a purely functional language. The initial interpreter should be 'obviously correct' (but might be inefficient – we don't care at this point). Fold-unfold transformations are then used to remove inefficiencies in the interpreter/abstract machine. We illustrate this by deriving (the equivalent of) the $\mathcal{E}$-scheme of the G-machine from (the equivalent of) the composition of $\mathcal{C}$ and the `EVAL` instruction. This is first done on a call-by-name (tree reduction) interpreter. To model sharing and the graph manipulation that goes on in a real graph reduction implementation, we use state monads. We do the same transformation of the state monadic interpreter. It is much less straightforward to transform the state monadic interpreter, as we have to lean heavily on the laws of the state monad. In return the state monadic interpreter can be said to better model a real implementation.

1 Introduction

Abstract machines, being the basis of real implementations of programming languages, functional or otherwise, are most often based on simple principles — but when confronted with the idiosyncrasies of every-day usage of the language and its compiler, often become quite complex in the hands of the implementor. This is both unsurprising and to be respected: implementors should spare no effort to improve on the efficiency of the cases that turn out to be frequent in daily use of the language and the compiler, in order not to waste other's or one's own cycles.

To mention a few examples: the Three Instruction Machine (TIM) [FW87] is indeed very simple (hence its name), but when used in a real implementation has considerably more instructions [Arg89, Arg90]. In the G-machine [Joh84] the basic compiled graph reduction scheme has been adorned with several other compilations schemes to deal with such matters as turning tail recursion into loops, and the efficient evaluation of basic valued expressions. The Spineless Tagless G-machine [PJS89, PJ92] has quite a cunning machinery for returning constructor values and to reduce the number of tag scrutinisations.

These abstract machines have all been constructed 'by hand', and it is not always easy to see that they implement what is intended, or whether all cases are covered.

The issues of complexity of abstract machines became particularly acute to this author when trying to define a variant of the G-machine, called the Optimistic G-machine, to do speculative evaluation of otherwise lazy arguments (see also section 6). Thus, the Optimistic G-machine performs not only 'normal' evaluation, but also speculative ones which stop when a certain amount of 'fuel' has been expended. The interplay between 'normal' evaluation, speculative evaluation, and as the last straw, sharing to implement call-by-need, was simply too mind-boggling to deal with in an ad hoc way and at the same time be confident that the machine did the right thing at all times.

Meanwhile, in other corners of computing science, more formal (and mech-anisable!) approaches to the improvement the efficiency of programs are taken; in particular we want to mention fold-unfold transformations [BD77].

It turns out that such transformations can be done on abstract machine too; and that is what this paper is about. Thus, what we advocate here is a more formal approach also to the optimisation of compilers and abstract machines, where an initial simple and 'obviously correct' (but possibly very inefficient) purely functional interpreter is transformed into a more efficient one, using fold-unfold transformations (here we take interpreters and abstract machines to be synonyms).

But rather than diving into the unknown waters of speculative evaluation and the Optimistic G-machine, in this paper we intend to stay on familiar grounds, and show how to recast a particular optimisation of the G-machine, the introduction of the $\mathcal{E}$-scheme, into the mold of fold-unfold transformations.

In modelling the graph manipulation needed to implement sharing and call-by-need, an interpreter needs to pass around a state (the heap) in a single-threaded manner. Monads [Wad92, Wad90, PJW93] and in particular state monads, have turned out to be very convenient formalism to do this. Thus, we also redo this exercise with a call-by-need interpreter written using a state monad. It turns out that the general monadic laws, i.e., the associative, left unit and right unit laws, are very helpful in doing so — in fact, *must* be used to proceed. These transformations constitute the main part of this paper.

Thus, this paper is organised as follows. In section 2 we recapitulate the motivations behind the introduction of the $\mathcal{E}$-scheme in the G-machine. In section 3 we describe the very simple language dealt with in this paper. In section 4 we derive the $\mathcal{E}$-scheme in a call-by-name setting using traditional fold-unfold methods. In section 5 we redo the entire exercise with a call-by-need interpreter using a state monad. In section 6 we say a bit more about the Optimistic G-machine, the motivation behind it, and how the techniques described in this paper help. Section 7 concludes.

2   Recapitulation: The $\mathcal{E}$-scheme in the G-machine

In the barest and most basic G-machine, evaluation of a function application proceeds by repeatedly *instantiating* the right hand side of the function defi-nition given the actual arguments of the function application. Thus the code for a function definition simply builds the graph of the right hand side, given a stack of pointers into the argument graphs, and re-applies EVAL to the result-ing graph. Figure 1 shows a (grossly simplified) fragment of such a compiler.

$$\mathcal{F}[\![f \; x_1 \; \ldots \; x_n = e]\!] = \mathcal{C}[\![e]\!] \; [n/x_1, \; \ldots \; 1/x_n] \; n; \; \text{EVAL}; \; \text{UPDATE\_RETURN} \; n$$

$$\mathcal{C}[\![x]\!] \; \rho \; n = \text{PUSH}(n - \rho \; x)$$
$$\mathcal{C}[\![f]\!] \; \rho \; n = \text{PUSHGLOBAL} \; f$$
$$\mathcal{C}[\![cons \; e_1 \; e_2]\!] \; \rho \; n = \mathcal{C}[\![e_2]\!] \; \rho \; n; \; \mathcal{C}[\![e_1]\!] \; \rho \; (n+1); \; \text{CONS}$$
$$\mathcal{C}[\![e_1 \; e_2]\!] \; \rho \; n = \mathcal{C}[\![e_2]\!] \; \rho \; n; \; \mathcal{C}[\![e_1]\!] \; \rho \; (n+1); \; \text{MKAP}$$
$$\ldots$$

Figure 1: Fragment of compiler to produce instantiating G-machine code

$$\mathcal{F}[\![f \; x_1 \; \ldots \; x_n = e]\!] = \mathcal{E}[\![e]\!] \; [n/x_1, \; \ldots \; 1/x_n] \; n; \; \text{UPDATE\_RETURN} \; n$$

$$\mathcal{E}[\![x]\!] \; \rho \; n = \text{PUSH}(n - \rho \; x); \; \text{EVAL}$$
$$\mathcal{E}[\![add \; e_1 \; e_2]\!] \; \rho \; n = \mathcal{E}[\![e_1]\!] \; \rho \; n; \; \mathcal{E}[\![e_2]\!] \; \rho \; (n+1); \; \text{ADD}$$
$$\mathcal{E}[\![cons \; e_1 \; e_2]\!] \; \rho \; n = \mathcal{C}[\![e_2]\!] \; \rho \; n; \; \mathcal{C}[\![e_1]\!] \; \rho \; (n+1); \; \text{CONS}$$
otherwise:
$$\mathcal{E}[\![e]\!] \; \rho \; n = \mathcal{C}[\![e]\!] \; \rho \; n; \; \text{EVAL}$$

$$\mathcal{C}[\![x]\!] \; \rho \; n = \text{PUSH}(n - \rho \; x)$$
$$\mathcal{C}[\![f]\!] \; \rho \; n = \text{PUSHGLOBAL} \; f$$
$$\mathcal{C}[\![cons \; e_1 \; e_2]\!] \; \rho \; n = \mathcal{C}[\![e_2]\!] \; \rho \; n; \; \mathcal{C}[\![e_1]\!] \; \rho \; (n+1); \; \text{CONS}$$
$$\mathcal{C}[\![e_1 \; e_2]\!] \; \rho \; n = \mathcal{C}[\![e_2]\!] \; \rho \; n; \; \mathcal{C}[\![e_1]\!] \; \rho \; (n+1); \; \text{MKAP}$$

Figure 2: Fragment of compiler to produce more 'direct evaluation' code

(Readers unfamiliar with the basics of the G-machine, see e.g. [PJ87].)

But we know by now that this is a needlessly inefficient evaluation method! Since the build/eval loop does not stop until a value has been reached, we might as well build the graph of the *value* as directly (and conventionally) as possible. This is what the $\mathcal{E}$-scheme in figure 2 does. The intuition behind the formulation of the $\mathcal{E}$-scheme is that $\mathcal{E}[\![\; e \;]\!] \; \rho \; n$ should have the same effect as (but be more efficient than!) $\mathcal{C}[\![\; e \;]\!] \; \rho \; n; \; \text{EVAL}$, i.e., push a pointer to the value of e into the stack.

What has been done in the past is to construct by hand the improved compilation schemes, leaving it to the compiler writer to make sure that the assertion is followed. However, it ought to be possible to do this more mechanically!

3   A tiny first order language

In the two examples of transformations in this paper, we assume a tiny first order language, where all values are integers and the only operator is +. Figure 3 shows the data types (abstract syntax) of this language. A program is a list of

```
data Expr   =   Int Int | Var Int | Plus Expr Expr
            |   Appl FunctionName [ Expr ]

type Program = [(FunctionName, Expr)]
```

Figure 3: A tiny first order functional language

pairs of function names and their corresponding right hand side. For example, the (concrete) program

```
f x y = y+1
g x = g x
main = f (g 2) 3
```

is represented by:

$$
\begin{array}{ll}
[& (\text{"f"}, \quad Plus(\textit{Var }2)(\textit{Int }1)), \\
  & (\text{"g"}, \quad Appl\ \text{"g"}\ [\textit{Var }1]), \\
  & (\text{"main"}, \quad Appl\ \text{"f"}\ [\ Appl\ \text{"g"}\ [\ \textit{Int }2],\ \textit{Int }3]) \\
]
\end{array}
$$

Since the language is first-order, all applications are 'saturated'. Variables are represented as follows: "f" for example, takes two arguments. Its two parameters x and y are represented by *Var* 1 and *Var* 2 in the right hand side. The value of the program is the value of main.

4   Transforming a call-by-name interpreter

Figure 4 shows a normal order interpreter for our tiny language. In the G-machine, EVAL reduces a graph to its value. Here, graphs correspond to *Expr* terms without free variables (*GroundExpr*) [1]. Hence, *Eval* takes a *GroundExpr* and returns a value. We will also write P_p, $Eval_p$ etc instead of $P\ p$, $Eval\ p$, to make equations slightly less verbose. The instantiation function C, which corresponds to the C-scheme of the G-machine, takes an expression, and a mapping of variables to their ground expressions (corresponding to the stack of argument pointers of the G-machine), and constructs a ground expression.

Like the bare G-machine, the interpreter in figure 4 is 'instantiating', i.e., to evaluate a function application it builds a term with the right hand side of the function instantiated with the argument expressions, which it continues to evaluate using *Eval*.

4.1   Improving the normal order interpreter: E

It is now common knowledge that instantiating evaluation is a needlessly inefficient evaluation method, which we can improve upon. Since the instantiated

---
[1] This is a situation in which subtypes would be useful.

```
type GroundExpr   =   Expr      —but not using Var
type Value        =   Expr      —but only using Int

P   ::   Program → Value
P p  =   Eval_p (rhsof_p "main")


Eval :: Program → GroundExpr  →   Value
Eval_p (Int i)                =   Int i
Eval_p (Plus e_1 e_2)         =   Int(getI(Eval_p e_1)+getI(Eval_p e_2))
Eval_p (Appl f a)             =   Eval_p (C a (rhsof_p f))

  C :: [GroundExpr] → Expr  →   GroundExpr
  C a (Int i)               =   Int i
  C a (Var v)               =   a↓v      —index in the list a
  C a (Plus e_1 e_2)        =   Plus(C a e_1)(C a e_2)
  C a (Appl f a')           =   Appl f (map (C a) a')
Auxiliary functions:
  getI(Int i)   =   i
  rhsof_p f     =   assoc f p      — the right hand side for f.
```

Figure 4: A normal order interpreter for the tiny language.

expression is evaluated right away, we might as well try to evaluate the instantiated expression more directly. This argument is made informally in [Joh84], where it is said that the code $\mathcal{E}[\![e]\!]r\ n$ yields the same result as the code $\mathcal{C}[\![e]\!]r\ n$ followed by an **EVAL** instruction and embodies said short-circuited evaluation.

This argument can be made precise, using fold/unfold transformations [BD77]. In figure 4 the case for $Eval$ of an $Appl$ is:

$$Eval_p\ (Appl\ f\ a)\quad =\quad Eval_p\ (C\ a\ (rhsof_p\ f))$$

This motivates us to define an evaluation function E:

$$E_p\ a\ e\quad \equiv\quad Eval_p\ (C\ a\ e)$$

We now instantiate e to the corresponding constructors of $Expr$, and apply fold/unfold transformations. First the Int case:

$$
\begin{aligned}
E_p\ a\ (Int\ i) \quad &=\quad Eval_p\ (C\ a\ (Int\ i)) \quad &\text{def of } E\\
&=\quad Eval_p\ (Int\ i) \quad &\text{unfold } C\\
&=\quad Int\ i \quad &\text{unfold Eval.}
\end{aligned}
$$

The Var case is also easy:

$$
\begin{aligned}
E_p\ a\ (Var\ v) \quad &=\quad Eval_p\ (C\ a\ (Var\ v)) \quad &\text{def of } E\\
&=\quad Eval_p\ (a↓v) \quad &\text{unfold } C.
\end{aligned}
$$

The case for $Plus$ is more interesting:

$$
\begin{array}{llll}
\textbf{type } GroundExpr & = & Expr & \text{—but not using } Var \\
\textbf{type } Value & = & Expr & \text{—but only using } Int
\end{array}
$$

$$
\begin{array}{lll}
P & :: & Program \to Value \\
P\ p & = & Eval_p\ (rhsof_p\ \texttt{"main"})
\end{array}
$$

$$
Eval :: Program \to GroundExpr \to Value
$$

$$
\begin{array}{lll}
Eval_p\ (Int\ i) & = & Int\ i \\
Eval_p\ (Plus\ e_1\ e_2) & = & Int(getI(Eval_p\ e_1) + getI(Eval_p\ e_2)) \\
Eval_p\ (Appl\ f\ a) & = & E_p\ a\ (rhsof_p\ f)
\end{array}
$$

$$
E :: Program \to [GroundExpr] \to Expr \to GroundExpr
$$

$$
\begin{array}{lll}
E_p\ a\ (Int\ i) & = & Int\ i \\
E_p\ a\ (Var\ v) & = & Eval_p\ (a{\downarrow}v) \\
E_p\ a\ (Plus\ e_1\ e_2) & = & Int(getI(E_p\ a\ e_1) + getI(E_p\ a\ e_2)) \\
E_p\ a\ (Appl\ f\ a') & = & E_p\ (map\ (C\ a)\ a')\ (rhsof_p\ f)
\end{array}
$$

$$
C :: [GroundExpr] \to Expr \to GroundExpr
$$

$$
\begin{array}{lll}
C\ a\ (Int\ i) & = & Int\ i \\
C\ a\ (Var\ v) & = & a{\downarrow}v \\
C\ a\ (Plus\ e_1\ e_2) & = & Plus\ (C\ a\ e_1)\ (C\ a\ e_2) \\
C\ a\ (Appl\ f\ a') & = & Appl\ f\ (map\ (C\ a)\ a')
\end{array}
$$

Auxiliary functions:

$$
\begin{array}{lll}
getI(Int\ i) & = & i \\
rhsof_p\ f & = & assoc\ f\ p \qquad \text{the right hand side for } f.
\end{array}
$$

Figure 5: The improved normal order interpreter for the tiny language.

$$
\begin{array}{lll}
E_p\ a\ (Plus\ e_1\ e_2) & & \\
\quad = Eval_p\ (C\ a\ (Plus\ e_1\ e_2)) & & \text{def of } E \\
\quad = Eval_p\ (Plus\ (C\ a\ e_1)(C\ a\ e_2)) & & \text{unfold } C \\
\quad = Int(getI(Eval_p\ (C\ a\ e_1)) + getI(Eval_p\ (C\ a\ e_2))) & & \text{unfold } Eval \\
\quad = Int(getI(E_p\ a\ e_1) + getI(E_p\ a\ e_2)) & & \text{fold def } E.
\end{array}
$$

The *Appl* case:

$$
\begin{array}{llll}
E_p\ a\ (Appl\ f\ a') & = & Eval_p\ (C\ a\ (Appl\ f\ a')) & \text{def of } E \\
& = & Eval_p\ (Appl\ f\ (map\ (C\ a)\ a')) & \text{unfold } C \\
& = & Eval_p\ (C\ (map\ (C\ a)\ a')\ (rhsof_p\ f)) & \text{unfold } Eval \\
& = & E_p\ (map\ (C\ a)\ a')\ (rhsof_p\ f) & \text{fold def } E.
\end{array}
$$

Figure 5 summarises the new improved interpreter.

It is possible to further transform the interpreter. For example, there is an inefficiency in how numbers are treated: when doing addition, *Eval* returns an *Int* object for each of the two subexpressions, which are then taken apart with *getI*, and the final result is again put in an *Int* ('boxed' arithmetic). This inefficiency can be removed by introducing functions *Beval*, and *B* such that:

$$
\begin{aligned}
Beval\ e &\equiv getI\,(Eval\ e) \\
B\ a\ e &\equiv getI\,(E\ a\ e)
\end{aligned}
$$

This is equivalent to the $\mathcal{B}$-scheme in the G-machine.

Another useful transformation towards a real implementation is to pass values on a (single-threaded) stack. This can be done by introducing

$$
\begin{aligned}
C'\ a\ e\ s &\equiv C\ a\ e : s \\
E'\ a\ e\ s &\equiv E\ a\ e : s \\
Eval'\ (x{:}e) &\equiv Eval\ x : e
\end{aligned}
$$

Applying fold/unfold transformation to the above equations, for instance for *Plus* we get:

$$
\begin{aligned}
C'\ a\ (Plus\ e_1\ e_2)\ s &= (mkPlus \circ C'\ a\ e_1 \circ C'\ a\ e_2)\ s \\
Eval'\ (Plus\ e_1\ e_2 : s) &= (add \circ Eval'_p\ e_1 \circ Eval'_p\ e_2)\ s \\
E'_p\ a\ (Plus\ e_1\ e_2)\ s &= (add \circ E'_p\ a\ e_1 \circ E'_p\ a\ e_2)\ s \\
\textbf{where}\ \ mkPlus\ (y{:}x{:}s) &= Plus\ x\ y : s \\
add\ (y{:}x{:}s) &= Int(getI\ x + getI\ y) : s
\end{aligned}
$$

(We omit the details for space reasons).

5   Dealing with sharing and state

We also want to model sharing and the graph manipulation that goes on in a real graph reduction implementation — for this we will use a *state monad* [Wad92, Wad90, PJW93]. Our intention is to play essentially the same trick as in the previous section, but with a call-by-need interpreter written in a monadic style. The state monad we will be using is defined in figure 6. The (;) operator is the same as 'bind' in [Wad92]. The state portion of the state monad consists of the graph (heap). The *store* operation stores a node in the graph and returns a pointer to where it was stored. *fetch* fetches a node from the graph given a pointer. *update* stores a node at a given location (previously obtained by *store*). To qualify as a monad, the three laws given in figure 7 must be satisfied. They will be used extensively in the transformations that follows, In particular the associative law, where we won't even bother to write the parentheses.

The initial, instantiating, call-by-need interpreter is given in figure 8. To avoid unnecessary clutter we have simply ignored the program argument that needs to be passed everywhere(p in the previous section).

The value returned by *Eval* and *Evalnode* is always an *Nint* node in our tiny language. *C* does basically the same thing as in the previous section, but now takes the expression to be instantiated and returns a pointer to the root of the graph instance. The environment argument a is now a list of pointers into the graph. *Eval* fetches the node pointed to, passes the node to the evaluation function proper *Evalnode*, and the value returned by *Evalnode* is updated onto the node pointed to by the argument p.

The *Evalnode* function is fairly straightforward. To evaluate a function application, the right hand side of the function is instantiated with the arguments, and *Eval* applied to the resulting graph:

$$
Evalnode\ (Nappl\ f\ ps) = C\ ps\ (rhsof\ f); \lambda p.Eval\ p
$$

This is the source of the same kind of inefficiency that we transformed away in the previous section. To attempt the same thing in this setting, we define

134

$$\textbf{type } S\ a = Graph \rightarrow (a,\ Graph)$$
$$\textbf{type } Pointer = ...$$
$$\textbf{data } Node = Nint\ Int\ |\ Nplus\ Pointer\ Pointer\ |\ Nappl\ FunName\ [Pointer]$$

$$unit:: a \rightarrow S\ a$$
$$unit\ x = \lambda g.(x,\ g)$$
$$(;):: S\ a \rightarrow (a \rightarrow S\ b) \rightarrow S\ b$$
$$k\ ;\ m = \lambda g.\textbf{let } (a_1,g_1) = k\ g$$
$$(b_2,g_2) = m\ a_1\ g_1$$
$$\textbf{in } (b_2,g_2)$$

$$store::Node \rightarrow S\ Pointer$$
$$store\ x = \lambda g.(newPointer\ g,\ updateGraph\ g\ x\ (newPointer\ g))$$

$$fetch::Pointer \rightarrow S\ Node$$
$$fetch\ p = \lambda g.(fetchfromGraph\ p\ g,\ g)$$

$$update::Node \rightarrow Pointer \rightarrow S\ ()$$
$$update\ x\ p = \lambda g.((),\ updateGraph\ g\ x\ p)$$

Figure 6: The state monad.

$$E::[Pointer] \rightarrow Expr \rightarrow S\ Node$$
$$E\ ps\ e \equiv C\ ps\ e;\lambda p.Eval\ p$$

We will now instantiate e to *Int*, *Var*, *Plus*, and *Appl*. First instantiate $e = Int$:

$E\ ps\ (Int\ i)$	=	$C\ ps\ (Int\ i);\lambda p.Eval\ p$	def of E
	=	$store(Nint\ i);\lambda p.Eval\ p$	unfold C
	=	$store(Nint\ i);\lambda p.fetch\ p;\lambda n.Evalnode\ n;\lambda n'.$	unfold Eval
		$update\ n'\ p;\lambda().unit\ n'$	

At this point we note that we store a node *Nint i* binding a pointer to it to p, only to fetch via p right away binding the fetched node to n ! Thus it seems fairly obvious that the following law, *the store-fetch law*, should hold:

$$store\ v;\lambda p.fetch\ p;\lambda v'.m = store\ v;\lambda p.m[v'/v] \qquad \text{store-fetch law}$$

Thus continuing,

	=	$store(Nint\ i);\lambda p.Evalnode\ (Nint\ i);\lambda n'.$	store-fetch law
		$update\ n'\ p;\lambda().unit\ n'$	
	=	$store(Nint\ i);\lambda p.unit\ (Nint\ i);\lambda n'.$	unfold Evalnode
		$update\ n'\ p;\lambda().unit\ n'$	
	=	$store(Nint\ i);\lambda p.update\ (Nint\ i)\ p;\lambda().unit\ (Nint\ i)$	left unit law.

At this point we note that we're storing a node to get a pointer, only to update

Left unit:

$$(unit\ e)\ ;\ k = k\ e \quad \text{or} \quad (unit\ e)\ ;\lambda a.k = k[e/a]$$

Right unit:

$$m\ ;\ unit = m \quad \text{or} \quad m\ ;\lambda x.unit\ x = m$$

Associativity:

$$
\begin{aligned}
& m\ ;\ (\lambda a.\quad (\quad (k\ a)\qquad ;\ h)) \\
= \quad & (\quad m\ ;\ (\lambda a.\qquad (k\ a)\quad)\quad ;\ h)
\end{aligned}
$$

or

$$(m\ ;\ \lambda a.\ k)\ ;\ \lambda b\ .\ h = m\ ;\ \lambda a.\ (\ k\ ;\ \lambda b\ .\ h\ )$$

(but c.f. name clashes)

Figure 7: General monad laws.

$$
\begin{aligned}
\textbf{data}\ Node\ =\ &\ Nint\ Int\ |\ Nplus\ Pointer\ Pointer \\
|\ &\ Nappl\ FunName\ [Pointer]
\end{aligned}
$$

$$
\begin{aligned}
C &:: [Pointer] \to Expr \to S\ Pointer \\
C\ a\ (Int\ i) &= store(Nint\ i) \\
C\ a\ (Var\ v) &= unit(a{\downarrow}v) \\
C\ a\ (Plus\ e_1\ e_2) &= C\ a\ e_1;\lambda p_1.C\ a\ e_2;\lambda p_2.store(Nplus\ p_1\ p_2) \\
C\ a\ (Appl\ f\ es) &= Cs\ a\ es;\lambda ps.store(Nappl\ f\ ps)
\end{aligned}
$$

$$
\begin{aligned}
Cs &:: [Pointer] \to [Expr] \to S\ [Pointer] \\
Cs\ a\ [\ ] &= unit\ [\ ] \\
Cs\ a\ (e{:}es) &= C\ a\ e;\lambda p.Cs\ a\ es;\lambda ps.unit(p{:}ps)
\end{aligned}
$$

$$
\begin{aligned}
Eval &:: Pointer \to S\ Node \\
Eval\ p &= fetch\ p;\lambda n.Evalnode\ n;\lambda n'.update\ n'\ p;\lambda().unit\ n'
\end{aligned}
$$

$$
\begin{aligned}
Evalnode &:: Node \to S\ Node \\
Evalnode\ (Nint\ i) &= unit(Nint\ i) \\
Evalnode\ (Nplus\ p_1\ p_2) &= Eval\ p_1;\lambda n_1.Eval\ p_2;\lambda n_2.unit(add\ n_1\ n_2) \\
Evalnode\ (Nappl\ f\ ps) &= C\ ps\ (rhsof\ f);\lambda p.Eval\ p
\end{aligned}
$$

$$
\begin{aligned}
add &:: Node \to Node \to Node \\
add\ (Nint\ i_1)\ (Nint\ i_2) &= Nint(i_1{+}i_2)
\end{aligned}
$$

Figure 8: The initial, instantiating, call-by-need interpreter.

it immediately. We might as well store the value of the update to begin with. Thus, the following law, *store-update law*, seems like a credible one:

$$store\ N;\lambda p.update\ N'\ p;\lambda().m = store\ N';\lambda p.m \qquad \text{store-update law}$$

Again continuing, we get:

$$= \quad store(Nint\ i);\lambda p.unit\ (Nint\ i) \qquad \text{store-update law}$$

At this point we are storing something which is not used, since the variable the pointer is bound to does not occur in the 'continuation', so we might as well not store it. Again we can express this as a law, *the garbage store law*:

$$store\ v;\lambda p.m \cong m \quad (p\ not\ free\ in\ m) \qquad \text{garbage store law}$$

We cannot say they are equal here, simply because they are not the same functions: they do different things to the store. However, they are equivalent in the sense that in all contexts where $store\ v;\lambda p.m$, simply using m will produce the same end result. Innocent as it may seem, this law has turned out to be very difficult to prove (at least to this author). Using this law, we finally get

$$= \quad unit\ (Nint\ i) \qquad \text{garbage store law}$$

which is probably what we expected from $E\ ps\ (Int\ i)$.

The case $E\ ps\ (Var\ v)$ is trivial:

$$
\begin{aligned}
E\ ps\ (Var\ v) \quad &= \quad C\ ps\ (Var\ v);\lambda p.Eval\ p & \text{def of E} \\
&= \quad unit(ps{\downarrow}v);\lambda p.Eval\ p & \text{unfold C} \\
&= \quad Eval\ (ps{\downarrow}v) & \text{left unit law}
\end{aligned}
$$

The case $E\ ps\ (Plus\ e_1\ e_2)$ is more interesting:

$E\ ps\ (Plus\ e_1\ e_2)$

$$
\begin{aligned}
&= \quad C\ ps\ (Plus\ e_1\ e_2);\lambda p.Eval\ p & \text{def of E} \\
&= \quad C\ ps\ e_1;\lambda p_1.C\ ps\ e_2;\lambda p_2.store(Nplus\ p_1\ p_2);\lambda p.Eval\ p & \text{unfold C} \\
&= \quad C\ ps\ e_1;\lambda p_1.C\ ps\ e_2;\lambda p_2.store(Nplus\ p_1\ p_2);\lambda p. & \text{unfold Eval} \\
&\quad\ fetch\ p;\lambda n.Evalnode\ n;\lambda n'.update\ n'\ p;\lambda().unit\ n' \\
&= \quad C\ ps\ e_1;\lambda p_1.C\ ps\ e_2;\lambda p_2.store(Nplus\ p_1\ p_2);\lambda p. & \text{store-fetch law} \\
&\quad\ Evalnode\ (Nplus\ p_1\ p_2);\lambda n'.update\ n'\ p;\lambda().unit\ n' \\
&= \quad C\ ps\ e_1;\lambda p_1.C\ ps\ e_2;\lambda p_2.store(Nplus\ p_1\ p_2);\lambda p. & \text{unfold Evalnode} \\
&\quad\ Eval\ p_1;\lambda n_1.Eval\ p_2;\lambda n_2.unit(add\ n_1\ n_2);\lambda n'. \\
&\quad\ update\ n'\ p;\lambda().unit\ n'
\end{aligned}
$$

At this point we seem to be stuck! We would like the $C\ ps\ e_1;\lambda p_1.$ and $Eval\ p_1$ adjacent to each other, and that p_1 does not occur elsewhere, so that we can fold this to an E term. To begin with, we take the liberty of moving the *store* operation forwards to the point where the result is first used — we express this as the *move store law*:

> move store law:
> $store\ e;\lambda p.m;\lambda x.k \cong m;\lambda x.store\ e;\lambda p.k$ $\quad (p \notin FV(m),\ x \notin FV(e))$

Again we cannot say the they are equal, since they do different things to the store if m does store operations, but they are equivalent in the same sense as for the garbage store law. Since C performs only store to the state, we should also be allowed to move C operations in the same way. Thus continuing, we finally get:

$$
\begin{aligned}
= &\ C\ ps\ e_1;\lambda p_1.Eval\ p_1;\lambda n_1.C\ ps\ e_2;\lambda p_2.Eval\ p_2;\lambda n_2. &&\text{rearrange terms}\\
&\ unit(add\ n_1\ n_2);\lambda n'.store(Nplus\ p_1\ p_2);\lambda p.\\
&\ update\ n'\ p;\lambda().unit\ n'\\
= &\ C\ ps\ e_1;\lambda p_1.Eval\ p_1;\lambda n_1.C\ ps\ e_2;\lambda p_2.Eval\ p_2;\lambda n_2. &&\text{left unit}\\
&\ store(Nplus\ p_1\ p_2);\lambda p.update\ (add\ n_1\ n_2)\ p;\lambda().\\
&\ unit\ (add\ n_1\ n_2)\\
= &\ C\ ps\ e_1;\lambda p_1.Eval\ p_1;\lambda n_1.C\ ps\ e_2;\lambda p_2.Eval\ p_2;\lambda n_2. &&\text{store-update law}\\
&\ store(add\ n_1\ n_2);\lambda p.unit\ (add\ n_1\ n_2)\\
= &\ E\ ps\ e_1;\lambda n_1.E\ ps\ e_2;\lambda n_2. &&\text{fold E (twice)}\\
&\ store(add\ n_1\ n_2);\lambda p.unit\ (add\ n_1\ n_2)\\
= &\ E\ ps\ e_1;\lambda n_1.E\ ps\ e_2;\lambda n_2.unit\ (add\ n_1\ n_2) &&\text{garbage store law.}
\end{aligned}
$$

No new law has to be invoked in the transformation of the *Appl* case:

$$
\begin{aligned}
&\ E\ ps\ (Appl\ f\ es)\\
= &\ C\ ps\ (Appl\ f\ es);\lambda p.Eval\ p &&\text{def of E}\\
= &\ Cs\ ps\ es;\lambda ps'.store(Nappl\ f\ ps');\lambda p.Eval\ p &&\text{unfold C}\\
= &\ Cs\ ps\ es;\lambda ps'.store(Nappl\ f\ ps');\lambda p. &&\text{unfold Eval}\\
&\ fetch\ p;\lambda n.Evalnode\ n;\lambda n'.update\ n'\ p;\lambda().unit\ n'\\
= &\ Cs\ ps\ es;\lambda ps'.store(Nappl\ f\ ps');\lambda p. &&\text{store-fetch law}\\
&\ Evalnode\ (Nappl\ f\ ps');\lambda n'.update\ n'\ p;\lambda().unit\ n'\\
= &\ Cs\ ps\ es;\lambda ps'.store(Nappl\ f\ ps');\lambda p. &&\text{unfold Evalnode}\\
&\ C\ ps'\ (rhsof\ f);\lambda p'.Eval\ p';\lambda n'.update\ n'\ p;\lambda().unit\ n'\\
= &\ Cs\ ps\ es;\lambda ps'.store(Nappl\ f\ ps');\lambda p. &&\text{fold E}\\
&\ E\ ps'\ (rhsof\ f);\lambda n'.update\ n'\ p;\lambda().unit\ n'\\
= &\ Cs\ ps\ es;\lambda ps'.E\ ps'\ (rhsof\ f);\lambda n'. &&\text{rearrange terms}\\
&\ store(Nappl\ f\ ps');\lambda p.update\ n'\ p;\lambda().unit\ n'\\
= &\ Cs\ ps\ es;\lambda ps'.E\ ps'\ (rhsof\ f);\lambda n'.store\ n';\lambda p.unit\ n' &&\text{store-update law}\\
= &\ Cs\ ps\ es;\lambda ps'.E\ ps'\ (rhsof\ f);\lambda n'.unit\ n' &&\text{garbage store law}\\
= &\ Cs\ ps\ es;\lambda ps'.E\ ps'\ (rhsof\ f) &&\text{right unit.}
\end{aligned}
$$

Figure 9 summarises the new improved interpreter.

6   Towards the Optimistic G-machine

As is well known, being lazy is not without its costs! It costs to build a closure to represent the unevaluated expression, and it costs to 'interpret' the closure to evaluate the argument if or when the argument is finally needed. Hence, much of the research in lazy functional language implementation has gone into reducing or eliminating this cost, most notably strictness analysis. However, strictness analysis is still in its infancy (except perhaps for first order programs with flat domains). What we propose here is a complement to strictness analysis:

$$
\begin{aligned}
C :: [Pointer] \to Rhs \quad &\to \quad S\ Pointer \\
C\ ps\ (Int\ i) \quad &= \quad store(Nint\ i) \\
C\ ps\ (Var\ v) \quad &= \quad unit(ps{\downarrow}v) \\
C\ ps\ (Plus\ e_1\ e_2) \quad &= \quad C\ ps\ e_1;\lambda p_1.C\ ps\ e_2;\lambda p_2.store(Nplus\ p_1\ p_2) \\
C\ ps\ (Appl\ f\ es) \quad &= \quad Cs\ ps\ es;\lambda ps'.store(Nappl\ f\ ps')
\end{aligned}
$$

$$
\begin{aligned}
Cs\ ps\ [\ ] &= unit\ [\ ] \\
Cs\ ps\ (e{:}es) &= C\ ps\ e;\lambda p.Cs\ a\ es;\lambda ps'.unit(p{:}ps')
\end{aligned}
$$

$$
\begin{aligned}
Eval::Pointer \quad &\to \quad S\ Node \\
Eval\ p \quad &= \quad fetch\ p;\lambda n.Evalnode\ n;\lambda n'.update\ n'\ p;\lambda().unit\ n'
\end{aligned}
$$

$$
\begin{aligned}
Evalnode::Node \quad &\to \quad S\ Node \\
Evalnode\ (Nint\ i) \quad &= \quad unit(Nint\ i) \\
Evalnode\ (Nplus\ p_1\ p_2) \quad &= \quad Eval\ p_1;\lambda n_1.Eval\ p_2;\lambda n_2.unit(add\ n_1\ n_2) \\
Evalnode\ (Nappl\ f\ ps) \quad &= \quad E\ ps\ (rhsof\ f)
\end{aligned}
$$

$$
add(Nint\ i_1)(Nint\ i_2)=Nint(i_1+i_2)
$$

$$
\begin{aligned}
E::[Pointer] \to Rhs \quad &\to \quad S\ Node \\
E\ ps\ (Int\ i) \quad &= \quad unit\ (Nint\ i) \\
E\ ps\ (Var\ v) \quad &= \quad Eval\ (ps{\downarrow}v) \\
E\ ps\ (Plus\ e_1\ e_2) \quad &= \quad E\ ps\ e_1;\lambda n_1.E\ ps\ e_2;\lambda n_2.unit\ (add\ n_1\ n_2) \\
E\ ps\ (Appl\ f\ es) \quad &= \quad Cs\ ps\ es;\lambda ps'.E\ ps'\ (rhsof\ f)
\end{aligned}
$$

Figure 9: The improved monadic interpreter.

limited speculative evaluation of lazy arguments. The reason this might be a win in terms of time efficiency is that in most programs, most lazy arguments are evaluated sooner or later anyway (or so we conjecture!). Thus if we do it sooner, in a manner similar to strict evaluation, we hope to avoid the cost of building and interpreting closures.

But we don't want to evaluate arguments completely strictly and change the semantics of the language! Thus, we have a notion of *fuel*, which is 'filled up' at the beginning of the evaluation of the argument. If evaluation of the argument terminated before the fuel is out, we have succeeded in the goal of passing a proper value. If fuel runs out, however, our speculative evaluator builds a graph of the computation as far as it got. The more likely it is that the value of a particular argument will be used, the more fuel we may profitably spend and still win in terms of speed.

But increasing the speed of an implementation of a lazy functional language is not just a matter of creating values instead of closures – it is also a matter of *where* the values are put! Compilers for traditional languages spend a great deal of effort in allocating locations for values to fast machine registers rather than slower memory. However, in functional languages in general and lazy ones in particular, values are too big to fit in registers: whereas we can profitably put an integer value in a fast machine register, this is impossible for an abritrarily big closure that represents an integer value. This is probably one major reason why implementations of traditional languages are faster than modern declarative ones! Our speculative evaluation effort should also be seen in this light: it increases the probability that the value of a particlular argument 'fits' into a fast register and that graph/heap manipulation will not have to be done at all.

But there is also a second, and perhaps more serious, reason why speculative evaluation might be very useful, and that is space efficiency and the plugging of space leaks. Röjemo [private communication] reports that eleven of the more closely studied programs from the **nofib** suite [Par93] had an obvious space leak — four of those were easily plugged with one well-placed **seq** to prematurely evaluate (in the lazy evaluation sense). Thus we conjecture that speculative evaluation in many cases will have the same beneficial effect on the space behaviour of lazy functional program.

How would fold-unfold transformations aid us in the development of the Optimistic G-machine? Very briefly, in the following way. Firstly, we add a component to the state monad corresponding to a fuel register. Secondly, we add evaluation functions *Seval* and *Sevalnode* to do the actual speculative evaluation. Thirdly, we derive a speculative evaluator

$$S \ ps \ e \equiv C \ ps \ e; \lambda p.Seval \ p$$

corresponding to a speculative compilation scheme applicable to arguments. S then becomes a combination of E and C, behaving like E when there is fuel left, and like C when out of fuel.

7 Conclusion

In this paper we have shown that it is possible to do fold-unfold transformations on state monadic programs that mirrors the transformations done on ordinary terms, but it turned out to be considerably more complicated and less elegant to do so. Apart from the general monadic laws of associativity and left and right unit, we also needed additional help from some laws particular to this state monad. Those laws were:

$store \ v; \lambda p.fetch \ p; \lambda v'.m = store \ v; \lambda p.m[v'/v]$	(store-fetch law)
$store \ N; \lambda p.update \ N' \ p; \lambda().m = store \ N'; \lambda p.m$	(store-update law)
$store \ v; \lambda p.m \cong m \quad (p \ not \ free \ in \ m)$	(garbage store law)
$store \ e; \lambda p.m; \lambda x.k \cong m; \lambda x.store \ e; \lambda p.k \quad (p \notin FV(m), \ x \notin FV(e))$	
	(move store law)

We have yet to prove these laws. However, the first two should involve only simple calculations inside an implementation of the state monad and thus should be easy to prove, since the heap does not change. However, the last two seem to require considerably more than that, as the heap is different before and after the application of the law.

However, the state monadic approach has the advantage of being closer to a real implementation, in that a monadic expression correspond to the sequentialisation that real implementation must do in the machine code.

140

Acknowledgements. I'm indebted to to Alex Bunkenberg, Sava Mintchev, and Colin Runciman for detailed comments and suggestions on this paper; and to the 'multigroup' for comments on earlier incarnations of this work.

References

[Arg89] G. Argo. Improving the three instruction machine. In *Proceedings of the 1989 Conference on Functional Languages and Computer Architecture*, pages 100–115, London, England, 1989.

[Arg90] G. M. Argo. *Efficient Laziness (under revision)*. PhD thesis, Glasgow University, 1990.

[BD77] R. M. Burstall and J. Darlington. A Transformation System for Developing Recursive Programs. *Journal of the ACM*, 24:44–67, 1977.

[FW87] J. Fairbairn and S. C. Wray. TIM: A simple, lazy abstract machine to execute supercombinators. In *Proceedings of the 1987 Conference on Functional Programming Languages and Computer Architecture*, Portland, Oregon, September 1987.

[Joh84] T. Johnsson. Efficient Compilation of Lazy Evaluation. In *Proceedings of the SIGPLAN '84 Symposium on Compiler Construction*, pages 58–69, Montreal, 1984.

[Par93] Will Partain. The **nofib** benchmark suite of haskell programs. In John Launchbury and Patrick Sansom, editors, *Proc. 1992 Glasgow Workshop on Functional Programming*, pages 195–202. Springer–Verlag, 1993.

[PJ87] S. L. Peyton Jones. *The Implementation of Functional Programming Languages*. Prentice Hall, 1987.

[PJ92] S. L. Peyton Jones. Implementing lazy functional languages on stock hardware: the Spineless Tagless G-machine. *Journal of Functional Programming*, 2(2), April 1992.

[PJS89] S. L. Peyton Jones and Jon Salkild. The Spineless Tagless G-machine. In *Proceedings of the 1989 Conference on Functional Programming Languages and Computer Architecture*, London, Great Britain, 1989.

[PJW93] S.L Peyton Jones and P. Wadler. Imperative Functional programming. In *Proceedings 1993 Symposium Principles of Programming Languages*, Charleston, N.Carolina, 1993.

[Wad90] P. Wadler. Comprehending Monads. In *Proceedings of the 1990 ACM Symposium on Lisp and Functional Programming*, Nice, France, 1990.

[Wad92] P. Wadler. The essence of functional programming. In *Proceedings 1992 Symposium on principles of Programming Languages*, pages 1–14, Albuquerque, New Mexico, 1992.

Functional Binomial Queues

David J. King

University of Glasgow*

Abstract

Efficient implementations of priority queues can often be clumsy beasts. We express a functional implementation of binomial queues which is both elegant and efficient. We also quantify some of the differences with other functional implementations. The operations `decreaseKey` and `delete` always pose a problem without destructive update, we show how our implementation may be extended to express these.

1 Functional priority queues

A crucial part of many algorithms is the data structure that is used. Frequently, an algorithm needs an abstract data type providing a number of primitive operations on a data structure. A priority queue is one such data structure that is used by a number of algorithms. Applications include, Dijkstra's [4] algorithm for single-source shortest paths, and the minimum cost spanning tree problem (see Tarjan [12] for a discussion of minimum spanning tree algorithms). See Knuth [8] and Aho *et al* [1] for many other applications of priority queues.

A priority queue is a set where each element has a key indicating its priority. The most common primitive operations on priority queues are:

`emptyQ`	Return the empty queue.
`isEmpty q`	Return `True` if the queue q is empty, otherwise return `False`.
`insertQ i q`	Insert a new item i into queue q.
`findMin q`	Return the item with minimum key in queue q.
`deleteMin q`	Delete the item with minimum key in queue q.
`meld p q`	Return the queue formed by taking the union of queues p and q.

In addition, the following two operations are occasionally useful:

`delete i q`	Delete item i from queue q.
`decreaseKey i q`	Decrease the key of item i in queue q.

There are numerous ways of implementing the abstract data type for priority queues. Using *heap-ordered* trees is one of the most common implementations. A tree is heap-ordered if the item at every node has a smaller key than its descendents. Thus the entry at the root of a heap has the earliest priority. A

---

*Author's address: Department of Computing Science, University of Glasgow, Glasgow G12 8QQ, Scotland. E-mail: `gnik@dcs.gla.ac.uk`. URL: `http://www.dcs.gla.ac.uk/~gnik`.

variety of different trees have been used including: heaps [8], splay trees [11], skew heaps [11], 2-3 trees [1]. In addition, lists (sorted or unsorted) are another possible implementation of queues, but will be less efficient on large data sets. For a comparative study of these implementations and others in an imperative paradigm see Jones [7].

There is very little in the literature on priority queues in a functional paradigm. Heaps are the most common functional implementation, see Paulson [9], for example. The disadvantage of using heaps, or balanced trees is that more bookkeeping is required for balancing. This extra bookkeeping adds to the amount of storage space needed by the queue, as well as making the implementation of the primitives more complex. We present a functional implementation of priority queues that is based on trees, but does not require as much storage space or balancing code as other implementations. The implementation is far more elegant than a typical imperative implementation, lending itself well to a formal proof of correctness.

Vuillemin [13] describes *binomial queues* which support the full complement of priority queue operations in $O(\log n)$ worst-case time. They are based on heap-ordered trees in that a priority queue is represented by a list of heap-ordered trees (that is, a forest), where each tree in the forest is a binomial tree. We present a purely functional implementation of binomial queues expressing the full complement of priority queue operations in Haskell (Hudak *et al* [6]).

2   Binomial trees

Binomial trees are general trees that have a regular shape. They are best presented diagrammatically:

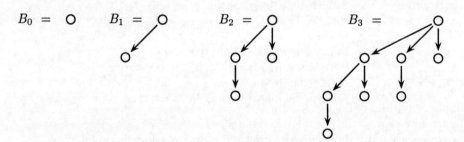

There are two equally good ways of expressing the general case, for $n \geq 1$.

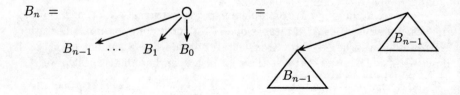

In Haskell we define a general tree with the datatype:

```
data Tree a = Node a [Tree a]
```

Then using this datatype we can define binomial trees inductively:

$$B_0 = Node\ x\ []$$
$$B_n = Node\ x\ [B_{n-1}, \ldots, B_1, B_0], \quad \text{for } n > 0$$

We may verify that a general tree is the binomial tree B_k with the following function:

```
isBinTree :: Int -> Tree a -> Bool
isBinTree k (Node x []) = k==0
isBinTree k (Node x ts) = and (zipWith isBinTree [0..]
                                         (reverse ts))
```

This works by checking that the last subtree is a B_0 tree, and then checking that the penultimate subtree is a B_1 tree, and so on for all subtrees.

Binomial trees have some very nice combinatorial properties. For instance, the binomial tree B_k has 2^k nodes, and $\binom{k}{d}$ nodes of depth d, hence their name. See Vuillemin [13] and Brown [3] for more properties.

3 Implementing binomial queues functionally

Vuillemin [13] represents a priority queue with a forest of binomial trees. It is important that a list of trees is used to represent the forest because the ordering is important (a set of trees would not do). The first tree in the binomial queue must either be a B_0 tree or just *Zero* meaning no tree, and the second a B_1 tree or just *Zero* so we have the following structure for a binomial queue:

$$[T_0, T_1, \ldots, T_n] \quad \text{where } T_k = Zero \mid B_k \text{ for } 0 \le k \le n.$$

Vuillemin [13] and others use an array to represent the forest, moreover, for simplicity binary trees are used to represent the binomial trees. Imperative implementations of linked structures of this kind usually turn out to be clumsy. Instead we express the primitives as recursive functions on a list of general trees, giving a very natural encoding.

So the following datatypes are used:

```
type BinQueue = [Maybe (Tree Item)]
data Maybe a  = Zero | One a
```

We use the standard `Maybe` datatype with constructors `Zero` and `One`, these names where chosen because the queue primitives are analogous with binary arithmetic.

Each item is a pair of entry and key:

```
type Item     = (Entry, Key)
```

So the projection functions on items are:

```
entry :: Item -> Entry
entry = fst

key :: Item -> Key
key = snd
```

The following functions may be used to verify that a list of trees has the right structure to be a binomial queue.

```
isBinQ :: BinQueue -> Bool
isBinQ q = isBinQTail 0 q

isBinQTail :: Int -> BinQueue -> Bool
isBinQTail k q = and (zipWith isTree [k..] q)
      where isTree m Zero    = True
            isTree m (One t) = isBinTree m t
```

The correctness of the queue primitives that follow may be shown by using the above functions. For example, the correctness of the meld function is shown by proving:

$$\forall p, q.\ \text{isBinQ } p \ \wedge\ \text{isBinQ } q \ \Rightarrow\ \text{isBinQ (meld } p \ q)$$

Now we can start to express the priority queue operations. Creating a new empty queue, and testing for the empty queue follow immediately:

```
emptyQ :: BinQueue
emptyQ = []

isEmpty :: BinQueue -> Bool
isEmpty q = null q
```

Taking the union of (or melding) two queues together is the most useful of all the primitive operations (because other primitives are defined with it) so we describe it next. There is a very strong analogy between meld and binary addition. Given two binomial queues $[P_0, P_1, \ldots, P_n]$ and $[Q_0, Q_1, \ldots, Q_m]$ melding is carried out positionally from left to right, using the property that two binomial trees B_k can be linked into a B_{k+1} binomial tree. First P_0 is melded with Q_0, giving one of four possible results. If both P_0 and Q_0 contain trees (that is, they are not Zero) they are linked to form a B_1 tree so that the heap-order property is maintained. With just one tree and one Zero the result is the tree, and given two Zero's the result is Zero. This process of linking is carried out on successive trees. If the result of melding P_k with Q_k results in a B_{k+1} tree then this is carried on (it is analogous to carry in binary arithmetic) and melded with P_{k+1} and Q_{k+1}.

```
meld :: BinQueue -> BinQueue -> BinQueue
meld p q = meldC p q Zero

meldC :: BinQueue -> BinQueue -> Tree Item -> BinQueue
meldC [] q Zero             = q
meldC [] q c                = meld [c] q
meldC p [] c                = meldC [] p c
meldC (Zero:ps) (Zero:qs) c = c:meld ps qs
meldC (One (Node x xs): ps) (One (Node y ys): qs) c
                            = let t =
                                 if key x < key y
                                    then Node x (Node y ys: xs)
                                    else Node y (Node x xs: ys)
                              in c:meldC ps qs (One t)
meldC (p:ps) (q:qs) c       = meldC (q:ps) (c:qs) p
```

The asymptotic complexity of meld is $O(\log n)$ (where n is the number of items
in the largest queue). We arrive at this by observing that two B_k trees can be
linked in constant time, and the number of these linking operations will be
equal to the size of the longest queue, that is $O(\log n)$. For a more detailed
analysis of the complexity of meld and the other queue operations see Brown
[3].

Inserting an item into the queue is most simply expressed by melding a B_0
tree holding the item, into the binomial queue.

```
insertQ :: Item -> BinQueue -> BinQueue
insertQ i q = meld [One (Node i [])] q

insertMany :: [Item] -> BinQueue
insertMany is = foldr insertQ [] is
```

As each binomial tree is heap-ordered the item with the minimum key will
be a root of one of the trees. This is found by scanning the list of trees. To
delete the item with minimum key we extract the tree that it is the root of,
and meld the subtrees back into the binomial queue. This melding is easy as
the subtrees themselves form a binomial queue, in reverse order. The subtrees
could be stored in reverse order, but this would make it more difficult to define
an efficient version of meld.

The extraction of the tree with minimum key is done in two steps. We first
traverse the forest returning the tree:

```
minTree :: BinQueue -> Maybe (Tree Item)
minTree q = foldl1 least q
     where
     Zero              'least' t     = t
     t                 'least' Zero  = t
     One (Node x xs) 'least' One (Node y ys)
                                     = if key x < key y
                                       then One (Node x xs)
                                       else One (Node y ys)
```

Then we delete the tree with the minimum key item from the binomial queue:

```
removeTree :: Item -> BinQueue -> BinQueue
removeTree i q = map match q
     where
     match Zero                    = Zero
     match (One (Node x xs)) | x==i = Zero
                             | x/=i = One (Node x xs)
```

These functions are combined and the subtrees of the extracted tree are melded back into the queue:

```
deleteMin :: BinQueue -> BinQueue
deleteMin q  = meld (map One (reverse ts)) (deleteTree i q)
     where
     One (Node i ts) = minTree q
```

The total running time of `minTree` and `removeTree` is $O(\log n)$. As both operations traverse a list of length $\log n$ carrying out constant time operations. The `deleteMin` operation carries out a meld, as well as `minTree` and `removeTree`. Since the subtrees being melding back into the queue are smaller, the melding will take $O(\log n)$ time. Hence `deleteMin` will run in $O(\log n)$ time.

We may also use `minTree` to express `findMin` which again runs in $O(\log n)$ time.

```
findMin :: BinQueue -> Item
findMin q = i
     where
     One (Node i ts) = minTree q
```

The two pass algorithm for `deleteMin` can be performed in one pass over the binomial queue (giving a constant time speed-up) by using the standard cyclic programming technique, see Bird [2]. A function is used that both takes the item to be removed as an argument and returns the item with minimum key, as well as the binomial queue without the item. As is usually the case with more efficient algorithms, the implementation becomes more cumbersome, so we omit it here.

4 Comparison with other priority queues

Imperatively binomial queues perform better than most other priority queue implementations, see Jones [7] for an empirical comparison. More recently Fredman and Tarjan [5] have developed Fibonacci heaps which are based on binomial queues. Fibonacci heaps have a better amortised complexity for many of the operations. Unfortunately, they make heavy usage of pointers, so do not lend themselves to a natural functional encoding.

Queue	insertQ		deleteMin		meld	
	Lines	Time	Lines	Time	Lines	Time
Binomial	1	$O(\log n)$	13	$O(\log n)$	12	$O(\log n)$
2-3 trees	16	$O(\log n)$	41	$O(\log n)$	26	$O(n)$
Sorted list	5	$O(n)$	1	$O(1)$	6	$O(n)$
Heaps	7	$O(\log n)$	17	$O(\log n)$	21	$O(n)$

Table 1: Differences between some Haskell implementations of priority queues

The usual functional implementation of priority queues is to use heaps, see Paulson [9], for example. The advantage of binomial queues over heaps is that the meld operation is more efficient. Imperatively Jones [7] reports that binomial queues are one of the most complex implementations. In Haskell the operations on tree and list data structures are far cleaner than in an imperative language. Functionally, binomial queues are in many ways more elegant than heaps. They are easier to program and understand, as well as being programmed in fewer lines of code. Similarly binomial queues have the same advantages over 2-3 trees, see Reade [10] for a functional implementation of 2-3 trees, and Aho *et al* [1] for a description of how they may be used for implementing priority queues. Sorted lists are the simplest of all implementations, and give the best performance for small queues. However, they have the worst complexity and will give slower running times for larger queues. Table 1 summarises the running times and lines of Haskell code for four different implementations.

5 Implementing decreaseKey and delete

The usual way in imperative languages to implement decreaseKey and delete is to maintain an auxiliary data structure which supports direct access, in constant time, to each item. Functionally such a data structure is not feasible. However, we do use an auxiliary data structure, a set. A set of all the items currently in the queue is maintained along with the queue.

```
type BinQueueExt = (BinQueue, Set Entry)
```

All the priority queue operations must do some extra bookkeeping to maintain the set.

```
emptyPQ :: BinQueueExt
emptyPQ = (emptyQ, emptySet)

isEmptyPQ :: BinQueueExt -> Bool
isEmptyPQ (q,s) = isEmptySet s
```

When inserting a new item we must also insert it into the set. Similarly, when two queues are melded we must take the union of their sets:

```
insertPQ :: Item -> BinQueueExt -> BinQueueExt
insertPQ i (q,s) = (insertQ i q, insSet (entry i) s)

meldPQ :: BinQueueExt -> BinQueueExt -> BinQueueExt
meldPQ (p,s) (q,t) = (meldQ p q, unionSet s t)
```

Deleting the minimum item must also delete it from the set:

```
deleteMinPQ :: BinQueueExt -> (Item, BinQueueExt)
deleteMinPQ (p,s)
       | not (isEmptySet s) = (i, (q, delSet (entry i) s))
                where
                   (i,q) = deleteMin p
```

The findMinPQ operation makes no change to the set and is just expressed in terms of findMinPQ. When decreasing the key for an item we simply insert the item into the queue with its new key. When deleting an item we delete it from the set.

```
decreaseKey :: Item -> BinQueueExt -> BinQueueExt
decreaseKey i pq | (entry i) 'elemSet' (snd pq) = insertPQ i pq
                 | otherwise                    = pq

delete :: Item -> BinQueueExt -> BinQueueExt
delete i (q,s) = (q, delSet (entry i) s)
```

Of course, maintaining a set has an impact on the time and space complexity of the priority queue operations. The set operations may be implemented with balanced trees for a reasonable complexity. The running times of decreaseKey and delete is $O(\log n)$. Both running times being dominated by the set operations. The other operations have the same worst-case complexity as before $O(\log n)$, except meldPQ which is now dominated by the complexity of the set union operation $O(n + m)$ (where n and m are the sizes of the two sets). Furthermore, because we never physically remove items from the queue the complexity of the operations is governed by the total number of inserts made. Constant factors may be improved by doing some garbage collection, that is, physically removing items that percolate to the roots of trees.

6 Conclusions

Binomial queues are both elegant and efficient. Our functional encoding is far more elegant than a typical imperative one (for instance the C code for meld is some four times larger). This is mainly because Haskell handles data structures like lists and trees very well. The implementation is also more elegant than other known efficient functional implementations of priority queues. It is hard to quantify elegance, but the code is smaller and I believe it's easier to understand and prove correct.

7 Acknowledgements

I am very grateful to the Workshop referees: Kieran Clenaghan, Simon Peyton Jones and Malcolm Wallace for their valuable comments. I am also grateful to the Glasgow FP group, especially those on the Workshop committee for their helpful feedback.

References

[1] Alfred V. Aho, John E. Hopcroft, and Jeffrey D. Ullman. *Data Structures and Algorithms*. Addison-Wesley, 1983.

[2] Richard S. Bird. Using circular programs to eliminate multiple traversals of data. *Acta Informatica*, 21(3):239–250, 1984.

[3] Mark R. Brown. Implementation and analysis of binomial queue algorithms. *SIAM Journal of Computing*, 7(3):298–319, 1978.

[4] Edsger W. Dijkstra. A note on two problems in connexion with graphs. *Numerische Mathematik*, 1:269–271, 1959.

[5] Michael L. Fredman and Robert E. Tarjan. Fibonacci heaps and their uses in improved network optimization algorithms. *Journal of the ACM*, 34(3): 596–615, July 1987.

[6] Paul Hudak, Simon L. Peyton Jones, Philip Wadler, Arvind, Brian Boutel, Jon Fairbairn, Joseph Fasel, María M. Guzmán, Kevin Hammond, John Hughes, Thomas Johnsson, Richard Kieburtz, Rishiyur S. Nikhil, Will Partain, and John Peterson. Report on the functional programming language Haskell, Version 1.2. *ACM SIGPLAN Notices*, 27(5), May 1992.

[7] Douglas W. Jones. An empirical comparison of priority-queue and event-set implementations. *Communications of the ACM*, 29(4):300–311, April 1986.

[8] Donald E. Knuth. *The Art of Computer Programming: Sorting and Searching*, volume 3. Addison-Wesley, Reading, Massachusetts, 1973.

[9] L. C. Paulson. *ML for the working programmer*. Cambridge University Press, Cambridge, 1991.

[10] Chris M. P. Reade. Balanced trees with removals: an exercise in rewriting and proof. *Science of Computer Programming*, 18:181–204, 1992.

[11] Daniel D. Sleator and Robert E. Tarjan. Self-adjusting binary trees. In *Proceedings of the 15th Annual ACM Symposium on Theory of Computing*, pages 235–245, Boston, Massachusetts, April 1983. ACM.

[12] Robert E. Tarjan. *Data Structures and Network Algorithms*. SIAM, 1983.

[13] Jean Vuillemin. A data structure for manipulating priority queues. *Communications of the ACM*, 21(4):309–315, April 1978.

Mechanized Reasoning about Functional Programs

Sava Mintchev

Department of Computer Science, University of Manchester

Manchester, UK

Abstract

This report describes a tool for reasoning about lazy functional programs written in a subset of Haskell. A first–order logic language for formulating theorems is defined. The syntax of the logic language is included in the functional language syntax; the semantics is classical. Structural induction and case analysis axioms are generated internally for suitable user–defined data types.

The logic language is given an operational semantics, which is implemented by the theorem proving tool. The operational semantics involves depth–first search, with limited backtracking. Proof can be goal–directed (backwards) or forward. Special care has been taken to restrict the search space. For example, induction is applied only where requested by the user. Pattern–matching is used instead of unification.

The theorem prover is in a sense 'automatic', as there is no user involvement in the proof of a goal. The approach taken can be called *declarative theorem proving*, since the user cannot manipulate a proof *state* using a sequence of tactics. The theorem prover can be regarded as an interpreter for a declarative language.

1 Introduction

Due to the absence of side effects, pure functional programs have a clean semantics, and are easier to reason about than imperative programs. It is tempting, therefore, to propose a framework for program development in a functional language. The framework should allow the formulation of program specifications, and offer means for ensuring that programs satisfy their specifications.

There are different approaches to functional–style provably correct program development. One possible way is to propose a calculus of functions within which programs with known properties can be derived, as e.g. in the Bird–Meertens formalism [1]. A second approach is that of constructive programming [9]: program specifications are existential statements in intuitionistic logic. Programs are not written, but are extracted from the constructive proofs of specifications. Finally, there is the conventional approach: after a program is written, a proof must be given in classical logic that the specification is satisfied. This approach is used, for example, in the Boyer–Moore theorem prover [2].

We have chosen the conventional, classical approach. The main reason for this conservative choice is the desire to build upon the existing programming practice, rather than propose a radically different programming methodology. The adoption of the constructive approach would replace programming by theorem proving, and programs by proofs. Another reason for preferring the conventional approach is that the power of classical reasoning increases the extent to which proofs can be automated.

Having selected the approach, we must choose a particular logic for reasoning about functional programs. Syntactically, logic formulae can be compatible with the object language, which makes it very easy to reuse parts of a compiler (parser, type checker) in the implementation of a theorem–proving tool. We have chosen a first–order logic language without existential quantification, with the hope of achieving a good compromise between expressiveness and realizability.

There is a wide variety of theorem proving techniques, involving different logics and object domains [7]. Since we want to reason about unbounded-state functional programs, we are concerned with proof–theoretic, rather than model–based methods.

One way of mechanizing reasoning about functional programs is to use a generic theorem prover. Such a prover must permit the formalization of programs with their precise semantics, and must be able to manipulate programs (i.e. reduce expressions). An example of a system that can meet these requirements is Isabelle [4].

A disadvantage of using a generic theorem prover is the need to provide a semantically equivalent formulation of functional programs in the prover's object language. Another drawback may be the low speed of generic provers: fast theorem proving is essential if reasoning about programs of a realistic size is to be attempted.

We have decided to build a specialized theorem prover, with the aim of achieving the following features:

Compatibility with Haskell. The theorem prover is to have two types of input — *modules* and *theories*. Modules contain function definitions written in *Core*, a subset of Haskell. Theories contain logic statements about Core functions.

Keeping Core programs separate from logic theories is rather convenient, because the programs can be processed by any Haskell compiler/interpreter. The same program can be executed and reasoned about, and there is no need for semantics–preserving translation before using the prover.

Simplicity of control. Theories have an operational as well as a denotational semantics. The theorem prover just implements the operational semantics, i.e. is an interpreter for theorems. There is no language of tactics and tacticals for guiding the proof.

By avoiding the introduction of a proof control language, we relieve the user of the task of learning yet another language.

Tractability. Search for proofs in large or infinite spaces is to be initiated only where specifically requested by the user. This applies, in particular, to the use of induction. At the cost of some extra complexity for the user, we can avoid having to apply induction heuristically, and consequently we can reduce the risk of excessively long or infinite computation.

Assistance in proof construction. A good theorem prover should not just verify the correctness of logic formulae; it should also help the user to gain insight into the proofs. The theorem prover must produce a readable trace of a proof attempt, enabling the user to see why a proof succeeds/fails.

A very important issue that must be addressed in the description of a theorem prover is that of *soundness*. This issue will not be considered here from a semantic viewpoint. Instead, reference will be made to appropriate well-known axioms, justifying the operation of the theorem prover.

Another important issue is *termination*. It has two aspects: i) termination of the reduction of Core expressions, and ii) termination of the proof of logic formulae. Ensuring termination is assumed to be a responsibility of the user, just as guaranteeing the termination of a program is a responsibility of the programmer.

The rest of this paper is organized as follows: Section 2 introduces the object and logic languages; Sections 3 and 4 present the operation of the theorem prover; Section 5 gives an example and discusses some pragmatic issues of proof construction.

2 The language

We start the description of the input language of the theorem prover with a brief overview of Core expressions – the terms in logic statements.

2.1 Terms (Core expressions)

Core expressions [6] (also referred to as *terms*) will be denoted by e, s, t. An expression can be a variable (v, x, y, z), data constructor (c), lambda abstraction (\xs -> e), application ($e_1 \cdots e_n$), case expression (case e of *alts*) or let expression (let *binds* in e). A sequence of syntactic objects is designated by appending an "s" to the name of the object, e.g. a sequence of variables *vs*.

Any function written in Core can be partial, and that is why the logic system must support reasoning about partial functions (The alternative approach was taken in the Boyer–Moore theorem prover [2], in which every function definition must be proved total before being accepted). To express partiality, the *undefined* expression Bot is introduced.

In subsequent sections we shall need applications of a restricted form. A restricted application *app* is a variable applied to zero or more restricted arguments. A restricted argument *arg* is a variable v, constructor c, Bot or an application of restricted arguments.

We shall assume that our Core programs have undergone dependency analysis and type checking [5]. As a result of dependency analysis, expressions are transformed so that each let expression contains as few binds as possible.

Figure 1 shows the function red which reduces Core expressions. The object language, Core, is a subset of the metalanguage used in Figure 1 and subsequent figures. In order to avoid confusion, Core keywords are written in typewriter font, while meta words are written without serifs.

red (e_1 e_2)	=	case red e_1 of	application
($\backslash x$ -> e)	$\rightarrow$	$e[e_2/x]$	
Bot	$\rightarrow$	Bot	
-	$\rightarrow$	(e_1 e_2)	
red (let *binds* in e)	=	$e[fs/vs]$	let expr
where			
(vs, es)	=	unzipBinds *binds*	
fs	=	map makeFix *binds*	
makeFix ($v = e$)	=	fix v ($\backslash xs$ -> $e[xs/vs]$) fs	
red (fix v ($\backslash xs$ -> e) fs)	=	red ($e[fs/xs]$)	fixpoint
red (case s of *alts*)	=	case red s of	case expr
c es	$\rightarrow$	red (selectAlt (c es) *alts*)	
Bot	$\rightarrow$	Bot	
-	$\rightarrow$	(case s of *alts*)	
red e	=	e	other

Figure 1: Reduction of Core terms

Let–expressions are reduced using a variant of the *fixpoint operator*. A new Core expression is introduced,

$$\text{fix } v \ (\backslash xs \text{ -> } e) \ fs$$

which allows recursive definitions to be unfolded one step at a time. The capacity for 'controlled unfolding' is essential to the operation of the theorem prover.

The function unzipBinds used in the reduction of let–expressions simply splits up a list of binds into a list of variables and a list of expressions to which the variables are bound. The function selectAlt chooses the appropriate alternative (c xs $-$ $>$ e) from *alts*, and $e[es/xs]$ is reduced. If there is no matching alternative, selectAlt returns Bot.

2.2 Logic formulae

Having described the object language, we now look at the logic language of the theorem prover. The syntax of logic formulae is shown in Figure 2. Atomic formulae can be built from Core expressions using the predicate (:==). The intended interpretation $\mathcal{F}[\![.]\!]$ of (:==) will be equivalence between the values of Core expressions:

(1) $\quad \mathcal{F}[\![e\ :==\ s]\!]\ \rho\ =\ (\mathcal{E}[\![e]\!]\ \rho\ \equiv\ \mathcal{E}[\![s]\!]\ \rho)$

The relation ($\equiv$) is undecidable in general (as expressions may denote functions), and it is convenient to use three–valued logic to accommodate the possibility that the procedure which implements (:==) may not be able to find an answer. Semantically, logic formulae are mapped onto a 3–point domain, whereby TT denotes *true*, FF denotes *false*, and UU denotes *bottom*, the least element in the domain.

Atomic	p, q, r	$\rightarrow$	TT	*true*
formulae		$\mid$	FF	*false*
		$\mid$	UU	*undefined*
		$\mid$	$app\ :==\ e$	equality
Logic	P, Q, R	$\rightarrow$	p	atomic formula
formulae		$\mid$	$P\ /\backslash\ Q$	conjunction
		$\mid$	$P\ \backslash/\ Q$	disjunction
		$\mid$	$[p_1,\ p_2,\ \cdots p_n]\ \text{->>}\ Q$	forward implication
		$\mid$	$[P_1,\ P_2,\ \cdots P_n]\ \text{-:}\ Q$	backwards implication
		$\mid$	All $(\backslash x\ \text{->}\ P)$	universal quantification
		$\mid$	Ind $(\backslash x\ \text{->}\ P)$	structural induction

Figure 2: Syntax of logic formulae

Complex formulae can be built from atomic ones using the connectives for conjunction, disjunction and implication. How do the connectives behave on unknown values (UU)? If both arguments of a connective are UU, the result is UU. When one of the arguments of a connective is unknown (UU), the result may still be known, e.g: (FF $/\backslash$ UU) is FF, (UU $/\backslash$ FF) is FF.

There are two forms of implication: forward (->>) and backwards (-:). They are the same denotationally, but differ operationally, as will be seen in Section 4.2.

Variables (Core expressions) occurring in logic formulae can be quantified either explicitly or implicitly. Explicit quantification is done by the universal quantifier All or by the structural induction quantifier Ind. Denotationally, All and Ind are the same, both representing universal quantification. The operational difference is discussed in Section 4.3.

All variables occurring free in a formula are implicitly universally quantified. The scope of quantification is always the smallest possible. For example,

$P(z)\ /\backslash\ Q(z)$ is All $(\backslash z\ \text{->}\ P(z)\ /\backslash\ Q(z))$, while
$P(x)\ /\backslash\ Q(y)$ is All $(\backslash x\ \text{->}\ P(x))\ /\backslash$ All $(\backslash y\ \text{->}\ Q(y))$

provided that x and y are distinct variables, y does not occur free in P, and x does not occur free in Q.

As a concrete example, consider the assertion that (++) is associative:

```
appAssoc:   Ind (\as ->
              ((as ++ bs) ++ cs) :== (as ++ (bs ++ cs)))
```

The variables **bs** and **cs** occur free in the above formula. Under the rule for implicit quantification with smallest scope, the formula will be interpreted in the same way as:

```
appAssoc:   Ind (\as -> All (\bs -> All (\cs ->
              ((as ++ bs) ++ cs) :== (as ++ (bs ++ cs)))))
```

Notice that append (++) has not been bound by a new universal quantifier, since it is a globally defined function.

2.3   Modules and theories

Modules are used in programming languages to facilitate programming in the large. Likewise, *theories* can be used to aid proof maintenance. Without going into a detailed description, we can enumerate the components of a theory:

- name of the theory;

- names of theorems which are exported from the theory (optional);

- names of imported Core modules;

- names of imported theories;

- named axioms (logic formulae which are assumed true);

- named theorems (logic formulae which must be proved).

The order of theorems is important — when proving a theorem, all preceding axioms and theorems (including imported ones) are assumed to hold. In other words, each theorem is in fact the conclusion of a backwards implication, in which all preceding axioms and theorems are premises.

3   Proving atomic formulae

Now we can describe the operation of the theorem prover. First, we consider the implementation of the atomic predicate (:==).

As already pointed out, we cannot implement a test (:==) which would satisfy (1); however, we would like to know that the implementation is sound. We need to define a function (:==), which, given any two Core expressions will return **TT** if in all environments they denote equal values, **FF** if in all environments the values are different[1], and **UU** if equality cannot be determined. It is also possible that the equality test may diverge. For a fully abstract model of Core expressions, the soundness condition can be expressed as:

(2) $\forall \rho, e, s. \mathcal{F}[\![e :== s]\!] \rho \sqsubseteq (\mathcal{E}[\![e]\!] \rho \equiv \mathcal{E}[\![s]\!] \rho)$

$(:==)$			$::$	Term $\to$ Term $\to$ Atomic	
c_1	$:==$	c_2			constructors
$\mid (c_1 == c_2)$			$=$	TT	
$\mid$ otherwise			$=$	FF	
v_1	$:==$	v_2			variables
$\mid (v_1 == v_2)$			$=$	TT	
$(\backslash x \to e_1)$	$:==$	$(\backslash x \to e_2)$	$=$	$e_1[z/x] :== e_2[z/x]$	lambdas (fresh z)
$\mathbf{fix}\ x\ f\ fs$	$:==$	$\mathbf{fix}\ y\ g\ gs$			fixpoints
$\mid$ all eq $(\mathrm{zip}\ fs\ gs)$			$=$	TT	
$\mid$ otherwise			$=$	UU	
where eq $(\mathbf{fix}\ x\ f\ fs, \mathbf{fix}\ y\ g\ gs)$			$=$	$\mathrm{isTT}(f\ zs :== g\ zs)$	(fresh zs)
$\mathbf{fix}\ v\ f\ fs$	$:==$	s	$=$	red $(f\ fs) :== s$	
e	$:==$	$\mathbf{fix}\ v\ f\ fs$	$=$	$e :== \mathrm{red}\ (f\ fs)$	
$(e_1 \cdots e_n)$	$:==$	$(s_1 \cdots s_m)$			applications
$\mid n == m$ && $\mathrm{isTT}\ (e_i :== s_i)$			$=$	TT	
$(e_1 \cdots e_n)$	$:==$	s	$=$	red $(e_1 \cdots e_n) :== s$	
s	$:==$	$(e_1 \cdots e_n)$	$=$	$s :== \mathrm{red}\ (e_1 \cdots e_n)$	
$\begin{array}{l}\mathbf{case}\ e_1\ \mathbf{of}\\ \quad alts_1\end{array}$	$:==$	$\begin{array}{l}\mathbf{case}\ e_2\ \mathbf{of}\\ \quad alts_2\end{array}$			case expr
$\mid \mathrm{isTT}(e_1 :== e_2)$ && all eq $(\mathrm{zip}\ alts_1\ alts_2)$			$=$	TT	
where eq $(\backslash c_1\ xs_1 \to e_1, \backslash c_2\ xs_2 \to e_2)$			$=$	$(c_1 == c_2)$ && $\mathrm{isTT}(e_1[zs/xs_1] :== e_2[zs/xs_2])$	(fresh zs)
$\begin{array}{l}\mathbf{case}\ e\ \mathbf{of}\\ \quad alts\end{array}$	$:==$	s	$=$	$\mathrm{red}\left(\begin{array}{l}\mathbf{case}\ e\ \mathbf{of}\\ \quad alts\end{array}\right) :== s$	
s	$:==$	$\begin{array}{l}\mathbf{case}\ e\ \mathbf{of}\\ \quad alts\end{array}$	$=$	$s :== \mathrm{red}\left(\begin{array}{l}\mathbf{case}\ e\ \mathbf{of}\\ \quad alts\end{array}\right)$	
e	$:==$	s	$=$	UU	other

Figure 3: Comparison of terms

A possible implementation is shown in Figure 3. The cases for constructors and variables are obvious. Note that distinct variables do not necessarily represent different values in all possible environments, and so the result of their comparison is undefined.

It is clear from inspection of Figure 3 that all variables are regarded as universally quantified. Universally quantified variables can be instantiated by pattern matching, as will be described in Section 4.1.

Lambda abstractions are compared using the axiom of weak extensionality [9]. The comparison of a pair of fixpoints is based on fixpoint induction; the function isTT returns True if its argument is TT, and False otherwise. If only one expression is a fixpoint, it is reduced, and the comparison is attempted again.

---

[1] in other words, TT if the equality is a valid formula, and FF if it is unsatisfiable

Two applications $(e_1 \; e_2 \; \cdots e_n)$ and $(s_1 \; s_2 \; \cdots s_n)$ are compared using a congruence axiom: if each e_i and s_i are equal, then the applications are equal. Note that the comparison is done left to right lazily (i.e. it is abandoned as soon as two terms e_i and s_i are found not to be equal). Failing a proof by congruence, an attempt is made to reduce each application before comparison.

Two **case** expressions are considered equal if the switch expressions are equal and all corresponding alternatives are equal. The alternatives in both expressions must be arranged in the same order, non-recursive alternatives first. The comparison of alternatives is again done lazily.

4 Proving complex formulae

Now we look at the tactics for proving complex formulae. Figure 4 presents the function to do that.

A formula paired with a *context* makes up a *goal*. The context contains in an appropriate form the assumptions which have been made during the proof of the formula. The precise structure of the context need not be discussed here.

The definition of prove clearly reflects the semantics of formulae. For example, an implication $(Ps \to\!\!> Q)$ or $(Ps -: Q)$ is handled by proving Q on the assumption that the premises Ps are true. A universally quantified formula $(\text{All } (\backslash x \to P))$ is proved by proving P after substituting in it a fresh variable for x.

```
prove :: (Context, Formula) → Atomic
prove (ctx, R) = case R of
   (P /\ Q)      →   prove (ctx, P) 'andT' prove (ctx, Q)    conjunction
   (P \/ Q)      →   prove (ctx, P) 'orT' prove (ctx, Q)     disjunction
   (Ps ->> Q)    →   prove (foldl (assume []) (ctx, Q) Ps)   fwd implic
                     'orT' prove (ctx , Q)
   (Ps -: Q)     →   prove (foldl (assume []) (ctx, Q) Ps)   bkw implic
                     'orT' prove (ctx , Q)
   All (\x -> P) →   prove (ctx, P[fresh z/x])               quantif
```

Figure 4: Basic proof tactic

The function assume (Figure 5) takes a list of goals gs, the current goal (ctx, Q), and an assumption P which is true provided that all gs hold. It returns the current goal modified so as to take the assumption into account.

4.1 Assumption of an atomic predicate

Let us look first at the case in which the assumption is an atomic predicate, $(app ::= e)$. The idea is to turn that into a rewrite rule for replacing instances of app by e.

The application app can be written as $(v \; arg_1 \; \cdots arg_n)$: a variable or a fixpoint, possibly applied to arguments of a restricted form. What assumeAtomic

assume ::	[(Context, Formula)] $\rightarrow$	new goals
	(Context, Formula) $\rightarrow$	goal
	Formula $\rightarrow$	assumption
	(Context, Formula)	new goal

```
assume gs (ctx, Q) P  =  case P of
  (app :== e)   →   assumeAtomic gs (ctx, Q) P                      atomic
  (P /\ R)      →   assume gs (assume gs (ctx, Q) P) R              conjunction
  (P \/ R)      →   assume gs (ctx, Q) ([[P] -: Q] -: R)           disjunction
  (Ps -: R)     →   assume (map addGoal Ps ++ gs)                   bkw implic
                       (ctx, Q) R
                  where addGoal P = (ctx, P)
  (Ps ->> R)    →   (assumeFwd gs ctx (Ps ->> R), Q)               fwd implic
  All(\x -> P)  →   assume gs (ctx, Q) P[fresh ?z/x]               quantif
  Ind(\x -> P)  →   assume gs (ctx, Q) P[fresh ?z/x]               induction
```

Figure 5: Assumptions

does is to provide a new topmost clause in the definition of v to be used in the proof of the current goal:

$$v\ arg_1 \cdots arg_n \mid \text{all (isTT . prove)}\ gs\ =\ e$$

The expressions $arg_1 \cdots arg_n$ are regarded as patterns, against which the actual arguments of v are matched. It is worth mentioning that the pattern matching involved here is an extension of the usual pattern matching algorithm, since fixpoints (in other words, bound variables) may be present in patterns.

The reader may find our way of dealing with atomic assumptions a little peculiar. The main motivation for turning atomic assumptions into rewrite rules is the desire to speed up the prover. A rewrite rule associated with a particular function is invoked only when the name of that function is encountered. Thus the number of rules that are applicable at each moment is limited.

When a universally quantified formula is assumed, a new *unknown* ($?z$) is substituted for the variable bound by the quantifier. The unknown can only be instantiated by pattern matching in the atomic assumptions derived from $P[?z/x]$.

4.2 Assumption of a conjunction, disjunction, implication

In the case of the assumption being a conjunction / disjunction, the appropriate propositional tautology justifies the action taken:

$$
\begin{array}{ll}
(P \wedge R) \Rightarrow Q \Leftrightarrow P \Rightarrow (R \Rightarrow Q) & \text{conjunction} \\
(P \vee R) \Rightarrow Q \Leftrightarrow ((P \Rightarrow Q) \Rightarrow R) \Rightarrow Q & \text{disjunction}
\end{array}
$$

When the assumption is a backwards implication (Ps -: R), the conclusion R is assumed, with new goals added for the premises Ps. If R is ever used in the proof, all the premises Ps will have to be proved. The following propositional tautology provides a justification:

$$(P \Rightarrow R) \Rightarrow Q \quad \Leftrightarrow \quad P \wedge (R \Rightarrow Q) \vee Q \quad \text{backwards implication}$$

When a forward implication is assumed, assumeFwd stores it into the context. Whenever a new atomic assumption is made, assumeAtomic attempts to infer other assumptions using the forward rules in the context.

The difference between forward and backwards implication is revealed here. Backwards implications are applied to Core expressions in the *current goal* to produce new goals, while forward implications are applied to *assumptions* to produce new assumptions.

Is it really necessary to have two different varieties of implication? Consider, for example, the assertion that the relation (<=) is transitive:

```
transLE:  All (\b -> [(a <= b) :== True, (b <= c) :== True]
               ->> ((a <= c) :== True))
```

Two problems would emerge if we used backwards (-:) instead of forward (->>) implication here. In the first place, the implication is left–recursive: the premises match the conclusion. In order to ensure termination, we would have to eliminate left recursion, in much the same way as in a Prolog program. Secondly, the premises contain a variable (b) which does not occur free in the conclusion.

Since full unification is not available, and pattern–matching is used instead, it is necessary that all free variables in the premises of a backwards implication occur free in the conclusion. Likewise, all free variables in the conclusion of a forward implication should occur free in the premises.

4.3   Structural induction

Structural induction is a powerful means for proving properties of functions. It is a built–in feature of this prover. Induction rules are produced internally for user–defined data types. Since they are second–order, however, they cannot be applied in the same way as (first–order) user–supplied axioms.

The use of induction is requested by a special quantifier, Ind, which has a type $(a \rightarrow \text{Formula})$ where a is a type variable. For each occurence of Ind the type inference mechanism must instantiate a to a concrete data type; if a is left uninstantiated, an error message is produced. The predicate to which Ind is applied should be inclusive, so that the result will be valid for infinite as well as finite data structures. Inclusivity is not enforced by the tool at present, however.

Suppose that the current goal is Ind ($\backslash$x -> P) where the type of x is $(tycon\ t_1 \cdots t_n)$. The goal is reduced to a conjunction of goals, one for every constructor alternative of $tycon$. For a constructor alternative $(c\ texp_1 \cdots texp_m)$ in which $texp_{i_1} \cdots texp_{i_k}$ are all $(tycon\ t_1 \cdots t_n)$, the new goal has the format:

$$[P\ [z_{i_1}/x],\cdots P\ [z_{i_k}/x]] \dashv:\ P\ [(c\ z_1\ \cdots z_m)/x]$$

where $z_1 \cdots z_m$ are fresh variables. In addition, the goal $P\ [\texttt{Bot}/x]$ must be proved to ensure that P holds for nonterminating or error expressions as well.

Going back to the example of the associativity of append, the goals which are generated for proof by induction are[2]:

```
(Bot ++ bs) ++ cs :== Bot ++ (bs ++ cs);
([] ++ bs) ++ cs :== [] ++ (bs ++ cs);
[All (\bs-> All (\cs-> (list0_2 ++ bs) ++ cs :==
                        list0_2 ++ (bs ++ cs)))] -:
    All (\bs-> All (\cs->
              ((a1 : list0_2) ++ bs) ++ cs :==
              (a1 : list0_2) ++ (bs ++ cs)))
```

The proof of these three goals is trivial.

4.4 Case analysis (disjoint sum types)

Case analysis can be viewed as structural induction on enumerated types (e.g. booleans). Hence the user can request case analysis explicitly (with $\texttt{Ind}$). However it is usually convenient to have case analysis applied automatically. For example, case analysis may be needed on variables which have been introduced by induction, and are not present in the original theorem. Moreover, case analysis may have to be performed not only on variables, but also on other expressions.

We restrict our attention to case analysis on function applications. For any application *app* of an enumerated type

$$\textbf{data}\ enumtype\ =\ c_1\ |\ c_2\ |\ \cdots |\ c_n$$

case analysis is encoded by the following axiom scheme:

$$app\ :==\ \texttt{Bot}\ \backslash/\ app\ :==\ c_1\ \backslash/\ \cdots\ app\ :==\ c_n$$

Case analysis axioms are generated internally. They are used only as a last resort, if an application *app* cannot be reduced to a constructor c_i.

5 Pragmatic issues in proof construction

In this section we briefly comment on the practical use of the theorem prover. We start by giving a simple example, both as an illustration of concepts introduced so far, and as a motivation for further discussion.

---

[2]Notice that in the third goal (the inductive step) the bs and cs in the premise (the inductive hypothesis) are different from the bs and cs in the conclusion. This is because in the theorem bs and cs are implicitly quantified *within* the scope of the induction quantifier Ind. In this particular example the order of quantifiers is unimportant, but in general it matters.

5.1 Example: a sorting algorithm

The problem is to prove the correctness of a simple sorting function (`sort ::
List Int -> List Int`).

Any sorting algorithm should satisfy two conditions: i) each element must
occur as many times in the result list as in the input list (i.e. the result must
be a permutation of the input); ii) the result list must be ordered. These
conditions constitute a specification for any sorting algorithm, and are stated
formally in the following theorem:

```
specSort: Ind (\xs -> occur y (sort xs) :== occur y xs)
       /\ Ind (\xs -> (ordered (sort xs) :== termL term xs))
```

The specification refers to the functions `termL`, `ordered` and `occur`, which
can be given Core definitions in the usual manner. Although the specification
as a whole (the theorem) is nonexecutable, the functions in terms of which it
is stated are.

```
term x = case x of        -- x terminates
            0 -> True
            _ -> True

termL term xs = case xs of
                  []   -> True
                  x:xs -> case term x of
                            True -> termL term xs

ordered xs = case xs of
               []   -> True
               y:ys -> case term y of
                         True -> (case ys of
                                    []    -> True
                                    z:zs  -> y <= z)
                                 && ordered ys

occur a xs = case xs of
               []   -> 0
               y:ys -> case a == y of
                         True  -> 1 + occur a ys
                         False -> occur a ys
```

The expression (`termL term xs`) evaluates to `True` if every element of the
list `xs` terminates. We cannot in general prove that (`ordered (sort xs) :==
True`), because the list `xs` may be infinite or may contain undefined elements.

The integer operations (`+`), (`<=`) and (`==`) are taken to be primitive. They
are not defined as Core functions, but are axiomatized. Any primitive operation
is strict (returns `Bot` if an argument is `Bot`) and terminating (terminates if both

arguments terminate). Furthermore, (<=) is antisymmetric and transitive (see example in Section 4.2).

The implementation of the insertion sort algorithm is straightforward:

```
insrt i xs = case xs of
                [] -> [i]
                y:ys -> case i <= y of
                            True -> i:xs
                            False -> y:insrt i ys

sort xs = case xs of
            [] -> []
            y:ys -> insrt y (sort ys)
```

Now we have to prove that **sort** satisfies the specification. We can attempt proving two separate goals. First we can try to prove that a sorted list is a permutation of the original:

```
occSort:    Ind (\xs -> occur y (sort xs) :== occur y xs)
```

The induction step won't go through, however, because an important fact about **insrt** is unknown: inserting an element **y** into a list **xs** results in a permutation of the list (**y:xs**). This fact can be proved by induction, but the theorem prover will not use induction on its own accord. Thus the following lemma must be proved first:

```
occInsrt:   Ind (\xs ->
                occur y (insrt x xs) :== occur y (x:xs))
```

The lemma is proved by induction on the list **xs**. The induction step involves automatic case analysis on (x <= a), (y == x) and (y == a), where a is the head of **xs**.

Proving the second part of the specification, namely that a sorted list is ordered, turns out to require two additional subgoals (because the function **ordered** looks at the first *two* elements of the input list):

```
ordIns1:    Ind (\xs -> [(x <= y) :== True] -:
            (ordered (x:insrt y xs) :== ordered (x:xs)))
ordIns:     Ind (\xs -> (ordered (insrt x xs) :==
                (case term x of True -> ordered xs)))
```

In the proof of **ordIns1**, the induction step requires case analysis on (y <= a), where a is the head of the list **xs**. In the proof of **ordIns**, the induction step again involves case analysis, and uses **ordIns1** instead of the induction hypothesis.

5.2 Axioms and abstract data types

Abstract data types are supported by Haskell's module system. They are also made available by the theorem prover. An abstract data type here is represented by type declarations for a collection of functions (as found in a Haskell interface), together with a theory which describes the properties of these functions. Abstraction is enforced by hiding the constructors of a datatype and/or hiding the definitions of the accessor functions. The type of integers, for example, can be regarded as abstract in the absence of definitions for primitive operations (<=, +, etc), although the data constructors (0, 1, etc) are visible.

Is it wise to permit user–supplied axioms in theories? After all, the axioms can make the theory inconsistent, and can be used in the proof of false statements. A safer approach would be to ban axioms, and insist on having Core definitions for all functions, so that the required properties can be formulated as theorems and proved.

Axioms are allowed in this theorem prover mainly in order to avoid the necessity of always appealing to 'first principles'. For example, building a theory of primitive arithmetic seems useless from a practical point of view, because primitive operations in a compiler are not implemented in the way we would define them. Furthermore, the user may want to refer to functions which are not definable in a sequential, deterministic functional language (e.g. parallel or).

5.3 Assistance in proof construction

An important practical question is: does the theorem prover make proof construction easier? For simple examples involving one application of structural induction (e.g. properties of standard functions like map, foldr, foldl, (++), etc) the answer is definitely 'yes', since proofs in those cases are found automatically. When a proof fails, however, the output of the theorem prover must be informative enough to help the user find the problem.

For example, consider an attempt to prove a modified version of the assertion that a sorted list is ordered:

```
specSort:  Ind (\xs -> ordered (sort xs) :== True)
```

The proof will fail (indeed it will produce FF) with a trace which presents a clear counterexample:

```
ordered (sort Bot)
not :==
True
```

As another example, let us try to prove ordIns in the absence of the lemma ordIns1. The prover informs us that it has been unable to go through the induction step

```
ordered (insrt x.3! (a1.1! : list1_2!))
```

```
??? :==
ordered (a1.1! : list1_2!)
```

in the particular case when ((x.3! <= a1.1!) :== False). At this point
we have to look at the definition of insrt and notice that what is needed is a
lemma like ordIns1.

Experience with this theorem prover suggests that having a single trace of
the proof is not enough. On the one hand, a high level trace is required for
documenting a successful proof attempt. On the other hand, a low level trace
may be necessary for the analysis of a failed proof attempt. Detailed tracing is
particularly needed when the prover enters an infinite loop, in order to avoid
falling into a silent 'black hole'. Being able to vary the degree of detail in a
proof trace is often useful. It seems desirable to have an extensive mechanism
for 'proof debugging'.

6   Conclusion

We have presented a tool for reasoning about functional programs. The tool
has been targeted at a subset of a particular lazy language — Haskell, although
the underlying ideas can be applied to reasoning about strict pure functional
languages as well.

The theorem prover has been designed as an interpreter for a declarative
language — the logic language used for formulating statements about functional
programs. The aim has been to avoid the use of obscure heuristics for guiding
the proof, and to avoid defining a separate language of tactics for proof–state
manipulation. The result of this design strategy is to hide proofs of theorems
in the theorems themselves.

There is ample scope for future work. First of all, the tracing mechanism of
the proving tool should be elaborated. Second, the input language of the prover
should be extended to include a larger subset of Haskell. Currently the input
is limited to Core. Since full Haskell can be transformed into Core, we have
reason to believe that upgrading the prover to cope with Haskell is feasible.
Still, some tricky questions can be expected, e.g. how to tie logic theories with
overloading.

Next, some of the restrictions on the syntax of logic formulae can perhaps
be relaxed. The power of the tool can be increased if higher–order pattern
matching is introduced. Higher–order pattern matching can for example facilitate reasoning about monads. Finally, other forms of induction can be provided
as primitive: fixpoint induction, well–founded induction.

Related work is reported in [3]. MetaMorph is a system for reasoning about
functional specifications. Functions in it are defined by equations with non-
overlapping patterns. A Prolog–like metalanguage is used for specifying tactics
to guide the proof. A transformational environment for lazy functional programming is described in [8].

Acknowledgements

I would like to thank Julian Seward for his comments and help. Thanks are due to the Glasgow FP people for giving me the opportunity to present this work, and to the referees for suggesting numerous improvements. The financial support of the CVCP, the Department of Computer Science at Manchester University and the Cyril and Methodius Foundation is gratefully acknowledged.

References

[1] R.S. Bird. A calculus of functions for program derivation. In David A. Turner, editor, *Research Topics in Functional Programming*, pages 287–308. Addison–Wesley, 1990.

[2] Robert Boyer and J. S. Moore. *A Computational Logic Handbook*. Academic Press, 1988.

[3] P.J. Brumfitt. Metamorph - a formal methods toolkit with application to the design of digital hardware. *Journal of Functional Programming*, 2(4):437–473, October 1992.

[4] Lawrence C. Paulson. The foundation of a generic theorem prover. *Journal of Automated Reasoning*, 5:363–397, 1989.

[5] S.L. Peyton Jones. *The Implementation of Functional Programming Languages*. Prentice-Hall International Series in Computer Science. Prentice-Hall International (UK) Ltd, London, 1987.

[6] S.L. Peyton Jones and D.R. Lester. *Implementing Functional Languages: A Practical Approach*. Prentice Hall International, Hemel Hempstead, UK, 1992.

[7] David A. Plaisted. Mechanical theorem proving. In R.B. Banerji, editor, *Formal Techniques in Artificial Intelligence*. Elsevier Science Publishers B.V., Amsterdam, The Netherlands, 1990.

[8] C. Runciman, I. Toyn, and M. Firth. An incremental, exploratory and transformational environment for lazy functional programming. *Journal of Functional Programming*, 3(1):93–117, January 1993.

[9] R. Turner. *Constructive Foundations for Functional Languages*. McGraw–Hill, London, 1991.

A Case Study in
Parallel Program Derivation:
the Heat Equation Algorithm

John O'Donnell   Gudula Rünger

University of Glasgow   Universität des Saarlandes

Glasgow, Scotland   Saarbrücken, Deutschland

Abstract

We investigate the application of functional specification and program transformation in a practical setting using a simple case study: the derivation of a parallel program for solving the heat equation. The main concerns here are: (1) how to write an initial specification of the algorithm using a notation appropriate to the subject area (partial differential equations), (2) the introduction of an intermediate algorithm specification using bidirectional mapping scan, and (3) the use of equational reasoning to transform the specification.

1   Introduction

Our long-term objective is to make it easier to write correct and efficient parallel programs. Our method is based on equational reasoning and program transformation in a higher order, nonstrict functional language. We selected this formal method because we hope to show that

1. The functional language is expressive enough to allow us to specify the original algorithm in a clear, readable, intuitive style, which ordinary programmers — not just functional programming researchers — would be willing to use.

2. The functional language is also expressive enough to allow various low level implementations to be specified close to the actual architecture models. It should be possible to compile the low level functional programs for execution on target machines, and we should also be able to predict the execution times.

3. Equational reasoning makes it feasible (although not trivial) to transform from (1) to (2) and to prove the correctness of the implementations.

The purposes of this paper are (1) to apply the method to a simple case study in order to identify its strengths and weaknesses, and (2) to state and prove some general lemmas relating two families of communication functions (scans and shifts).

The heat equation is a partial differential equation that can be solved numerically by a particularly simple algorithm. This makes it suitable for a preliminary case study, but showing that a programming methodology can handle the heat equation does not establish that it will be useful for more challenging problems.

We begin by specifying the problem in a form appropriate to the subject area, so we'll specify the heat equation and its numerical solution using conventional mathematical notation, and then convert this to a functional specification which is as similar as possible.

There are several reasons for deriving an intermediate representation for the algorithm, rather than going directly from the initial specification to the implementations:

- It may be easier to do two shorter derivations rather than one long one; if the goal is far from the initial specification, then our derivation may be aimless instead of moving systematically toward the goal.

- The intermediate representation can be chosen to express abstractly those properties of the algorithm that all implementations will share (for example, restrictions on the communications) while avoiding overspecification (for example, expressing constraints that will exist for some architectures but not for others).

We use a bidirectional mapping scan for the intermediate representation, since this represents the communication requirements very explicitly (which are inherent in the problem) and says nothing about the actual timing of events (which will be vary across different architectures). The bidirectional scans are not easy to understand, so they will often be unsuitable for initial specifications of algorithms.

The final result of our transformation is a low-level functional program which is suitable for execution on a parallel mesh architecture. We intend to extend this work by transforming the intermediate representation into different implementations for alternative architectures, including a sequential machine (using techniques similar to those in [1]) and a parallel tree machine [5].

This paper contains several Haskell implementations of the heat equation algorithm, although a number of straightforward definitions are omitted. An extended version of the paper containing a complete Haskell program and an appendix with additional proofs is available on the WWW at

```
http://www.dcs.gla.ac.uk/~jtod/
```

2 Case study: one-dimensional heat equation

This section states the mathematical definition of the one-dimensional heat equation and the abstract numerical solution from which we will derive a parallel implementation.

2.1 Mathematical statement of the problem

We consider the one-dimensional heat equation

$$\frac{\partial u}{\partial t} = \frac{\partial^2 u}{\partial x^2}, \quad x \in (0,1), \quad t > 0$$

with boundary value condition $u(0,t) = u_1(t), \quad u(1,t) = u_2(t), \quad t > 0$, and initial condition $u(x,0) = u_0(x), \quad x \in [0,1]$. For the numerical solution we discretize in both space and time at the grid points

$$x_j = jh, \quad j = 0,\ldots,n+1, \quad t_i = ik, \quad i = 0,1,\ldots$$

with spatial stepsize $h = \frac{1}{n+1}$ and constant stepsize k for the time steps. The term $u_{i,j}$ denotes the approximation of the solution u at the grid point (x_j, t_i). The replacement of the partial derivatives by finite difference approximations results in the system

$$u_{i+1,j} = u_{i,j} + \frac{k}{h^2}[u_{i,j+1} - 2u_{i,j} + u_{i,j-1}], \quad j = 1,\ldots,n \quad i = 1,2,\ldots$$

$$u_{i,0} = u_1(t_i), \quad u_{i,n} = u_2(t_i), \quad i = 1,2\ldots$$

and

$$u_{0,j} = u_0(x_j), \quad j = 0,\ldots,n+1$$

2.2 The grid function

The heat equation uses the following function $heatGridFcn$ to calculate the new approximation $s' = u_{i+1,j}$ for time t_{i+1} at position x_j given left neighbor $l = u_{i,j-1}$, current value $s = u_{i,j}$ and right neighbor $r = u_{i,j+1}$. Combining the (l,s,r) arguments into a tuple will simplify the notation later on.

$$heatGridFcn :: Float \rightarrow (Float, Float, Float) \rightarrow Float$$
$$heatGridFcn\ \alpha\ (l,s,r)\ =\ s + \alpha * (l - 2*s + r)$$
$$\alpha = k/h^2$$

For one particular grid we'll work with a partial application of $heatGridFcn$ with the parameter α specified, and call this special function $heat$.

$$heat\ ::\ (Float, Float, Float) \rightarrow Float$$
$$heat\ =\ heatGridFcn\ \alpha_0$$

2.3 The inputs

For given input data the discretized heat equation entirely specifies how to compute the approximation values $u_{i,j}$. The input data are:

- the data specifying the grid, i.e. the stepsize k and the number n of discrete spatial positions (grid points) which also determines h,

- an initial vector of spatial values $init_j = u_0(x_j), 1 \le j \le n$. The whole initial vector is denoted $inits = [init_1,\ldots,init_n]$.

- and sequences of the left boundary values $\{u_1(t_i)\}_{i=1,2,\ldots}$ and the right boundary values $\{u_2(t_i)\}_{i=1,2,\ldots}$.

2.4 The outputs

The system of equations defines a two-dimensional array of values $u_{i,j}$. We can organize these in several ways, including

1. **Vector (Stream Float).** The outputs of the computation are the n result streams

$$p_j :: Stream\ Float$$
$$p_j = [init_j,\ u_{1,j},\ u_{2,j},\ u_{3,j}\ldots]$$

where p_j describes the temporal development of the function u at the grid point x_j where $1 \leq j \leq n$. The entire output of the system of equations is a vector of such streams:

$$result\_vs = [p_1, \ldots p_n].$$

2. **Stream (Vector Float).** Here we view the $u_{i,j}$ as a stream of vectors

$$q_i :: Vector\ Float$$
$$q_0 = inits$$
$$q_i = [u_{i,1},\ u_{i,2},\ \ldots,\ u_{i,n}]$$

Now the result of the system of equations is the stream

$$result\_sv = [q_0,\ q_1,\ q_2,\ \ldots].$$

These two views define the same values in different data structures, and we can use whichever form is more convenient. The important point is that the choice should be made for the convenience of the application area, not for the convenience of the implementor. Many other views are possible (for example, the polytope model [2] can be used to transform the problem into many other views) but we will not consider those in this paper.

3 Developing an initial algorithm

This section transforms the mathematical statement of the numerical solution into an executable functional program, going through several intermediate versions.

3.1 Functional sequences

The first step is to change notation from mathematical sequences to functional streams. The mathematical notation uses sequences of $u_{i,j}$ to *structure* the values and a general equation $u_{i,j} = \cdots$ to *define* the values. In contrast, the functional specification uses map3 (a combination of map with zip3) to express how the values are defined as well as how they are structured, and it introduces a cons operator (:) to initialize stream p_j with $init_j$. This specification uses subscripts to express the relationships among the streams, following closely the style of the original mathematical specification.

$$p_0 = [u_{0,0}, u_{1,0}, u_{2,0} \ldots]$$
$$p_j = init_j : \text{map3 } heat\ p_{j-1}\ p_j\ p_{j+1} \quad \text{for } 1 \leq j \leq n$$
$$p_{n+1} = [u_{0,n+1}, u_{1,n+1}, u_{2,n+1} \ldots]$$

with the following definition (Haskell code will be typeset in tt font).

```
map3 g xs ys zs = map g (zip3 xs ys zs)
```

3.2 Making the inputs explicit

Now the specification is transformed to make explicit which inputs are required to calculate each output stream. The key point here is that in order to calculate p_j, only the left and right neighbor streams p_{j-1} and p_{j+1} and the initial singleton $init_j$ are required, along with the function $heat$. We can write an equation defining p_j with those values, using a new (unknown) operator op to be defined shortly. The left and right boundary stream inputs are vs and ws.

$$p_0 = vs$$
$$p_j = op\ heat\ init_j\ p_{j-1}\ p_{j+1} \quad \text{for } 1 \leq j \leq n$$
$$p_{n+1} = ws$$

It is straightforward to define op in Haskell:

```
op :: ((a,a,a)->a) -- function to compute new value
   -> Stream a      -- left neighbor stream
   -> a             -- initial value
   -> Stream a      -- right neighbor stream
   -> Stream a      -- result is self stream

op g ls x rs = ss
 where ss = x : map3 g ls s rs
```

3.3 combineSub: an executable program

Now we can write the *initial functional specification* of the problem, which defines the entire system of streams (not just the j'th stream). In order to make this specification as close as possible to the mathematical specification, it uses subscripts corresponding to those in the mathematics.

```
combineSub
  :: ((a,a,a) -> a)
  -> Stream a
  -> Vector a
  -> Stream a
  -> Vector (Stream a)

combineSub g vs inits ws = zss
  where ps = [vs] ++ zss ++ [ws]
```

```
zss = [op g (ps!!j-1) (inits!!j-1) (ps!!j+1)
       | j <- [1..n]]
n = length inits
```

4 Communication functions: shift and mscan

Before transforming combineSub into an efficient parallel implementation, it is necessary to define suitable communication primitives. This section defines two families of communication operators: the *shift* functions provide fast nearest-neighbor communication, while the *scan* functions provide a very general and abstract way to express communication.

4.1 Expressing restricted communication: shifting

If the spatial data points are stored in a sequence of processors, then interprocessor communication corresponds to shifting information across the sequence. Therefore it is useful to define a family of abstract shifting functions; they can also be defined using the communication primitives on a parallel machine. Only the types and examples are given here. The most general shift functions are shiftR and shiftL.

```
shiftR :: a  -> Vector a -> (Vector a, a)
shiftL :: Vector a -> a -> (a, Vector a)
```

For example,

```
shiftR 1 [ ]        = ([ ], 1)
shiftR 1 [2,3,4,5]  = ([1,2,3,4], 5)
shiftL [ ] 9        = (9, [ ])
shiftL [5,6,7,8] 9  = (5, [6,7,8,9])
```

Sometimes we're interested only in the shifted vector, or in the output from the end of a shift. The following four projection functions return just the vector output (...*vec*) or the singleton output (...*out*) from a shift.

```
shiftRvec :: a -> Vector a -> Vector a
shiftRout :: a -> Vector a -> a
shiftLvec :: Vector a -> a -> Vector a
shiftLout :: Vector a -> a -> a
```

For example,

```
shiftRvec 1 [2,3,4,5]  = [1,2,3,4]
shiftRout 1 [2,3,4,5]  = 5

shiftLvec [5,6,7,8] 9  = [6,7,8,9]
shiftLout [5,6,7,8] 9  = 5
```

The following sections will use these simple properties of the shift functions (for proofs, see the Appendix):

```
shiftLout [] w              = w
shiftLout (x:xs) w          = x
shiftRout v []              = v
shiftRout v (x:xs)          = shiftRout x xs

head (shiftRvec v (x:xs)) = v
tail (shiftRvec v (x:xs)) = shiftRvec x xs
head (shiftLvec (x:xs) w) = shiftLout xs w
tail (shiftLvec (x:xs) w) = shiftLvec xs w
```

4.2 General communication: Bidirectional mapping scan

It is convenient to use a bidirectional mapping scan [4] to express both the communications and the calculations. This approach is useful because

- The scans can express general patterns of communication, making them suitable for a wide class of algorithm.

- Several quite different implementations can be derived from scan functions, including sequential algorithms and algorithms for parallel tree and mesh architectures.

```
mscan
  :: ((a,c,b) -> (b,d,a))    -- discrete point function
  -> a                       -- left boundary input
  -> Vector c                -- vector input
  -> b                       -- right boundary input
  -> (b, Vector d, a)        -- (left out, vector', right out)

mscan f v [] w =  (w,[],v)

mscan f v (x:xs) w = (w'',y:ys,v'')
  where (w'',y,v')  =  f (v,x,w')
        (w',ys,v'') = mscan f v' xs w
```

The following diagram illustrates the communications defined by mscan.

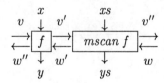

4.3 The MScan–Shift lemma

The advantage of mscan is its generality; the advantage of shift is its efficiency. When the auxiliary function g meets certain constraints, then mscan g can be implemented by a shift.

The heat equation algorithm requires *nearest neighbor communication*. To implement this, each processor must output its own data value to its left and right neighbors, and it must also read data values from its neighbors. The commNN function ("communicate with nearest neighbors") does this by reading v from the left neighbor, reading w from the right neighbor, and supplying the local data value x to both neighbors in the result tuple. It uses its argument function g to calculate the new data value. Thus commNN specifies both the communication and computation to be performed by the processor holding one spatial component x_j.

```
commNN g (v,x,w) = (x, g(v,x,w), x)
```

The following lemma says that if g performs a calculation that depends only on the immediate left and right neighbors, then mscan (commNN g) is equivalent to the algorithm that reads the neighbors and then computes the result. (Recall that in general mscan performs unbounded communication.)

Lemma. *(Nearest-neighbor mscan.)*

```
mscan (commNN g) v xs w
  = (shiftLout xs w,
     map3 g (shiftRvec v xs) xs (shiftLvec xs w),
     shiftRout v xs)
```

Proof by induction over the length of xs.

Base case.

```
mscan (commNN g) v [] w
  = (w, [], v)
  = (w, map g [], v)
  = (shiftLout [] w,
     map3 g (shiftRout v []) [] (shiftLout [] w),
     shiftRout v [])
```

Inductive case. Assume the inductive hypothesis for lists xs of length n. The goal is to prove the lemma for lists of length $n + 1$, so let $x : xs$ a list where xs has length $n > 0$. We proceed by simplifying both sides of the equation to the same term. First we simplify the left hand side for the list $x : xs$.

```
mscan f v (x:xs) w
  = (w'',y:ys,v'')
    where (w'',y,v') = f (v,x,w')
          (w',ys,v'') = mscan f v' xs w

  = (w'',y:ys,v'')
    where (w'',y,v') = (x , g (v,x,w') , x)
          (w',ys,v'') = (shiftLout xs w,
                           map3 g (shiftRvec v' xs)
                                 xs
                                 (shiftLvec xs w),
                           shiftRout v' xs)

  = (x,
```

```
    g (v, x, shiftLout xs w)
      : map3 g (shiftRvec x xs) xs (shiftLvec xs w),
    shiftRout x xs)
```

Now we simplify the right hand side to the same term.

```
(shiftLout (x:xs) w,
 map3 g (shiftRvec v (x:xs))
        (x:xs)
        (shiftLvec (x:xs) w),
 shiftRout v (x:xs))

 = (x,
     g v x (shiftLout xs w)
      : map3 g (shiftRvec x xs) xs (shiftLvec xs w),
     shiftRout x xs)
```

This completes the proof of the lemma.

5   Implementing communications with shifts

Now that the general communication primitives have been presented, we return
to the heat equation algorithm. The subscripts in the `combineSub` function
cause several difficulties:

1. They lead to inefficient communication if implemented naively.

2. They are difficult to manipulate during program transformation.

3. They make it hard to see what communications are required in combine-
   Sub. It is necessary to examine the *values* of the subscripts, and to realize
   that the $(j-1)$ and $(j+1)$ inputs are required by the j'th stream, in
   order to deduce that only nearest-neighbor communication is required.

The aim of this section is to use the family of shift functions to express the
communication explicitly.

5.1   combineShift

Before implementing the heat equation algorithm with shift functions, we need
two auxiliary definitions.
    The `lift3` function takes an argument function g over a triple of singletons
and lifts it to operate over lists.

```
lift3 :: ((a,a,a) -> a)
      -> (Stream a, Stream a, Stream a)
      -> Stream a

lift3 g ([],xs,ws) = []
lift3 g (vs,[],ws) = []
lift3 g (vs,xs,[]) = []
lift3 g (v:vs,x:xs,w:ws) = g (v,x,w) : lift3 g (vs,xs,ws)
```

An individual stream p_j must be initialized by attaching $init_j$ to its front. Similarly, a vector of streams *zss* can be initialized with a vector *xs* by attaching each element of *xs* to the corresponding stream in *zss*. The `putfront` function does this, and it's also carefully designed to be lazy in the structure of *zss*. This ensures that the top level structure of the result list can be constructed just using *xs*, without needing any of the structure of *zss*. That makes it possible to define *zss* recursively without deadlock (for example, see the definition of `combineShift` below).

```
putfront :: Vector a
         -> Vector (Stream a)
         -> Vector (Stream a)

putfront [] zss = []
putfront (x:xs) zss = (x : head zss) : putfront xs (tail zss)
```

The `combineShift` function implements the stream equations using shifting primitives to do the communications, instead of relying on subscripts. The shift functions are easy to implement using nearest-neighbor channels on a mesh machine, so we are getting closer to an efficient parallel program.

```
combineShift
  :: ((a,a,a) -> a)
  -> Stream a
  -> Vector a
  -> Stream a
  -> Vector (Stream a)

combineShift g vs xs ws = zss
  where zss = putfront xs
                (map3 (lift3 g) (shiftRvec vs zss)
                                zss
                                (shiftLvec zss ws))
```

5.2   The "subscript — shift vector" lemma

The following lemma says that `combineShift`, implemented with the efficient parallel shift operator, computes the same result as `combineSub`, the initial functional program which is based on the mathematical specification.

Lemma *(Subscript–shift.)* For all g, vs, xs and ws,

```
combineSub g vs xs ws  = combineShift g vs xs ws
```

Proof by induction over the structure of xs.

Base case. We simplify the left hand side of the equation for xs=[] and get `combineSub g vs [] ws = []`. Furthermore, by the definition of `putfront`, the right hand side `combineShift g vs [] ws = []`.

Inductive case. Assume the inductive hypothesis yss=zss for lists xs, yss and zss of length n where

```
yss = combineSub g vs xs ws
zss = combineShift g vs xs ws
```

The goal is to prove

```
ys : yss = zs : zss
```

assuming that the lists xs, yss, zss have length n, and where

```
ys:yss = combineSub g vs x:xs ws
zs:zss = combineShift g vs x:xs ws
```

First we simplify the left hand side:

```
combineSub g vs xs ws = (ys:yss)
  where ps = [vs] ++ (ys:yss) ++ [ws]
        (ys:yss) = [op g (ps!!j-1) ((x:xs)!!j-1) (ps!!j+1)
                    | j <- [1 .. length (x:xs)]]
```

The stream ys is simplified as follows:

```
ys = op g (ps!!0 ((x:xs)!!0)) (ps!!2)
   = op g vs x (shiftLout yss ws)
   = x : map3 g vs ys (shiftLout yss ws)
```

The vector of streams yss can be simplified using the inductive hypothesis.

```
yss = [op g (ps!!j-1 ((x:xs)!!j-1)) (ps!!j+1) | j <- [2..n]]
    = [op g (qs!!j-1) (xs!!j-1) (qs!!j+1)| j <- [1 .. length xs]]
      where qs = [ys] ++ yss ++ [ws]
    = combineShift g ys xs ws
```

For the simplification of the right hand side we use the definition of shiftRvec, sfiftLout, map3 and putfront.

```
(zs:zss)

 = putfront (x:xs)
     (map3 (lift3 g) (shiftRvec vs (zs:zss))
                     (zs:zss)
                     (shiftLvec (zs:zss) ws))
 = putfront (x:xs)
     (map3 (lift3 g) (vs : shiftRvec zs zss)
                     (zs:zss)
                     (shiftLout zss ws : shiftLvec zss ws))

 = putfront (x:xs)
             (map3 g vs zs (shiftLout zss ws)
               : map3 (lift3 g) (shiftRvec zs zss)
                                zss
                                (shiftLvec zss ws))

 = (x : map3 g vs zs shiftLout zss ws)
```

```
          : putfront xs
            (map3 (lift3 g) (shiftRvec zs zss)
                            zss
                            (shiftLvec zss ws))
```

According to the definition of `combineShift` we get

```
combineShift g vs (x:xs) ws  =  zs:zss
  where zs = x : map3 g vs zs (shiftLout zss ws)
        zss =  combineShift g zs xs ws
```

This finishes the proof.

6 Looping over time

The previous implementations have focused on the stream produced by each
processor. This viewpoint is suitable for systolic array architectures. However,
on many other architectures it's better to transpose the implementation, creating an outer loop over time where each iteration computes the next spatial
vector.

6.1 combineLoopMScan

We begin by defining some functions for expressing such loops.

```
loop
  :: (a -> Vector a -> a
        -> Vector a)      -- step function
  ->  Stream a            -- left boundary stream
  ->  Vector a            -- current spatial vector
  ->  Stream a            -- right boundary stream
  ->  Stream (Vector a)   -- stream of spatial vectors

loop f [] xs ws = [xs]
loop f vs xs [] = [xs]
loop f (v:vs) xs (w:ws) = xs : loop f vs (f v xs w) ws
```

In every time step the approximation of the function u at the all spatial
grid points x_j, $j = 1, \ldots, n$ is computed according to the same operation which
we call `step`. The `step` function is composed of `mscan` applied to the `commNN`
function.

```
step
  :: ((a,a,a) -> b) -- spatial point transition function
  -> a              -- left boundary value
  -> Vector a       -- spatial vector
  -> a              -- right boundary value
  -> Vector b       -- spatial result vector

step g v xs w = snd (mscan (commNN g) v xs w)
```

The `combineLoopMScan` algorithm computes the time stream of the approximation vectors $[u_{i,1}, \ldots, u_{i,n}]$. It starts with the initial values `inits` and consecutively applies the time `step` function.

```
combineLoopMScan
  :: ((a,a,a) -> a)
  -> Stream a
  -> Vector a
  -> Stream a
  -> Stream (Vector a)

combineLoopMScan g vs inits ws = loop (step g) vs inits ws
```

6.2 The "Shift Vector — Loop MScan" lemma

Now we should prove that the loop implementation calculates the same values as the stream implementations; the result of one can be transposed to produce the other. Define

```
transVS :: Vector (Stream a) -> Stream (Vector a)
transVS xss = map head xss : transVS (map tail xss)
```

Lemma *Shift–Loop MScan*

```
loop (step g) vs xs ws = transVS (combineShift g vs xs ws)
```

Proof by induction over time, i.e. the structure of streams vs and ws.

Base case. We prove the lemma for vs = ws = []. First consider the left hand side.

```
loop (step g) [] xs [] = [xs]
```

To simplify the right hand side, we use the following lemma (whose proof by induction appears in the appendix):

```
combineShift g vs xs []) = map (:[]) xs
```

Now the RHS can be simplified directly:

```
RHS = trans (putfront xs
               (map3 (lift3 g) (shiftRvec [] zss)
                               zss
                               (shiftLvec zss [])))
    = trans (map (:[]) xs)
    = map head (map (:[]) xs) : trans (map tail (map (:[]) xs))
    = xs : []
    = [xs]
```

Inductive case. The goal is to prove

```
loop (step g) (v:vs) xs (w:ws)
  = transVS (combineShift g (v:vs) xs (w:ws))
```

We begin with the right hand side. Let

```
zss = putfront xs
         (map3 (lift3 g) (shiftRvec (v:vs) zss)
                         zss
                         (shiftLvec zss (w:ws)))
```

Using the definition of transVS we get

```
transVS (combineShift g (v:vs) xs (w:ws))
  = map head zss : transVS (map tail zss)
```

It is easy to calculate that map head zss = xs using the definition of putfront.
Next we calculate zss' = map tail zss using the definitions of shiftRvec,
shiftLvec and map3.

```
zss'

  = map3 (lift3 g) (shiftRvec (v:vs) zss)
                   zss
                   (shiftLvec zss (w:ws))

  = putfront
     (map3 g (shiftRvec v (map head zss))
                     (map head zss)
                     (shiftLvec (map head zss) w))
     (map3 (lift3 g) (shiftRvec vs (map tail zss))
                     (map tail zss)
                     (shiftLvec (map tail zss) ws))

  = putfront
     (map3 g (shiftRvec v xs )
             xs
             (shiftLvec xs w))
     (map3 (lift3 g) (shiftRvec vs zss')
                     zss'
                     (shiftLvec zss' ws))
```

The *nearest–neighbor mscan* lemma and the definition of step are used to
transform the first argument of putfront

```
(map3 g (shiftRvec v xs ) xs (shiftLvec xs w))
  = (snd (mscan (commNN g) v xs w))
  = (step g v xs w)
```

Thus

```
(map3 (lift3 g) (shiftRvec vs zss') zss' (shiftLvec zss' ws))
  = combineShift g vs (step g v xs w) ws
```

Because of the definition of combineshift

```
zss'
  = putfront (step g v xs w)
      (map3 (lift3 g) (shiftRvec vs zss')
                      zss'
                      (shiftLvec zss' ws))

  = combineShift g vs (step g v xs w) ws
```

Now we can apply the inductive hypothesis to the right hand side of the goal, transforming it into the left hand side.

```
transVS (combineShift g (v:vs) xs (w:ws))
  = map head zss : trans (map tail zss)
  = xs : transVS (combineShift g vs (step heat v xs w) ws)
  = xs : loop (step g) vs (step g v xs w) ws
  = loop (step g) (v:vs) xs (w:ws)
```

This completes the inductive case and the proof.

7   The abstract Mesh-1D architecture

A linear mesh architecture consists of a sequence of processors zs with a left port v and right port w. The architecture provides two operations: a *communication* causes each processor to read a value from its two neighbors, while a *map* causes each processor to apply a function to its local store.

We can express the communication of such an architecture using the shift functions. Since the architecture is specified using an `mscan`, just like the algorithm, the final program `combineAbstMesh` doesn't appear to be a step forward. However, it is because

- With suitable auxiliary definitions (see [3]) the `mesh1D` specification specifies the hardware precisely, and can indeed be used to fabricate the hardware.

- In the previous algorithms, the definitions of `shiftL` and `shiftR` are irrelevant. Now, however, they correspond directly to parallel machine instructions.

The `mesh1D` architecture is SIMD—it receives a stream of instructions to be executed in parallel on all processing elements.

```
mesh1D
  :: Stream ((a,a,a) -> (a,a,a))
  -> Stream a
  -> Vector a
  -> Stream a
  -> Stream (a, Vector a, a)

mesh1D [] vs xs ws = []
mesh1D xs (g:gs) (v:vs) (w:ws) =
  (w',xs',v') : mesh1D xs' gs vs ws
  where (w',xs',v') = mscan (commNN g) v xs w
```

```
combineAbstMesh
  :: ((a,a,a) -> a)
  -> Stream a
  -> Vector a
  -> Stream a
  -> Stream (a, Vector a, a)
```

It is now easy to implement the heat equation algorithm on the abstract mesh machine. Since the abstract machine performs the g computation on each step, the program is simply a stream of commNN g instructions.

combineAbstMesh g vs xs ws = mesh1D xs (repeat (commNN g)) vs ws

We stop at this point, although it would be useful to go one step further: defining a concrete mesh architecture, deriving a program for it (which will be more complex than just repeat (commNN g), showing how to represent the lists in the hardware, and proving the correctness of the concrete mesh program.

8 Conclusions

Many papers on program transformation start with an algorithm and transform it into another algorithm that is better in some way. Our goals go beyond this:

1. We begin with a problem statement in the application area, rather than a program. We finish with a specification that shows precisely how the architecture will execute the algorithm. Thus we start at a higher level and finish with a lower level than usual.

2. We intend to derive several different implementations from the same specification, although this paper presents only one.

3. We use an intermediate form (based on bidirectional mapping scan) to represent the algorithm in a way that will support derivations of distinct parallel implementations.

Experience from this derivation suggests the following conclusions and problems.

1. The initial specification of a problem should be as close as possible to what people in the subject area would normally write. Therefore we used the normal mathematical $u_{i,j}$ form in this case study. We can move from the mathematical notation, based on subscripts, to an algorithmic notation using exactly the same kind of equational reasoning required for transforming programs.

2. There are likely to be many final targets for the implementation, corresponding to different machine architectures. These targets are inevitably machine dependent. It is possible to write functional specifications of such implementations.

3. Because there can be several quite different implementations for one algorithm, it is useful to transform the initial specification into an intermediate form. The intermediate form should explicitly state properties that all implementations must share, but should be abstract about properties that differ across implementations. In the case study, the intermediate form using *mscan* shows formally how we can exploit the data dependencies in the original equations. It does this by stating explicitly what communications will be required by *every* parallel implementation without specifying the particular way the program is executed.

4. Ideally we don't want to prove things like the scan–subscript lemma for each problem. Instead, we should develop a library of lemmas relating standard forms of systems of equations with standard intermediate implementations. The idea is that the mathematician should be able to look in a library of lemmas to see how to implement a system of equations. Scientists commonly work this way. For example, difficult integrals often arise in the physical sciences, and the best way to approach them is to learn how to transform a particular integral into a form that is already in an integral table. In a similar way, we're trying to develop a library of parallel function definitions corresponding to different patterns of equations.

References

[1] A. Bunkenburg and S. Flynn, "Expression refinement: deriving Bresenham's algorithm," *Functional Programming: Glasgow 1994*, Springer-Verlag Workshops in Computing.

[2] C. Lengauer, "Loop parallelization in the Polytope Model," *Proc. CONCUR* (1993).

[3] J. O'Donnell, "Generating netlists from executable circuit specifications in a pure functional language," *Functional Programming Glasgow 1992*, Springer-Verlag Workshops in Computing 178–194.

[4] J. O'Donnell, "Bidirectional fold and scan," *Functional Programming: Glasgow 1993*, Springer Workshops in Computing (1994).

[5] J. O'Donnell, "A correctness proof of parallel scan," *Parallel Processing Letters* (Sept. 1994).

Compilation by Transformation in the Glasgow Haskell Compiler

Simon Peyton Jones   André Santos*

University of Glasgow†

Abstract

In this paper we describe the full set of local program transformations implemented in the Glasgow Haskell Compiler. The transformations are presented as source to source transformations in a simple functional language. The idea is that by composing these simple and small high level transformations one can achieve most of the benefits of more complicated and specialised transformations, many of which are often implemented as code generation optimisations.

1   Motivation

Quite a few compilers use the *compilation by transformation* idiom. The idea is that as much as possible of the compilation process is expressed as correctness-preserving transformations, each of which transforms a program into a semantically-equivalent program that (hopefully) executes more quickly or in less space. Functional languages are particularly amenable to this approach because they have a particularly rich family of possible transformations. Examples of transformation-based compilers include the Orbit compiler ([9]), Kelsey's compilers ([8],[7]), the New Jersey SML compiler ([1]), and the Glasgow Haskell compiler ([15]). Of course many, perhaps most, other compilers also use transformation to some degree.

Compilation by transformation uses automatic transformations; that is, those which can safely be applied automatically by a compiler. There is also a whole approach to programming, which we might call *programming by transformation*, in which the programmer manually transforms an inefficient specification into an efficient program. This development process might be supported by a programming environment which does the book keeping, but the key steps are guided by the programmer. We focus exclusively on automatic transformations in this paper.

Automatic program transformations seem to fall into two broad categories:

- **Glamorous transformations** are global, sophisticated, intellectually satisfying transformations, sometimes guided by some interesting kind of analysis. Examples include: lambda lifting ([6]), full laziness ([5],[17]),

---

*Sponsored by the Brazilian agency CAPES under contract 2323/91-5.

†Department of Computing Science, University of Glasgow, Glasgow G12 8QQ, Scotland. E-mail: {simonpj,andre}@dcs.gla.ac.uk. URL: http://www.dcs.gla.ac.uk.

closure conversion ([2]), deforestation ([19],[3],[11],[4]), transformations based on strictness analysis ([16]), and so on. It is easy to write papers about these sorts of transformations.

- **Humble transformations** are small, simple, local transformations. Individually they look very trivial. Here are two simple examples:

```
let x = y in E[x]                    ===>  E[y]

case (x:xs) of (y:ys) -> E1[y,ys]  ===>  E1[x,xs]
               []      -> E2
```

The notation `E[]` stands for an arbitrary expression with zero or more holes. The notation `E[e]` denotes `E[]` with the holes filled in by the expression `e` (All transformations throughout the paper assume renaming is performed to avoid name capture problems. We discuss this in section 5.2). Transformations of this kind are almost embarrassingly simple. How could anyone write a paper about them?

This paper is about *humble transformations*, and how to implement them. Although each individual transformation is simple enough, there is a scaling issue: there are a large number of candidate transformations to consider, and there are a very large number of opportunities to apply them.

In the Glasgow Haskell compiler, all humble transformations are performed by the so-called *simplifier*. Our goal in this paper is to describe the complete set of transformations used by the simplifier and present measurements of their usefulness. It is important to notice that not all of the transformation were immediately obvious to us, but derived from close inspection of the intermediate code of the compiler.

2   The Core language

The simplifier performs transformations on the Core language (Figure 1), which is a desugared version of Haskell, i.e. a simpler language with things like list comprehensions and pattern matching already transformed out to simpler constructs.

The concrete syntax we use is conventional: parentheses are used to disambiguate; application associates to the left and binds more tightly than any other operator; the body of a lambda abstraction extends as far to the right as possible; the usual infix arithmetic operators are permitted; the usual syntax for lists is allowed, with infix constructor ":" and empty list []; and, where the layout makes the meaning clear, we allow ourselves to omit semicolons between bindings and `case` alternatives.

Notice that the bindings in `let` expressions are all simple; that is, the left hand side of the binding is always just a variable. Function bindings are expressed by binding a variable to a lambda abstraction (although we permit ourselves the small liberty of sometimes writing the arguments of function bind-

Program	$Prog$	$\rightarrow$	$Binding_1$; ... ; $Binding_n$ $n \geq 1$	
Bindings	$Binding$	$\rightarrow$	$Bind$	
		|	rec $Bind_1 \ldots Bind_n$	
	$Bind$	$\rightarrow$	$var = Expr$	
Expression	$Expr$	$\rightarrow$	$Expr\ Atom$	Application
		|	$Expr\ ty$	Type application
		|	$\lambda\ var_1 \ldots var_n$ -> $Expr$	Lambda abstraction
		|	$\Lambda\ ty$ -> $Expr$	Type abstraction
		|	case $Expr$ of $Alts$	Case expression
		|	let $Binding$ in $Expr$	Local definition
		|	$con\ var_1 \ldots var_n$	Constructor $n \geq 0$
		|	$prim\ var_1 \ldots var_n$	Primitive $n \geq 0$
		|	$Atom$	
Atoms	$Atom$	$\rightarrow$	var	Variable
		|	$Literal$	Unboxed Object
Literal values	$Literal$	$\rightarrow$	$integer \mid float \mid \ldots$	
Alternatives	$Alts$	$\rightarrow$	$Calt_1 ; \ldots ; Calt_n ; Default$	$n \geq 0$
		|	$Lalt_1 ; \ldots ; Lalt_n ; Default$	$n \geq 0$
Constr. alt	$Calt$	$\rightarrow$	$Con\ var_1 \ldots var_n$ -> $Expr$	$n \geq 0$
Literal alt	$Lalt$	$\rightarrow$	$Literal$ -> $Expr$	
Default alt	$Default$	$\rightarrow$	var -> $Expr$	

Figure 1: Syntax of the Core language

ings to the left of the = sign). Similarly, the patterns in case expressions are all simple; nested pattern matching has been compiled to nested case expressions.

Other important points about the Core Language are:

- It is based on the Second order lambda calculus (i.e. with type abstractions and type applications), extended with lets and cases.

- Arguments are atomic, i.e. variables or literals. In section 5.1 we will discuss the reasons for this decision.

- it supports unboxed data types, and unboxed cases ([16]).

- Constructors and primitives are always saturated.

- The Core language has a direct operational reading: allocations are represented by lets and evaluation by cases.

3   Transformations

This section lists all the transformations implemented by the simplifier. Because it is a complete list, it is a long one. We content ourselves with a brief statement of each transformation, augmented with forward references to Section 4 which gives examples of the ways in which the transformations can compose together.

3.1   Beta reduction

If a lambda abstraction is applied to an argument, we can simply beta-reduce. This applies equally to ordinary lambda abstractions and type abstractions:

```
(\x  -> E[x]) arg     ===>     E[arg]
(/\a -> E[a]) ty      ===>     E[ty]
```

There is no danger of duplicating work because the argument is guaranteed to be a simple variable or literal.

3.2   Floating applications inward

Applications can be floated into a `let` or `case` expression. This is a good idea, because they might find a lambda abstraction inside to beta-reduce with:

```
(let Bind in E) arg   ===>     let Bind in (E arg)
```

```
(case E of {P1 -> E1;...; Pn -> En}) arg
===>
case E of {P1 -> E1 arg; ...; Pn -> En arg}
```

Notice that the second version might cause a minor increase in code size, as the argument is duplicated in each branch.

3.3   Floating `let` out of `let`

It is sometimes useful to float a `let` out of a `let` right-hand side:

```
let x = let(rec) Bind in B1            let(rec) Bind in
in B2                         ===>      let x = B1
                                        in B2
```

```
letrec x = let(rec) Bind in B1         let(rec) Bind
in B2                         ===>                x = B1
                                        in B2
```

This is particularly good if

- B1 is in head normal form (x becomes a non-updatable closure)

- x is strict in B2, and therefore we know that `Bind` would be allocated anyway.

188

3.4 `let` to `case`

The `let`-to-`case` transformation can be done whenever we have a strict `let` that is not already in normal form, that is a `let` that is guaranteed to be demanded during the evaluation of its body and is not bound to a constructor or lambda expression:

```
let v = E1 in E2  ===> case E1 of v -> E2
```

The idea here is that in the original expression we are allocating a closure for v in the heap which only later will be evaluated (as it is strict) and possibly updated (if v's closure was updatable). After the transformation we evaluate E1 first and bind it to v, therefore saving the cost of the update and some heap allocation if the update was not done originally in place. Notice that the semantics of `case`s in Core mean that E1 *is* evaluated, whereas in Haskell this would not be the case, and therefore this transformation would be not valid in Haskell.

Actually there is an extra restriction for doing this transformation: the `let` must *not* have a function type (that is, it must not be a function). This restriction is due to implementation details, as `case`s cannot scrutinise objects which have a function type.

3.5 Unboxing `let-to-case`

The unboxing `let-to-case` transformation is similar to the `let` to `case` transformation, but it has the advantage of exposing the structure of the expression, by explicitly exposing its constructor. To avoid code duplication this is only used when the type of the `let` binding is a single constructor data type, like n-tuples, boxed integers etc.

If v is of a constructor type and E2 is strict in v then

```
let v = E1 in E2  ===> case E1 of C a b -> let v = C a b in E2
```

The extra advantage here compared to the previous transformation is that as the structure is made explicit transformations like the `case` of known constructor (Section 3.7) can be exposed. Also often the `let` binding introduced by the transformation is later eliminated.

3.6 Floating `case` out of `let`

`case`s may be floated out of strict `let`s:

```
let v = case E1 of              case E1 of
          C a b -> E2  ===>       C a b -> let v = E2
in E3                                     in E3
```

where E3 is strict in v and v is not a free variable in E1.

Thsi transformation increases the scope of the `case`, and therefore it might expose transformations, such as `case` of known constructor, in E3. It is also good if E2 is a head normal form expression, as v will no longer be a thunk and therefore no updates will be performed on it.

If the `case` has multiple branches we can still do the transformation but we would have some code duplication, as E3 would occur in each of the branches.

This can be avoided by using a similar technique to the one we use for the `case` of `case` transformation (Section 3.11), where we create a new `let` binding (which we call a *join point*):

```
let v = case E1 of                let j v = E4
          C1 a b -> E2    ===>     in case E1 of
          C2 a b -> E3                   C1 a b -> let v = E2 in j v
    in E4                                C2 a b -> let v = E3 in j v
```

This avoids duplicating E4 in each of the branches. The newly-created `let` can be implemented very efficiently (as we discuss in Section 4.3) and therefore does not introduce any major efficiency or allocation costs. Although we lose the benefit of increasing the scope of the `case` to include E4, we will still benefit in the cases in which E2 or E3 are head normal form expressions (no updates then).

Notice that even if one is already using the `let-to-case` transformation, which would remove many of the opportunities for this transformation, this transformation is still useful in cases when the `let-to-case` transformation cannot be used, like when the `let` rhs has a functional type.

Also, there is an interesting optimisation that uses the `case` floating from `let` transformation, but without the restriction on the `let` being strict: for *cheap, non-failing* cases. These are `cases` evaluating some primitive operations on unboxed values, such as primitive `Int` addition, subtraction, multiplication, and similar operations for `Floats` and `Doubles`. An example of this is

```
let v = case x# +# 1# of      case x# +# 1# of
          r# -> I# r#    ===>    r# -> let v = I# r#
    in E                       in E
```

where names with `#` are unboxed values and `I#` is the constructor for boxed integers. In this case `v` is now bound to a constructor, therefore no updates are performed. Although this is doing some eager evaluation that might be unnecessary, the cost of the operation is small and the expression could end up being evaluated anyway. This transformation is sometimes called "cheap eagerness".

3.7 Case of known constructor

If a `case` expression scrutinises a constructor, the `case` can be eliminated. This transformation is a real win: it eliminates a whole `case` expression.

```
case (C a1 ... an) of
                          ===>    E[a1...an]
  ...
  C b1 ... bn -> E[b1...bn]
  ...
```

If none of the constructors in the alternatives match, then the default is taken:

```
case (C a1 ... an) of                let y = C a1 ... an
  ...[no alt matches C]...    ===>    in E
    y -> E
```

In this case

- we eliminate dead code.

- we save the cost of entering an expression that is already in head normal form.

- y may be used by the constructor reuse transformation.

The first two benefits also happen in the first example.

There is an important variant of this transformation when the `case` expression scrutinises a *variable* which is known to be bound to a constructor. This situation can arise for two reasons:

- An enclosing `let` binding binds the variable to a constructor. For example:
  ```
  let x = C p q in ... (case x of ...) ...
  ```

- An enclosing `case` expression scrutinises the same variable. For example:
  ```
  case x of ...
             C p q -> ... (case x of ...) ...
        ...
  ```

This situation is particularly common, as we discuss in Section 4.1.

In each of these examples, x is known to be bound to C p q at the inner `case`. Assuming x is bound to C a1 ... an The general rules are:
```
case x of {...; C b1 ... bn -> E[b1...bn]; ...} ===> E[a1...an]

case x of {...[no alts match C]...; y -> E[y]}  ===> E[x]
```

3.8   Dead alternative elimination

Dead alternative elimination is similar to the `case` of known constructor transformation, but deals with the case when all we know about a variable is that it in *not* bound to some constructors. Assuming x is *not* bound to constructor C, we have:
```
case x of C a ... z -> E      ===>  case x of ...[other alts]...
          ...[other alts]...
```
We might know that x is not bound to a particular constructor because of an enclosing `case`:
```
case x of C a ... z -> E1
          other -> E2
```
Inside E1 we know that x is bound to C. However inside E2 all we know is that x is *not* bound to C.

This applies to unboxed `cases` also, in the obvious way.

3.9   Case elimination

If we can prove that x is not bottom, then the following rule applies:
```
case x of y -> E[y]            ===>  E[x]
```
We might know that x is non-bottom because:

- x has an unboxed type.

- There's an enclosing `case` which scrutinises x.

- It is bound to an expression which provably terminates.

If we apply this transformation even when x is not provably non-bottom we can only improve termination; therefore we provide a compiler flag to enable it all the time if the user does not worry about turning a non terminating program into a terminating one.

3.10 Floating `lets` out of a `case` scrutinee

A `let` binding can be floated out of a `case` scrutinee:
```
case (let(rec) Bind in E) of Alts  ===>  let(rec) Bind
                                          in case E of Alts
```
This increases the likelihood of a `case` of known constructor transformation, because E is not hidden from the `case` by the `let`.

3.11 Floating `case` out of `case` (`case of case`)

Analogous to floating a `let` from a `case` scrutinee is floating a `case` from a `case` scrutinee. We have to be careful, though, about code size. If there's only one alternative in the inner `case`, things are easy:
```
case (case E of {P -> R}) of  ===>  case E of {P -> case R of
Q1 -> S1                                        Q1 -> S1
...                                             ...
Qm -> Sm                                        Qm -> Sm}
```
If there's more than one alternative there's a danger that we'll duplicate S1...Sm, which might be a lot of code. Our solution is to create a new local definition for each alternative:
```
case (case E of {P1 -> R1; ...; Pn -> Rn}) of Q1 -> S1
                                                 ...
                                              Qm -> Sm

===>
let s1 = \x1 ... z1 -> S1
    ...
    sm = \xm ... zm -> Sm
in case E of
      P1 -> case R1 of {Q1 -> s1 x1...z1;...; Qm -> sm xm...zm}
      ...
      Pn -> case Rn of {Q1 -> s1 x1...z1;...; Qm -> sm xm...zm}
```
Here, x1 ... z1 are that subset of variables bound by the pattern Q1 which are free in S1, and similarly for the other si.

Is this transformation a win? After all, we have introduced m new functions! Section 4.3 discusses this point.

3.12 Case merging

```
case x of                              case x of
   ...[some alts]...          ===>       ...[some alts]...
   other -> case x of                    ...[more alts]...
               ...[more alts]...
```

Any alternatives in [more alts] which are already covered by [some alts] should first be eliminated by the dead-alternative transformation.

3.13 Eta expansion

We perform general η-expansion when we have an expression with a functional type that has arity greater than the number of lambdas enclosing it:

```
v = \ a b -> f a b      ===>   v = \ a b c -> f a b c
```

(assuming f has arity 3). This improves the efficiency as instead of creating a partial application of f when v is entered, (if it is being called with 3 arguments) f will be called directly. This also saves an argument satisfaction check (to check if enough arguments are already available during the call) in some implementations.

Notice that the notion of arity in this case is a bit different from the usual notion, as we do not intend to lose laziness by adding extra arguments to a function. We do not, for example, perform the following transformation:

```
v = \a b -> let x = e    ===>   v = \a b c -> let x = e
              in f x b                          in f x b c
```

as although it can receive 3 arguments (as we assume that f receives 3 arguments), if it is partially applied to two arguments it would have very different behaviours in the two expressions above:

- in the first one a closure for x is allocated and would be shared by the partial application (if the partial application was applied multiple times), while

- in the second one, as it only does any work after receiving the 3 arguments, the closure for x would be allocated and evaluated as many times as the partial application was applied, thus losing laziness.

Therefore the concept of arity we use is not directly related to the maximum number of arguments that a function may receive, but to the number of lambdas in its definition, i.e. the number of arguments that can be passed to the function before it performs any actual "work", like evaluate a case or a let expression for example.

Actually we sometimes do perform the η-expansion when we have a case expression in some circunstances. Let us analyse this case in more detail. assuming $e_1 \dots e_n$ have a functional type:

```
case e of  p1 -> e1           \y -> case e of p1 -> e1 y
              ...      ===>                      ...
           pn -> en                           pn -> en y
```

- It is a bad idea to do this if *e* is not a simple variable, because it pushes a redex *e* inside a lambda. Even if *e* is a variable, doing this transformation moves an evaluation inside a lambda, which loses a small amount of work for each call of the lambda.

- If any of the e_i are redexes, it would also probably be a bad idea, for the same reason.

But if the two problems above do not occur, in particular if the scrutinee is a variable and therefore the (possible) work duplication is restricted to entering the variable, it is sometimes a very useful transformation.

Therefore the strategy is to do it for `cases` if

- the rhss have functional type

- e is a variable

- all the rhss are manifestly HNFs

3.14   case of error

`error` is a built-in function of the Glasgow Haskell Compiler, usually associated with pattern matching failures and other sorts of run-time errors. Its semantic value is the same as $\bot$.

Due to transformations like `case` of `case`, for example, we may end up with `error` as a `case` scrutinee, to which we can apply the following transformation

```
case (error ty E) of Alts   ===>   error ty' E
```

where `ty'` is the type of the whole `case` expression.

3.15   Constructor reuse

The constructor reuse transformation tries to avoid allocating new objects (constructors) when there is an identical object in scope:

```
case x of                   ===>   case x of
a:as -> let y = a:as in E1          a:as -> E1[x/y]
```

This transformation may occur in two circunstances:

- there was an identical constructor expression bound by a `let`.

- there was an identical constructor expression bound by a `case` scrutinee.

The main points about this transformation are

- it avoids that an identical object is allocated and built in the heap when an already existing object in the heap can be used instead.

- it may increase the lifetime of objects.

3.16   Default binding elimination

```
case v1 of v2 -> e        ===> case v1 of v2 -> e[v1/v2]
```

Usually the code generator can generate better code if the default variable is not used in its rhs (it does not need to bind the result of the `case` evaluation to the default variable).

3.17   Inlining

The inlining transformation is simple enough:

```
let x = R in B[x]   ===>   B[R]
```

Inlining is more conventionally used to describe the instantiation of a function body at its call site, with arguments substituted for formal parameters. We treat this as a two-stage process: inlining followed by beta reduction (Section 3.1). Since we are working with a higher-order language, not all the arguments may be available at every call site, so separating inlining from beta reduction allows us to concentrate on one problem at a time.

The choice of exactly *which* bindings to inline has a major impact on efficiency. Specifically, we need to consider the following factors:

- Inlining a function at its call site, followed by some beta reduction, very often exposes opportunities for further transformations. We inline many simple arithmetic and boolean operators for this reason.

- Inlining can increase code size.

- Inlining can duplicate work, e.g. if a redex is inlined at more than one site. Duplicating a single expensive redex can ruin a program's efficiency.

Our inlining strategy depends on the form and size of R and on the places and number of occurrences of x. The algorithm can be described as follows: We inline an occurrence of x by R in B if and only if

- The occurrence is not in an argument position (unless R is itself an atom, as arguments can only be atoms)

- if R is manifestly a HNF

  − either x only occurs once in B

  − or R is small enough to duplicate

- if R is not an HNF

  − no occurrences of x are inside a non-linear lambda abstraction

  − either x occurs only once in B

  − or x occurs only once in any control path and R is small enough to duplicate

The notion of "small enough" is entirely arbitrary, and can be set by a flag to the compiler. It is mostly based on the syntactical size of the expression, but takes into account other characteristics of the expression.

By control path we mean `case` branches, that is if R is small enough and has only one occurrence in different `case` branches we may inline it, as it can only be evaluated once (only one `case` branch will be taken). Notice that if a `case` branch has another `case` expression with R occurring only once in each branch it is still only a single occurrence in a given control path.

Linear lambdas are lambdas that the compiler can guarantee (by means of a program analysis) that will only be applied (entered) st most once. This allows non HNF expressions to be inlined in some lambda expressions, otherwise non HNF cannot be inlined into lambda expressions due to the risk that the inlined expression will be evaluated multiple times (losing laziness) if the lambda expression is applied (evaluated) multiple times.

3.18   Dead code removal

If a `let`-bound variable is not used the binding can be dropped:

```
let x = E in B          ===>              B
```

supposing x is not used in B. A similar transformation applies for `letrec`-bound variables. Programmers seldom write dead code, of course, but bindings often become dead when they are inlined.

4   Composing transformations

The really interesting thing about humble transformations is the way in which they compose together to carry out substantial and useful transformations. This section gives a collection of motivating examples, all of which have shown up in real application programs.

4.1   Repeated evals

The expression `x+x` (where x is of type `Int`) in the source code generates the following code in the compiler:

```
case x of
  I# x# -> case x of
              I# y# -> case x# +# y# of r# -> I# r#
```

due to the inlining of the (boxed) operator `+`, which unboxes its two arguments, applies the primitive (unboxed) operator `+#` to them and finally boxes the resulting value. In this case it unboxes x twice, but the `case` of known constructor transformation can eliminate the second evaluation of x and generate the code we expect:

```
case x of I# x# -> case x# +# x# of r# -> I# r#
```

The transformations in this case are making use of the notion of unboxed data types, as presented in [16].

196

4.2 Lazy pattern matching

Lazy pattern matching is very inefficient. Consider:

```
let (x,y) = E in B
```

which desugars to:

```
let t = E
    x = case t of (x,y) -> x
    y = case t of (x,y) -> y
in B
```

This code allocates three thunks! However, if B is strict in *either* x *or* y, then the strictness analyser will easily spot that the binding for t is strict, so we can do an unboxing let-to-case transformation:

```
case E of (x,y) -> let t = (x,y) in
                   let x = case t of (x,y) -> x
                       y = case t of (x,y) -> y
                   in B
```

whereupon the case of known constructor transformation eliminates the case expressions in the right-hand side of x and y, and t is then spotted as being dead, so we get

```
case E of (x,y) -> B
```

4.3 Join points

One motivating example is this:

```
if (not x) then E1 else E2
```

After desugaring the conditional, and inlining the definition of not, we get

```
case (case x of True -> False; False -> True}) of
     True  -> E1
     False -> E2
```

Now, if we apply our case of case transformation we get:

```
let e1 = E1 ; e2 = E2
in case x of True  -> case False of {True -> e1; False -> e2}
             False -> case True  of {True -> e1; False -> e2}
```

Now the case of known constructor transformation applies:

```
let e1 = E1 ; e2 = E2
in case x of True  -> e2
             False -> e1
```

Since there is now only one occurrence of e1 and e2 we can inline them, giving just what we hoped for:

```
case x of {True -> E2; False -> E1}
```

The point is that the local definitions introduced by the case of case transformation will often disappear again.

4.3.1 How join points occur

But what if they don't disappear? Then the local definitions will play the role of "join points"; they represent the places where execution joins up again, having forked at the `case x`. The "calls" to the local definitions should really be just jumps. To see this more clearly consider the expression

    if (x || y) then E1 else E2

A C compiler will "short-circuit" the evaluation if x turns out to be `True`, generating code like:

```
        if (x) {goto l1};
        if (y) {goto l1};
        goto l2;
l1:  ...code for E1...; goto l3}
l2:  ...code for E2...
l3:  ...
```

In our setting, here's what will happen. First we desugar the conditional, and inline the definition of `||`:

    case (case x of {True -> True; False -> y}) of True -> E1
                                                   False -> E2

Now apply the `case of case` transformation:

    let e1 = E1 ; e2 = E2
    in case x of True -> case True of {True -> e1; False -> e2}
                 False -> case y   of {True -> e1; False -> e2}

Unlike the not example, only one of the two inner `case`s simplifies, and we can therefore only inline e2, because e1 is still mentioned twice[1]

    let e1 = E1
    in case x of True -> e1
                 False -> case y of {True -> e1; False -> E2}

The code generator produces essentially the same code as the C code given above. The binding for e1 turns into just a label, which is jumped to from the two occurrences of e1.

4.4 case of error

The `case of error` transformation is often exposed by the `case of case` transformation. Consider

    case (hd xs) of {True -> E1; False -> E2}

After inlining hd, we get

    case (case xs of [] -> error "hd"; (x:_) -> x) of True -> E1
                                                       False -> E2

(we have omitted the type argument of `error` for simplicity). Now doing `case of case` we get

    let e1 = E1 ; e2 = E2
    in case xs of
          []   -> case (error "hd") of { True -> e1; False -> e2 }
          (x:_) -> case x   of { True -> e1; False -> e2 }

---

[1] Unless the inlining strategy decides that E1 is small enough to duplicate; it is used in separate case branches so there's no concern about duplicating work. Here's another example of the way in which we make one part of the simplifier (the inlining strategy) help with the work of another (case-expression simplification).

198

Now the case-of-error transformation springs to life, after which we can inline
e1 and e2 to get the efficient result
```
case xs of []      -> error "hd"
            (x:_) -> case x of {True -> E1; False -> E2}
```

4.5   Nested conditionals combined

Sometimes programmers write something which could be done by a single `case`
as a sequence of tests:
```
if x==0::Int then E0 else
if x==1      then E1 else E2
```
After eliminating some redundant evals and doing the `case` of `case` transformation we get
```
case x of I# x# -> case x# of 0#    -> E0
                              other -> case x# of 1#    -> E1
                                                  other -> E2
```
The case-merging transformation puts these together to get
```
case x of I# x# -> case x# of 0#    -> E0
                              1#    -> E1
                              other -> E2
```
Of course many programmers would write a `case` rather than a sequence of
conditions in the first place, but sometimes the sequence of tests cannot be
eliminated from the source code because of overloading:
```
f :: Num a => a -> Bool
f 0 = True
f 3 = True
f n = False
```
The overloading forces `f` to be compiled to a sequence of conditionals, but if
`f` is specialised to `Int` (a common situation) we will get the previous example
again.

4.6   Error tests eliminated

The elimination of redundant alternatives, and then of redundant cases, arises
when we inline functions which do error checking. A typical example is this:
```
if (x 'rem' y) == 0 then (x 'div' y) else y
```
Here, both `rem` and `div` do an error-check for `y` being zero. The second check
is eliminated by the transformations. After transformation the code becomes:
```
case y# of 0# -> error "rem: zero divisor"
           _  -> case x# rem# y# of
                     0# -> case x# div# y# of r# -> I# r#
                     _  -> y
```

5   Design Issues

5.1   Atomic arguments

At this point it is possible to appreciate the usefulness of the Core-language syntax requirement that arguments are atomic. For example, suppose that arguments could be arbitrary expressions. Here is a possible transformation (supposing f is strict in its argument):

```
f (case x of (p,q) -> p)      ===>  case x of (p,q) -> f p
```

Doing this transformation would be useful, because now the argument to f is a simple variable rather than a thunk. However, if arguments are atomic, this transformation becomes just a special case of floating a case out of a strict let:

```
let a = case x of (p,q) -> p  ===>  case x of
in f a                              (p,q) -> let a=p in f a
```

which is further simplified to

```
case x of (p,q) -> f p
```

There are many examples of this kind. For almost any transformation involving let there is a corresponding one involving a function argument. The same effect is achieved with much less complexity by restricting function arguments to be atomic.

5.2   Renaming and cloning

Every program-transformation system has to worry about name capture. For example, here is an erroneous transformation:

```
let y = E                     =/=>  let y = E
in (\x -> \y -> x + y) (y+3)        in (\y -> (y+3) + y)
```

The transformation fails because the originally free-occurrence of y in the argument y+3 has been "captured" by the \y-abstraction. There are various sophisticated solutions to this problem but we adopted a very simple one: we uniquely rename every locally-bound identifier on every pass of the simplifier. Since we are in any case producing an entirely new program (rather than side-effecting an existing one) it costs very little extra to rename the identifiers as we go.

So our example would become

```
let y = E                     ===>  let y1 = E
in (\x -> \y -> x + y) (y+3)        in (\y2 -> (y1+3) + y2)
```

The simplifier accepts as input a program which has arbitrary bound variable names, including "shadowing" (where a binding hides an outer binding for the same identifier), but it produces a program in which every bound identifier has a distinct name.

5.3   Confluence and Termination

The set of transformations we have presented can be seen as a set of term rewiriting rules. We would like the set of transformations we use to be

- confluent: that we can apply the transformations in any order (when more than one is applicable) and we still get the same result. This is important to make sure that we are not losing transformations or generating worse code by choosing to apply one transformation before another one, when both are applicable.

- terminating: that the process of simplification terminates, meaning that we always get to a point where no transformation is applicable. One has to be particularly careful that one transformation cannot generate code that can be transformed back to the original code by other transformations; that no transformations undo the work of other transformations.

Although we tried to maintain these two properties and experimentally we have verified they are maintained we had no proofs of these properties for quite sometime.

As the transformations are in a very simple left to rigth form with very few side conditions they are good candidates to be treated as rewrite rules in a term rewriting system. In [13] a proof of confluence and termination of a subset of the rules was obtained, using the order-sorted equational theorem proving system MERILL [12], developed at Glasgow University. Initially the system was used to prove confluence and termination for the subset of the rules containing the `let` and `case` floating rules. Later the set was extended to include the constructor reuse, beta reduction and inlining, retaining the same properties.

6 Implementation of the simplifier

The basic algorithm followed by the simplifier is:

1. Analyse: perform occurrence analysis and dependency analysis.

   The occurrence analyser collects information about binders' occurrences, in particular the number of occurrences and their place. This will be used for inlining decisions (Section 3.17). This is "Global" information, therefore it could not be gathered while the simplifier pass is being run.

   Dependency Analysis is needed because while floating `lets` out of `lets` (Section 3.3) we may leave recursive bindings that are not necessarily recursive. As all the information that is needed for performing dependency analysis is already gathered when performing the Occurrence Analysis, we do it together with the Occurrence Analysis.

2. Simplify: apply as many transformations as possible.

3. Iterate: perform the above two steps repeatedly until no further transformations are possible. (A compiler flag allows the programmer to bound the maximum number of iterations.)

We make an effort to apply as many transformations as possible in Step 2. To see why this is a good idea, just consider a sequence of transformations in which each transformation enables the next. If each iteration of Step 2 only performs one transformation, then the entire program will have to be re-analysed by Step 1, and re-traversed by Step 2, for each transformation of the sequence. Sometimes this is unavoidable, but it is often possible to perform a sequence of transformations in a single pass.

7 Measurements

In Table 1 we have a raw count of the number of times some of the transformations we discussed are performed during the compilation of some programs from the *real* part of the **nofib** Benchmark suite ([14]). Knowing the benefits that each transformation presents individually, this gives some idea of the overall effect on the programs.

programs	a	b	c	d	e	f	g	h	i	j
compress	547	35	17	5	3	7917	1	26	2	4
fluid	2391	627	42	71	56	1408	46	520	187	170
gg	810	384	55	36	21	514	54	384	135	187
hidden	509	263	13	9	39	165	33	115	148	33
hpg	2059	408	26	18	4	781	9	287	52	47
infer	585	164	5	10	13	126	7	148	33	25
lift	2023	137	87	7	26	2189	8	151	57	27
maillist	177	39	3	5	2	4	2	49	0	5
parser	4595	265	52	760	22	2359	63	451	49	298
prolog	640	114	20	14	5	139	20	118	28	32
reptile	1553	220	56	30	70	620	31	260	79	130
rsa	97	47	2	10	3	38	2	30	5	9

Table 1: Transformation Count

a	number of lines
b	inlining (Section 3.17)
c	constructor reuse (Section 3.15)
d	floating case out of let (Section 3.6)
e	case of case(Section 3.11)
f	floating lets out of let (Section 3.3)
g	floating lets out of case scrutinees (Section 3.10)
h	floating applications inward (Section 3.2)
i	case of known constructor (Section 3.7)
j	let-to-case (Sections 3.4 and 3.5)

Notice that there are many opportunities for transformations like `case` of known constructor, although they are rarely explicitly written in the source code. This is true for many of the transformations, that is they are generated by the compilation process after desugaring and inlining of expressions take place.

Actually many of these transformations were chosen by directly inspecting the intermediate code generated by the compiler.

In Table 7 we can see the effect of the transformations on various programs from the **nofib** Benchmark suite. We measure the number of instructions executed as this is a more reliable and reproducible number than run time. They were measured on a SparcStation 10. As the compiler relies on the use of some of the transformations we presented during the process of desugaring, the base line actually still includes *one* traversal of the code by the simplifier, which will perform a minimal set of transformations, e.g. inlining trivial expressions like `let a = b in E` (where a and b are variables). These numbers also exclude any benefits from strictness analysis, which is exploited by the compiler using the `let-to-case` and `case` floating from `let` transformations, therefore their effect (which is essentially the effect of strictness analysis as presented in [18]) is not reflected in these measurements.

	Simplified	
	No	Yes
infer	383,582,881	0.61
maillist	89,490,841	0.71
parser	269,289,414	0.75
prolog	9,298,035	0.76
reptile	64,101,111	0.77
hpg	826,552,571	0.77
fluid	50,675,650	0.80
compress	1,701,504,670	0.84
lift	3,155,801	0.85
veritas	2,756,900	0.86
gg	96,702,693	0.86
hidden	9,390,241,691	0.87
rsa	1,146,617,118	1.00
Minimum		0.61
Maximum		1.00
Median (13 programs)		0.80
Geometric Mean (13 programs)		0.80

Table 2: Total Instructions Executed

8 Conclusions

We have presented the complete set of local transformations performed by the simplifier pass of the Glasgow Haskell Compiler.

We believe this set of transformations, together with the overall design of the simplifier and the Core Language allows complex transformations to be performed by means of composing simpler transformations.

References

[1] A. Appel. *Compiling with Continuations*. Cambridge University Press, 1992.

[2] A. Appel and T. Jim. Continuation-passing, closure-passing style. In *ACM Conference on Principles of Programming Languages*, pages 293–302, January 1989.

[3] W. N. Chin. *Automatic Methods for Program Transformation*. PhD thesis, Imperial College, London, March 1990.

[4] A. Gill, J. Launchbury, and S. Peyton Jones. A short cut to deforestation. In *Functional Programming Languages and Computer Architecture*, pages 223–232, Copenhagen, June 1993. ACM Press.

[5] R. J. M. Hughes. *The Design and Implementation of Programming Languages*. PhD thesis, Programming Research Group, Oxford University, July 1983.

[6] T. Johnsson. Lambda lifting: Transforming programs to recursive equations. In *Functional Programming Languages and Computer Architecture*, number 201 in LNCS, pages 190–203, Nancy, September 1985. Springer-Verlag.

[7] R. Kelsey and P. Hudak. Realistic compilation by program transformation. In *ACM Conference on Principles of Programming Languages*, pages 281–292, January 1989.

[8] R. A. Kelsey. *Compilation by Program Transformation*. PhD thesis, Yale University, Department of Computer Science, May 1989. YALEU/DCS/RR-702.

[9] D. A. Kranz. *ORBIT - an optimising compiler for Scheme*. PhD thesis, Yale University, Department of Computer Science, May 1988.

[10] J. Launchbury and P. M. Sansom, editors. *Functional Programming, Glasgow 1992*, Ayr, Scotland, 1992. Springer Verlag, Workshops in Computing.

[11] S. Marlow and P. Wadler. Deforestation for higher-order functions. In Launchbury and Sansom [10], pages 154–165.

[12] B. Matthews. MERILL: An equational reasoning system in Standard ML. In *5th International Conference on Rewriting Techniques and Applications*, number 690 in LNCS, pages 414–445. Springer-Verlag, 1993.

[13] B. Matthews. Analysing a set of transformation rules using completion. 1994.

[14] W. Partain. The nofib benchmarking suite. In Launchbury and Sansom [10].

[15] S. Peyton Jones, C. Hall, K. Hammond, W. Partain, and P. Wadler. The Glasgow Haskell compiler: a technical overview. In *UK Joint Framework for Information Technology (JFIT) Technical Conference*, Keele, March 1993.

[16] S. Peyton Jones and J. Launchbury. Unboxed values as first class citizens. In *Functional Programming Languages and Computer Architecture*, pages 636–666, September 1991.

[17] S. Peyton Jones and D. Lester. A modular fully-lazy lambda lifter in Haskell. *Software – Practice and Experience*, 21(5):479–506, May 1991.

[18] S. Peyton Jones and W. Partain. On the effectiveness of a simple strictness analyser. In *Functional Programming, Glasgow 1993*, Ayr, Scotland, 1993. Springer Verlag, Workshops in Computing.

[19] P. Wadler. Deforestation: Transforming programs to eliminate trees. *Theoretical Computer Science*, 73:231–248, 1990.

Experience of developing a cervical cytology scanning system using Gofer and Haskell

Ian Poole and Derek Charleston

MRC Human Genetics Unit

Crewe Rd.

Edinburgh EH4 2XU

Scotland

Abstract

We present as a case study, the development of an application in automated image microscopy, using the functional programming languages Gofer and Haskell. Gofer is used as a formal specification language and subsequently for animation. I/O is sequenced by an I/O monad similar to that proposed for Haskell 1.3. The final implementation is in Haskell 1.2, although pragmatically, a C–coded image processing library is exploited.

1 ILDAS – a demonstration cervical cytology system

As part of a collaborative project[1] we are developing part of a cervical cytology scanning system, dubbed "ILDAS", using the functional programming languages Gofer [3] and Haskell[2]. Our purpose is to investigate the costs and benefits in using functional languages and elements of formal methods in our particular field — medical diagnostic imaging.

The following sections describe the three phases of development — formal specification in Gofer, animation also in Gofer, and final system implementation in Haskell. Fragments of Gofer/Haskell[2] code from ILDAS are given in the appendix.

ILDAS controls a microscope equipped with motorised stage and a digital camera to scan slides of monolayer preparations from cervical scrape material, identifying likely dyskaryotic cells, and delivering for each slide a final specimen-level decision — *sign-out* as clear of abnormality or send for *review* by conventional manual screening. HGU has been involved in the automation of cervical cytology for almost two decades and our latest C–coded prototype ('Cytoline') is now being developed commercially. Thus, ILDAS represents a partial re-engineering of an existing system.

ILDAS functions in two scanning passes — a "search" pass at low magnification, to identify suspicious cells, followed by a "rescan" at higher resolution

---

[1] *SADLI – Safety Assurance in Diagnostic Laboratory Imaging* is part funded by the DTI within its *Safety-critical Systems Programme*. The three collaborators on the project are The Centre for Software Engineering Ltd (CSE), Cambridge Consultants Ltd (CCL) and the MRC Human Genetics Unit (HGU)

[2] We'll write "Gofer/Haskell" to refer to code which is valid in either language

for a closer analysis of the most suspicious objects. However, due to limited project resources, only the rescan pass has been implemented in Gofer/Haskell, the search pass implementation being borrowed directly from Cytoline.

Briefly, the following ILDAS functionality is implemented in Gofer/Haskell:

- Relocation and re-analysis at higher magnification of each cell identified by the low magnification "search" pass as being suspicious. This involves:
    - control of the motorised stage and camera for stage location and auto focusing;
    - frame capture, correction to optical density and segmentation of individual nuclei;
    - identification of the target cell from constellation information provided by the search pass;
    - feature measurement and computation of posterior probability over object class (*leukocyte, normal cell, "suspicious" cell, artefact*).

- A simple teletype style, menu driven user interface;

- Graphic display of each captured frame showing segmentation and relocation match;

- Ordering of target records by posterior probability of correct classification;

- Specimen classification using a Bayesian model[8], classifying each specimen as *sign—out* or *review*;

- Graphic display of a "rogues' gallery" of the top ranked suspicious objects, together with normal cells for reference;

- Comprehensive simulation of microscope hardware (camera, lamp, stage, objective turret, etc.) to allow development and testing in the absence of external hardware.

Thus, the system addresses a broad range of practical issues: user interaction, hardware control, image processing, image display, statistical pattern recognition and interface to existing software. Implementation involved four people across across two sites — two at HGU in Edinburgh and two at CSE in Flixborough. The CSE team had no prior experience of functional programming whilst HGU had only a little such experience. None of us had experience in formal methods. For these reasons, we believe it represents a realistic (if small-scale) case study.

2   "Formal specifications" in Gofer

The formal specification (FS) of ILDAS was developed in three stages:

1. "Statement of Need" — a top-level wish-list in 18 pages,

2. "Software Requirements Specification"[10] — 50 pages of informal description including considerable detail of the algorithms to be used, and

3. "Software Formal Specification" [11] — 127 pages of Gofer with English commentary.

The following sub-sections highlight some techniques which we found useful in developing the FS in Gofer.

2.1 Implicit specifications

A key element of formal specification is the use of implicit definitions to state "post-conditions" of functions rather than giving full constructive forms.

By declaring the class **Universe** with the method **universe** to stand for the universal set of all values of a type, it is possible to construct an infrastructure which allows expression in Gofer of universal ($\forall$) and existential ($\exists$) quantification, and so record implicit specifications.

We leave some issues unresolved, however. As written, **implicit** insists on a unique solution, but one of the purposes of implicit specifications is to allow ambiguous specification. Does the universal set of functions of a given type include partial functions? What is the meaning of equality between partial functions (the definition below has such equality undefined)?

```
> class (Eq a) => Universe a where
>     universe :: Set a    -- Set of all values of type a

> instance Universe a where
>     universe = error "universal not executable in general"

> instance Eq a where (==) = error "(==) catch-all instance"

> instance (Universe a, Universe b) => Eq (a->b) where
>     f == g = forall (\x -> g x == f x)

> forall, exists :: (Universe a) => (a -> Bool) -> Bool
> forall pred = allSet pred universe
> exists pred = anySet pred universe

> implicit :: (Universe a) => (a -> Bool) -> a
> implicit spec =
>     case (card solutions) of
>         0           -> error "implicit: no solution"
>         1           -> singletonSet solutions
>         otherwise -> error "implicit: multiple solutions"
>     where
>         solutions = filterSet spec universe
```

The catch-all instances (allowed by Gofer) of **Eq** and **Universe** allow our specifications to be checked by the interpreter for syntax, type-correctness and closure. So for example we can write:

Def. maxGauss: *Given three points close to the peak of a Gaussian curve, return the position of the peak.*

```
> maxGauss :: (Int,Int) -> (Int,Int) -> (Int,Int) -> Double
> maxGauss (xi,ai) (yi,bi) (zi,ci) =
>     let (fitMean, fitSigma)::(Double, Double) =
>         implicit (\(m, s, c) ->
>             c * gauss (m,s) xi == ai &&
>             c * gauss (m,s) yi == bi &&
>             c * gauss (m,s) zi == ci)
>     in fitMean  -- Since the mean of a gaussian is also the mode.
```

By providing tongue-in-cheek instances of `Universe` for the types `Int`, `Double`, `String` etc., propositions involving `forall` and `exists` can be "executed", which has saved us on several occasions from searching for the proof of a false proposition! This latter gimmick is of course no substitute for symbolic proof.

2.2   Formal specification of image operations

It's in this area that we found formal specification to be of greatest value. We have developed an image analysis environment, "F-Woolz" (see [7]) which provides a collection of imaging related datatypes and associated operations. As will be seen in section 3.1, these types and operations are ultimately implemented via a C–coded image processing library. However, we have found that the semantics of these operations can be succinctly stated in Gofer. The following is an abbreviated summary; further details may be found in [9].

2.2.1   Image representations

F-Woolz provides (amongst others) the abstract data types `BIm` and `GIm`.

Decl. BIm: *Binary images are isomorphic with a set of points from the discrete plane, which we call a* domain.

```
> type BIm = Domain
> type Domain = Set (Crd2 Int)
> plane = universal :: Domain   -- Set of all points on the plane
```

Decl. GIm: *Greyscale images consist of a domain as above, paired with a pixel function which must be defined for every point in the domain.*

```
> data GIm = GIm Domain PixFunc
> type Pix = Int
> type PixFunc = (Crd2 Int -> Pix)
```

To the F-Woolz programmer, `BIm` and `GIm` are primitive types; neither the `GIm` constructor function nor the type synonym `BIm = Domain` are valid in application programs.

Decl. class Dom: *Collects types which represent a spatial domain.*

```
> class Dom a where
>    toBIm  :: a -> BIm              -- convert to BIm
>    shift  :: (Crd2 Int) -> a -> a  -- translation
>    mask   :: a -> BIm -> a         -- select a subset
>    nullIm :: a                     -- the empty dom.
```

It is important that the `mask` method for `GIm` is defined with care.

Def. maskGIm: *Select a sub-region of an image, providing the region is wholly included in the original.*

```
> maskGIm:: GIm -> BIm -> GIm
> maskGIm (GIm d1 gf) d2 =
>    | d2 'subset' d1 = GIm d2 gf
>    | otherwise      = error "maskGIm: d2 falls outside d1"
```

2.2.2 Som F-Woolz operations

Def. area,mass: *Basic image statistics.*

```
> area :: Dom a => a -> Int
> area = cardSet . toBim

> mass :: GIm -> Int
> mass GIm d gf = sum [gf p | p <- unset d]
```

Def. threshold: *Select only those points of an image with values* >= `th`.

```
> threshold :: Int -> GIm -> GIm
> threshold th (GIm d gf) = GIm d' gf
>        where
>        d' = filterSet (\p -> gf p >= th) d
```

2.2.3 Propositions about image primitives

It can be useful to record properties of functions, to serve as a resource when proving further results for an application. They also reinforce understanding of the functions concerned. Here's a trivial example:

Proposition (thThreshold): *A lower threshold may be applied prior to a higher one with no effect.*

```
> thThreshold =
>        forall (\(a,b) -> a >= b ==>
>                threshold a . threshold b == threshold a
>                )
```

Proof follows directly from the definition of `threshold`.

3   Animation in Gofer

In the animation phase, all implicit specifications were translated to constructive forms, with minimal attention to efficiency, in order to generate an executable Gofer prototype. However, special attention was given to the F-Woolz primitives.

3.1   Implementation of F-Woolz for Gofer

Whilst most F-Woolz specifications are in constructive form, the chosen representation is clearly highly inefficient, being unworkable even for prototyping purposes. Although efficient functional language implementations of image processing primitives have been proposed (see eg [5]), we chose not to take this route. Instead we have constructed bindings to an existing C–coded image processing library, known as "C-Woolz"[6]. Obviously the name of "F-Woolz" derives from this library, as does its broad semantics — the notion of an arbitrary shaped domain and separate pixel values is central to C-Woolz. However, C-Woolz representations are highly efficient, being based on interval coding.

The F-Woolz --> C-Woolz bindings are implemented via a *Woolz server* process, communicating with the Gofer interpreter through a Unix socket. Image data is held by the server in C-Woolz structures and processed by C-Woolz functions as demanded by Gofer via the socket. Image identifiers are transmitted across the socket as string encoded integers. To ensure referential transparency, image operations must generate new structures. This is not so inefficient as it might seem, since C-Woolz structures are designed to allow sharing; for example `threshold` generates a new (interval coded) domain, but shares the original pixel values. Never-the-less, large amounts of image data are allocated which are never freed, thus restricting Gofer based F-Woolz to prototyping work. This shortcoming is addressed in the Haskell based system described later.

These implementation details are hidden from the Gofer programmer, who sees only a library of functions and abstract data types, with semantics exactly (we hope!) equivalent to the Gofer specifications.

3.2   Input/Output

3.2.1   State monad

We have adopted an I/O monad (see eg [4]) with built in exception handling. Our Gofer implementation derives from Andy Gordon [1], being simulated on top of a Gofer/Haskell `Dialogue`. The package has common ancestry with the I/O monad proposed for Haskell 1.3. To this monad we have added general purpose state, allowing operations to transform the state *type*. Thus our monad is `Job s1 s2 a`, where `s1` and `s2` are the initial and final state type respectively, and `a` is the return type. Primitive operations on this monad are:

```
> (>>>=) :: Job s1 s2 a -> (a -> Job s2 s3 b) -> Job s1 s3 b

> val :: a -> Job s s a
```

```
> setState :: s2 -> Job s1 s2 ()
> getState :: Job s s s
```

This can be entertaining. For example, it's possible to work with a type heterogeneous *stack* of states, implemented as nested 2-tuples, so that a job can *push* its own local state and *pop* it off before returning:

```
> pushState :: top -> Job s (top,s) ()
> pushState st = getState >>>= (\s -> setState (top,s))

> popState :: Job (top,s) s top
> popState = getState >>>= (\(top,s) setState s >>>= (\_-> val st))
```

It's satisfying that such operations are fully exposed to the type system, so that a job of type `Jobs s s A` cannot modify the state in any way, though it may *push/pop* its own local state in a balanced fashion. Similarly, a job of type `Job s S A` may set the state but not read from it.

Unfortunately, however, state type transformation interacts poorly with exceptions, since if the first `Job` fails with an exception then the state must become undefined, as there is no way that a value of type `s3` can be obtained. This fact forces us to use a restricted binding operator in most cases:

```
> (>>=) :: Job s1 s2 a -> (a -> Job s2 s2 b) -> Job s1 s2 b
```

Thus the state type transforming monad has not turned out to be particularly useful in practice — we more-or-less work with a fixed state type throughout an application.

3.2.2 Access to microscope, camera and display

It is a simple matter to establish bindings, via the Woolz server, to a C–coded library to control our hardware. Thus the Gofer/Haskell programmer sees functions such as:

```
> pfDisplay      :: (Dom a) => Picframe -> a -> Job s s ()
>                    -- display an image
> cameraCapture  :: CamParams -> Job s s GIm
>                    -- capture an image
> moveStageAbs   :: (Crd3 Int) -> Job s s ()
>                    -- move the microscope stage
> lampLevelTo    :: Int -> Job s s ()
>                    -- set transmission illumination
> positionSlide  :: Job s s (Crd3 Int)
>                    -- return current stage position
```

where the type `Picframe` is an ADT representing image to display transformation (scale, translation, reflection and intensity look-up map), and the type `CamParams` represents camera parameters such as image window, exposure and sub-sampling ratio. These functions may **raise** exceptions if, for example, the camera hardware indicates an error, or an attempt is made to move the stage beyond its end-stops.

3.2.3 Simulation

A parallel library provides simulations for the camera and stage functions, in Gofer/Haskell. Camera simulation uses a file of pre-captured in-focus images at selected stage locations. An image is selected according to the current (x, y) stage position and masked according to the camera window. It's then blurred according to the current stage **z** position and sub-sampled as necessary. Finally it is adjusted in intensity according to the requested exposure setting and current lamp level. Stage simulation addresses issues such as the use of slide-relative coordinates and exception behavior at end-stops. The necessary simulation state is carried by the monad, so that the simulation functions have a more specialised type signature, e.g.,

```
> cameraCapture :: CamParams -> Job (SimState, s) (SimState, s) GIm
```

The free type parameter **s** allows a higher level application to define its own state (*c.f.* state stacks described earlier).

The simulation environment was essential to allow our collaborators, CSE, to work without access to real hardware. It yielded a subsidiary benefit in recording the intended semantics, in Gofer/Haskell, of our hardware environment.

4   Translation to Glasgow Haskell

The Gofer animation was modified to compile with Glasgow Haskell (**ghc** version 0.22) in order to take advantage of compiled execution and to address the problem of image deallocation (see below). We were also keen to use Haskell's module system — Gofer's simple "project files" provide no mechanism for controlling the name-space.

Translation was simple enough, the two languages being very similar. It was further simplified since the Gofer animation used a 'Haskellised' prelude (from Andy Gill, Glasgow). With some use of conditional compilation in low-level modules (we modified Gofer to pipe its source and project files through **cpp**), our sources remain executable via Gofer and Glasgow Haskell. This required us to maintain an acyclic module referencing structure as enforced by Gofer, though we believle this to be good practice in any case.

4.1   Monads and `ccall`

The `Job` monad was implemented on top of Glasgow's primitive `PrimIO` monad, adding state then exceptions:

```
> data StateMonad s1 s2 a = StateMonad (s1 -> PrimIO (s2, a))
> data Job s1 s2 a         = Job (StateMonad (E a))
> data E a                 = Is a | Fail String
```

Note that the exception monad must be built on top of the state monad, not the other way round, or the state could not propagate across exceptions.

The Woolz server was replaced by a compiled library, the Haskell --> C bindings being achieved via ghc's ccall mechanism. It's satisfying that for the most part it was possible to ccall *directly* to C–Woolz library functions, without the annoyance of intervening wrappers.

4.2   Image deallocation

As mentioned above, the Gofer implementation of F-Woolz did not allow image memory to be freed — a serious deficiency. Ghc solves this problem by providing the special type MallocPtr to represent a pointer to *externally allocated* memory. When the garbage collector recovers a value of type MallocPtr it calls a programmer-provided C function to free whatever external resources are associated with that value. We consider this to be an important practical provision; just as ccall allows primitive functions to be implemented externally, so MallocPtr allows similar extensibility with regard to datatypes. This facility was added to ghc by Alistair Reid, and is described elsewhere in this volume.

We have yet to undertake the planned final phase of the implementation — optimisation of the Haskell code. However, the current version executes with acceptable efficiency — only slightly (around 30%) slower than the C–coded Cytoline system. This is of no great surprise, since the processor intensive pixel processing remains in C.

4.3   Haskell shortcomings

Following are some minor points of the Haskell language which we feel need attention.

- Absence of record types — we found pattern matching on datatypes with dozens of elements to be tedious, ugly and error-prone.

- A method toDouble :: Real a => a -> Double needs adding to class Real. Whilst it is possible to define this as fromRational . toRational, this is outrageously inefficient, especially when used, as it often is, at type Int -> Double (*i.e.* fromInt) or Double -> Double (*i.e.* id)!

- There seems to be no prelude function for controlling the printed precision of floating point numbers.

5   Conclusions

Our impressions of the value of formal specification, as we employed it, are mixed. The specification was highly algorithmic in style, being in places little short of an untested program. In part this was due to the nature of our problem domain — it's hard to define *what* is a dyskaryotic (abnormal) cell, easier to evolve a recipe to find one. Given the pre-existing Cytoline implementation, we doubtless fell into reverse-engineering the Gofer specification from C code! Even without these difficultes and shortcommings, it seems to us inevitable that the fully formal specification of a large and complex system will be large and complex — there's no free lunch. That said, formal specification of the image

214

processing primitives was found to be clearly beneficial, and in fact helped us to identify several deficiencies in their C implementations.

Using Gofer as the specification language had the advantage that a syntax and type checker was readily available, and allowed smooth progression from specification to animation. Thus, although the FS turned out rather too detailed and algorithmic, at least little effort was wasted towards achieving the animated prototype.

In conclusion, we have demonstrated that a diagnostic imaging system, incorporating image processing and hardware control can be developed in a functional language, provided a pragmatic approach is adopted to low level pixel processing. Gofer was found to be serviceable as a formal specification language. The monadic style of I/O was a delight to use. The type security and modularity provided by Gofer/Haskell were of great benefit in preventing blunders as code was exchanged between sites. Given the infra-structure we now have in place, we believe that a novel application in automated microscopy could be developed in Gofer/Haskell with benefits in reliability and development effort, at an acceptable efficiency cost.

Acknowledgments

We are grateful for assistance provided by the functional programming group at Glasgow, particularly Will Partain, Kevin Hammond, Alistair Reid and Andy Gill. Andy Gordon (University of Cambridge), introduced us to, and tutored us in, monadic I/O. Mark Jones (University of Nottingham) gave us generous support in the use and modification of Gofer. Thanks also to our collaborators at CSE — Jenny Butler and Mary McGeachin.

A Example Gofer/Haskell code from ILDAS

Following is code from an ILDAS module, demonstrating the monadic style of I/O, including use of exceptions.

Code is layed-out with the aid of LaTeX macros. These also allow sources to be input to higher level documents with correct attention to section numbering. If the "bird-track" literate style is accepted as standard Gofer/Haskell, then our source files are simultaneously valid to LaTeX, Gofer and Haskell without pre-processing. The only disadvantage is that the raw source is rather ugly.

A.1 Auto-focus

This concerns the focusing on each relocated cell, and assumes the slide is already in approximate focus. Focus will usually be found in just three captures.

Def. focus3Point: *Measure the focus value at three equally–spaced points, and look for a trend. If none is visible, then try again with a bigger stepsize, up to a maximum of 3 times.*

```
> type IJob a = Job (SimState, IldasState) (SimState, IldasState) a

> focus3Point :: FocusParams -> Int -> Int -> IJob Bool
```

```
> focus3Point fp tries z =
>         doIt 'handle' report
>         where
>
>         doIt =
>                 moveStageZAbs z >> measure
>             >>= \b -> moveStageZAbs (z-step) >> measure
>             >>= \a -> moveStageZAbs (z+step) >> measure
>             >>= \c -> interp3Point measure z step a b c
>             >>= \ok ->
>                 if ok then val True
>                 else if tries >= 3 then val False
>                 else focus3Point fp (tries+1) z
>
>         step        = tries * fineFocusStepSize fp
>         measure     = measureFocus fp
>         report estr = raise ("focus3Point: exception:\n " ++ estr)
```

Def. interp3Point: *Interpret the focus values given for 3 equally-spaced points* a, b, c, *and look for a trend. If the trend indicates that the peak is between points* a *and* c, *then interpolate to estimate the position of maximum focus, and move there. If the trend is uphill or downhill, then follow the slope and measure a new focus value. If no trend is visible then return false. A valley is treated as a dire exception.*

```
> interp3Point :: IJob Int -> Int -> Int -> Int -> Int -> Int ->
>                 IJob Bool
> interp3Point measure z step a b c =
>     case (trend a b c) of
>     "<>" -> nearPeak    -- straddling peak, interpolate
>     "<<" -> upHill      -- on the slope, need to increase z
>     "=<" -> upHill      -- at foot of slope, need to increase z
>     ">>" -> downHill    -- on the slope, need to decrease z
>     ">=" -> downHill    -- at foot of slope, need to decrease z
>     "<=" -> nearPeak    -- approaching the brow
>     "=>" -> nearPeak    --    "  "       "  "
>     "==" -> val False   -- flat, no trend, give up
>     "><" -> raise "interp3Point: found valley in focus profile"
>     where
>
>     nearPeak =  -- close enough to interpolate
>         let finalZ = round (maxGauss (z - step, a)
>                                      (z, b)
>                                      (z + step, c))
>         in
>                 putLine ("interp3Point: finalZ==" ++ show finalZ)
>         >>      moveStageZAbs finalZ
>         >>      val True
>
```

```
>       upHill =    -- need to increase z
>               moveStageZAbs (z + (2*step))
>           >>    measure
>           >>= \d -> interp3Point measure (z+step) step b c d
>
>       downHill =  -- need to decrease z
>               moveStageZAbs (z - (2*step))
>           >>    measure
>           >>= \d -> interp3Point measure (z-step) step d a b
```

Note that the *specification* of maxGauss has been given in section 2.1.

Def. trend: *The configuration of three points* a, b *and* c *is represented by two characters, each of which may be* <, > *or* =. *For example, "<>" indicates a peak, "><" a valley, "<<" the left slide of a hill and "=<" near the foot of the left side of a hill*

```
> trend :: Int -> Int -> Int -> String
> trend a b c =
>     let
>         tolerance = 0.05 :: Double
>         (<<), (>>) :: Int -> Int -> Bool
>         a << b = a < b - round (tolerance * (fromInt b))
>         a >> b = a > b + round (tolerance * (fromInt b))
>         comp :: Int -> Int -> Char
>         a 'comp' b =
>             if a >> b then '>'
>                 else if a << b then '<'
>                 else '='
>     in
>         [a 'comp' b, b 'comp' c]
```

References

[1] Andy Gordon. Functional programming and input/output. Master's thesis, University of Cambridge Computer Laboratory, August 1992.

[2] Paul Hudak et al. *Report on the programming language Haskell (V1.2)*. University of Glasgow, 1993.

[3] Mark P Jones. *An introduction to Gofer*, 1992.

[4] Simon L Peyton Jones and Philip Wadler. Imperative functional programming. In *ACM Conference on the Principles Of Programming Languages*, pages 71–84, 1993.

[5] Y Kozato and G P Otto. Geometric transformations in a lazy functional language. In *11th International Conference on Pattern Recognition*, pages 128–132, 1992.

[6] J Piper and D Rutovitz. Data structures for image processing in a C language and a Unix environment. *Pattern Recognition Letters*, pages 119–129, 1985.

[7] Ian Poole. A functional programming environment for image analysis. In *11th International Conference on Pattern Recognition*, volume IV, pages 124–127, 1992.

[8] Ian Poole. A statistical model for classifying cervical monolayers. Research Note RN94-003, Pattern Recognition and Automation Section, MRC Human Genetics Unit, Edinburgh, UK, October 1993.

[9] Ian Poole and Derek Charleston. Formal specification of image processing primitives in a functional language. In *Accepted for the 12th International Conference on Pattern Recognition*, 1994.

[10] Ian Poole, Derek Charleston, and Jenny Butler. ILDAS: Software requirements (Issue 3). DTI deliverable D2.1 for the SADLI project IED4/1/9042, February 1994.

[11] Ian Poole, Derek Charleston, Jenny Butler, and Mary McGeachin. ILDAS: Software formal specification (Issue 1.1). DTI deliverable D2.2 for the SADLI project IED4/1/9042, April 1994.

Binding-time Improvement and Fold/Unfold Transformation

Colin Runciman

Department of Computer Science, University of York

York YO1 5DD, England

colin@minster.york.ac.uk

Abstract

Binding-time improvement (BTI) is an important preliminary stage in partial evaluation. Some BTI rules can be automated, but the state of the art is that many improvements are still made "by hand" using an ordinary text editor. Mechanically assisted fold/unfold transformation could provide a more systematic framework for BTI.

1 Introduction

In Chapter 17 of their book[5] Jones *et.al.* stress the advantages of full automation that *partial evaluation* offers over more general *fold/unfold transformation*. They remark:

> A recurring problem with [more general transformation] systems is incomplete automation, resulting in the need for a user to read (and evaluate the efficiency of!) incompletely transformed programs.

However, partial evaluation is not entirely free of such problems. The full potential of a partial evaluator usually cannot be realised by applying it to a program *as originally written*. Most partial evaluators work well only if programs supplied to them are first reformulated to maximise opportunities for static computation. Modification with this purpose is called *binding-time improvement* (BTI) and it can greatly enhance the performance of residual programs. As Chapter 12 of [5] explains, some rules for BTI can be automated within a partial evaluator itself. But many improvements are made "by hand" using an ordinary text editor, guided by rules of thumb and the need to eliminate observed deficiencies in residual programs. This latter approach to BTI has clear disadvantages:

1. Because BTI usually involves making the program structure more complicated there is a risk that the function computed by a program will be changed by mistake — perhaps in a subtle way that's hard to trace.

2. Even if no such mistakes are made, the risk of making them may deter the programmer from attempting some of the more ambitious improvements.

3. There is no systematic way of recording a series of changes; so there is nothing to help the programmer deriving alternative variants of the same program, or making similar improvements in other programs.

4. The programmer has "to read and evaluate incompletely transformed programs" — the disappointing residual outputs of first attempts at partial evaluation.

Fold/unfold program transformation [2, 7], carried out using an interactive system that checks and applies each step, is an "intermediate technology" between text editing and fully automated program derivation. Using a fold/unfold system for BTI could in principle avoid or reduce all the above-listed disadvantages of BTI by manual editing.

1. Changing a program only by valid fold/unfold steps eliminates almost all risk of unintentionally altering the function it computes. Safe transformation of simple specifications into more complex derived programs was part of the original motivation for fold/unfold.

2. Use of mechanically applied transformations, with suitable support for exploratory working and recovery of earlier positions, could encourage rather than deter the programmer in their BTI work.

3. Changes expressed using fold/unfold rules lend themselves to systematic record-keeping, and mechanical checkers can "replay" these records on request — perhaps with variations specified by the programmer.

4. Since partial evaluation is itself a specialised form of fold/unfold transformation, the programmer using fold/unfold for BTI has a means of exploring the consequences of changes they make. They can anticipate the later automated stages of transformation, exploring critical parts of it by hand-driven tests.

This paper investigates the idea of fold/unfold BTI to see whether it is feasible in practice: §2 reviews fold/unfold transformation and partial evaluation; §3 explains the need for BTI and some standard BTI techniques; §4 looks at two examples of BTI expressed as a fold/unfold transformation; §5 discusses some issues arising when a mechanised fold/unfold system is used; §6 concludes.

2 Fold/unfold and partial evaluation

2.1 Fold/unfold transformation

The ideas of fold/unfold program transformation were first put forward in the 70's by Burstall and Darlington[2]. Expressing programs as first-order recursion equations, they suggested that program development could proceed as a series of transformational steps. The starting point is a program written as simply as possible, ignoring efficiency concerns. Subsequent transformation preserves the

220

extensional meaning of a program, but may alter its computational workings significantly. The final program is typically more complex than the original, but also more efficient. The big advantage of the transformational approach is its in-built correctness argument: the final program is reached by series of meaning-preserving steps starting from an original program sufficiently clear and simple to serve as a specification.

Example By way of reminder or introduction to the fold/unfold rules, here is the derivation of a list-reversing function that works by accumulation, starting from an original naive definition using list concatenation. The naive definition is:

$$reverse \quad [] \quad = \quad []$$
$$reverse \quad (x\!:\!xs) \quad = \quad reverse\ xs \mathbin{+\!\!+} [x]$$

A so-called *eureka step* introduces a more general function:

$$reverseInto\ xs\ ys \quad = \quad reverse\ ys \mathbin{+\!\!+} xs$$

The *primitive law* $xs \mathbin{+\!\!+} [] = xs$ justifies the embedding:

$$reverse\ xs \quad = \quad reverseInto\ []\ xs$$

The next step is to *instantiate* the *reverseInto* definition for $ys = []$ and $ys = (z\!:\!zs)$.

$$reverseInto \quad xs \quad [] \quad = \quad reverse\ [] \mathbin{+\!\!+} xs$$
$$reverseInto \quad xs \quad (z\!:\!zs) \quad = \quad reverse\ (z\!:\!zs) \mathbin{+\!\!+} xs$$

Now *unfold* the applications of *reverse*, appealing to its original definition.

$$reverseInto \quad xs \quad [] \quad = \quad [] \mathbin{+\!\!+} xs$$
$$reverseInto \quad xs \quad (z\!:\!zs) \quad = \quad (reverse\ zs \mathbin{+\!\!+} [z]) \mathbin{+\!\!+} xs$$

Appeal to the associativity of $\mathbin{+\!\!+}$ then unfold $\mathbin{+\!\!+}$ in both equations.

$$reverseInto \quad xs \quad [] \quad = \quad xs$$
$$reverseInto \quad xs \quad (z\!:\!zs) \quad = \quad reverse\ zs \mathbin{+\!\!+} (z\!:\!xs)$$

Finally, in the second equation introduce a recursive application of *reverseInto*, by *folding* the right-hand side — it is an instance of the original specification for *reverseInto*.

$$reverseInto \quad xs \quad [] \quad = \quad xs$$
$$reverseInto \quad xs \quad (z\!:\!zs) \quad = \quad reverseInto\ (z\!:\!xs)\ zs$$

The value of mechanical assistance in such transformations was soon recognised [3]. However, *no full automation* of the fold/unfold scheme seemed possible. The transformational development of any but the most modest programs still required a great deal of effort on the part of programmers. Also, fold/unfold transformation is only effective where some larger idea determines a strategy for its use: in particular, the success of fold/unfold often depends on the timely introduction of *eureka* definitions.

2.2 Partial evaluation

As Jones *et.al.*[5] explain, *partial evaluation* can be regarded as a special purpose implementation of fold/unfold transformation under the control of an algorithmic strategy. A *partial evaluator* takes as input a source program and some but not all of its input data. The given data is termed *static*, the remainder is termed *dynamic*. If we identify program inputs with the arguments of a main function, the starting point for transformation is a specialised *instance* of the main function with the given values "frozen in" in place of static arguments. The aim is to do as much computation as possible given the static values. This goal drives subsequent unfolding and folding, and the generation of specialised instances of needed auxiliary functions in further *eureka* steps. The result of partial evaluation is a specialised *residual program* that requires only the dynamic data as input. Since all the evaluation that depends only on static data has been performed at partial evaluation time, the residual program often runs much faster than the orginal program of which it is a specialised version.

Example A simple introductory example is a function to raise numbers to natural powers.

$$power \quad 0 \quad\quad x \;=\; 1$$
$$power \quad (n+1) \quad x \;=\; x \times power\; n\; x$$

A partial evaluator can specialise this definition for fixed powers. If 3 is supplied as the static value of the first argument, the residual program is:

$$power3\; x \;=\; x \times x \times x \times 1$$

A partial evaluator *cannot* derive the accumulating definition of *reverse* as a residual program given naive *reverse* as the original program (even if accompanied by *reverseInto*). Such rearrangement of a computation by judicious appeal to an associative law is beyond the scope of partial evaluation. However, partial evaluation does have a wide range of applications. Its *forte* is specialisation of interpretive systems: partial evaluation can turn interpreters into compilers (static program, dynamic input); generic parsing algorithms into parser-generators (static grammar, dynamic text); and so on.

3 Binding-time improvement

The workings of a (simple, off-line) partial evaluator depend on a *binding-time analysis* of the program supplied to it: as a result of this analysis each argument of each function is labelled as either static or dynamic. The result of a function application is static only if *all* the arguments the result depends on are static. As a corollary, in a basic partial evaluator a data structure is static only if all its components are – though more sophisticated systems can exploit "partially static" values.

Consider as an example a simple interpreter with two arguments, s the source program and d its data. A large part of the interpreter's work lies in the manipulation of *environments* mapping names to values. If partial evaluation is applied to the interpreter, since all the names are drawn from s, the static program, one might hope that a good deal of this work could be done by the partial evaluator. But if the environment is represented as a single data structure (eg. an association list) its components also include values derived from d, the dynamic data. So the environment as a whole is treated as dynamic, and no work on it is attempted by the partial evaluator. Hence the first heuristic for BTI:

1. *Separate static and dynamic structures.*

A remedy for the interpreter's environment is to unzip it into a static list of names and a dynamic list of values. But this poses another problem: what about functions whose *result* is an environment? To avoid this problem, there is a second heuristic.

2. *Recast functions in continuation-passing style.*

In a continuation-passing interpreter environments are never returned as results, only supplied as arguments to continuations.

Figure 1 illustrates the result of applying these two BTI heuristics for the interpreter example. It shows a typical environment-manipulating function before and after BTI. The original $bind_1$ binds a name to a value in a given environment yielding a new environment; its replacement for purposes of partial evaluation, $bind_2$, does the same job but with a separated environment and in continuation-passing style.

$$
\begin{array}{llllll}
bind_1 & [\,] & n' & v' & = & [(n', v')] \\
bind_1 & ((n, v)\!:\!env) & n' & v' & = & \textbf{if } n{=}{=}n' \textbf{ then } (n, v')\!:\!env \\
& & & & & \quad \textbf{else } (n, v)\!:\!bind_1 \; env \; n' \; v' \\
bind_2 & [\,] & [\,] & n' \; v' \; k & = & k \; [n'] \; [v'] \\
bind_2 & (n\!:\!ns) & (v\!:\!vs) & n' \; v' \; k & = & \\
\multicolumn{6}{l}{\quad \textbf{if } n{=}{=}n' \textbf{ then } k \; (n\!:\!ns) \; (v'\!:\!vs)} \\
\multicolumn{6}{l}{\quad \textbf{else } bind_2 \; ns \; vs \; n' \; v' \; (\lambda ns'. \lambda vs'. k \; (n\!:\!ns') \; (v\!:\!vs'))}
\end{array}
$$

Figure 1: Separating static names from dynamic values.

But what if the interpreter is for a *reflective* language, in which names are first class citizens? A *computed* name is surely dynamic; does this spoil things once again? Since even computed names are only dynamic within the bounds of *static variation* a further heuristic — known as *The Trick* — provides a remedy.

3. *The Trick: for a dynamic variable substitute an equal static one.*

So instead of applications such as $f \; (lookup \; ns \; dn)$, where ns is a static name list but dn is a dynamic name, the application of f is moved *inside* the *lookup* function where The Trick can be used to provide a static argument.

4 Examples

4.1 String matcher

String matching is a standard example in partial evaluation. An initial program is shown in Figure 2. One string p matches another s simply if p occurs somewhere in s, a test performed by checking whether p is a prefix of s or of some recursive tail of s. It is easy to see that this program is rather inefficient, $O(\#p \times \#s)$, as no information obtained when testing prefixes of s is retained to save work in recursive searches in tails of s. The aim is to generate an efficient specialised matcher for some fixed p, but a residual $match_p$ generated from the program in Figure 2 only inherits its inefficiency.

Intuitively, it should be possible to use The Trick to obtain an efficient, $O(\#s)$, residual program because the prefix test only re-traverses sections of the dynamic string previously found equal to some portion of the static one. For this observation to be exploited, however, the matching program must undergo substantial modifications. Figure 3 shows the matching program after appropriate binding-time improvements have been made: compared with Figure 2 the program is certainly more complex, and it is harder to see how it works. Assuming static p and dynamic s arguments to $match$, only the third arguments of $matchtail$ and $prefix$ are dynamic; so inefficient-looking expressions such as $(km + [pc])$ do not occur in residual programs.

$$
\begin{array}{lllll}
match & p & s & = & prefix\ p\ s \parallel matchtail\ p\ s \\[2mm]
matchtail & p & [] & = & False \\
matchtail & p & (sc{:}s) & = & match\ p\ s \\[2mm]
prefix & [] & s & = & True \\
prefix & (pc{:}p) & [] & = & False \\
prefix & (pc{:}p) & (sc{:}s) & = & \textbf{if}\ pc{==}sc\ \textbf{then}\ prefix\ p\ s\ \textbf{else}\ False
\end{array}
$$

Figure 2: String-matching program before BTI.

Main lines of a fold/unfold derivation

This version of the string-matching example is taken from lecture notes written by John Hughes. To explain the BTI process, John gives intermediate program versions, with informal arguments for the validity of successive changes. To test the idea of BTI by fold/unfold transformation, three questions seem appropriate:

1. Can fold/unfold transformation be used to formalise the derivation of the program in Figure 3 from the program in Figure 2? *Answer: Yes.*

$$
\begin{array}{llll}
match & p & s & = & prefix\ p\ [\,]\ s\ p\ [\,] \\[6pt]
matchtail & p & [\,] & [\,] & = & False \\
matchtail & p & [\,] & (dc:ds) & = & prefix\ p\ [\,]\ ds\ p\ [\,] \\
matchtail & p & (sc:ss) & ds & = & prefix\ p\ ss\ ds\ p\ [\,] \\
prefix & [\,] & ss & ds & kp & km & = & True \\
prefix & (pc:ps) & [\,] & [\,] & kp & km & = & matchtail\ kp\ km\ [\,] \\
prefix & (pc:ps) & [\,] & (dc:ds) & kp & km & = \\
\end{array}
$$

$\qquad$ **if** $pc == dc$ **then** $prefix\ ps\ [\,]\ ds\ kp\ (km +\!\!+ [pc])$

$\qquad$ **else** $matchtail\ kp\ km\ (dc:ds)$

$prefix\quad (pc:ps)\quad (sc:ss)\quad ds\qquad kp\quad km\ =$

$\qquad$ **if** $pc == sc$ **then** $prefix\ ps\ ss\ ds\ kp\ (km +\!\!+ [pc])$

$\qquad$ **else** $matchtail\ kp\ (km +\!\!+ sc:ss)\ ds$

Figure 3: String-matching program after BTI.

$$
\begin{array}{lllllll}
prefix_1 & p & s & & k & & = & k\ (prefix\ p\ s) \\
prefix_2 & p & s & & kp & ks & = & prefix_1\ p\ s\ (\|\ matchtail\ kp\ ks) \\
prefix_3 & p & s & & kp & km & = & prefix_2\ p\ s\ kp\ (km +\!\!+ s) \\
prefix_4 & p & ss & ds & kp & km & = & prefix_3\ p\ (ss +\!\!+ ds)\ kp\ km \\
\end{array}
$$

Figure 4: Eureka steps in the transformation from Figure 2 to Figure 3.

2. Can the derivation follow the overall sequence of steps that was found natural in the informal explanation? *Answer: Yes.*

3. Can the derivation be carried out conveniently using a mechanised system? *Answer: Maybe. See discussion in §5.*

A fold/unfold derivation can be based on four successive versions of the *prefix* function. Each version is specified in terms of its predecessor by a single *eureka* equation, as shown in Figure 4. With reference to the binding-time improvement heuristics noted in §3: $prefix_1$ introduces continuation-passing; $prefix_2$ generalises, paving the way for arguments in the recursive call other than the whole pattern and the entire tail of the text being searched; $prefix_3$ alters the way information is split across two arguments, preparing for use of The Trick; $prefix_4$ splits the original dynamic string argument into static and dynamic parts, using The Trick to transfer originally dynamic text to the static part.

As each new version is formulated, the definition of *match* is changed to use it. The series of foldings is:

$$match\ p\ s\ =\ prefix_1\ p\ s\ (\|\ matchtail\ p\ s)$$

$$= prefix_2\ p\ s\ p\ s$$
$$= prefix_3\ p\ s\ p\ []$$
$$= prefix_4\ p\ []\ s\ p\ []$$

Transforming successive $prefix_n$ definitions to directly recursive form follows the standard strategy [2]: case instantiation, then unfolding and re-arrangement to achieve folding. The necessary pattern of case instantiation is simply determined by that of the previous version of $prefix$.

Use of laws: a few details

The only laws considered in [2] were about primitives (with no equational definitions to fold or unfold). But all kinds of equivalence laws about programmer-defined functions could also be used to justify transformation steps. So what kinds of laws are needed for the string-matcher BTI?

Rearrangements with the aim of bringing together the body of a recursive call, often involve simple *promotion laws* [1]. For example, the rule for promoting a strict function application through a conditional

$$f \perp = \perp\ \vdash\ f\ (\textbf{if } c \textbf{ then } x \textbf{ else } y)\ =\ \textbf{if } c \textbf{ then } f\ x \textbf{ else } f\ y$$

is used repeatedly to achieve directly recursive definitions of the $prefix_i$ functions. The Trick is also cast as a law about conditionals:

$$(\textbf{if } x\!==\!y \textbf{ then } f\ x \textbf{ else } z)\ =\ (\textbf{if } x\!==\!y \textbf{ then } f\ y \textbf{ else } z)$$

This law is used, for example, to replace the boxed sc by pc in the recursive $prefix_3$ equation:

$$prefix_3\ (pc\!:\!ps)\ (sc\!:\!ss)\ kp\ km\ =$$
$$\textbf{if } pc\!==\!sc \textbf{ then } prefix_3\ ps\ ss\ kp\ (km \mathbin{+\!\!+} [\,\boxed{sc}\,])$$
$$\textbf{else } matchtail\ kp\ (km \mathbin{+\!\!+} sc \mathbin{+\!\!+} ss)$$

A few laws are needed that express simple algebraic properties such as associativity or identity. For example, when the s argument is finally split into ss and ds in $prefix_4$, it is necessary to make a corresponding change in $matchtail$ using the *eureka* equation:

$$matchtail_4\ p\ ss\ ds\ =\ matchtail\ p\ (ss \mathbin{+\!\!+} ds)$$

The choice of arguments when the time comes to fold using this equation is critical. Consider the boxed expression in the following $prefix_4$ equation:

$$prefix_4\ (pc\!:\!ps)\ (ssc\!:\!sss)\ ds\ kp\ km\ =$$
$$\textbf{if } pc\!==\!ssc \textbf{ then } prefix_4\ ps\ sss\ ds\ kp\ (km \mathbin{+\!\!+} [pc])$$
$$\textbf{else } \boxed{matchtail\ kp\ (km \mathbin{+\!\!+} ssc\!:\!(sss \mathbin{+\!\!+} ds))}$$

Incautiously folding this into the application

$$matchtail_4\ kp\ km\ (ssc\!:\!(sss \mathbin{+\!\!+} ds))$$

would ignore the static nature of *ssc* and *sss*, including them as part of the dynamic argument to $matchtail_4$. Instead we must appeal to the definition and associativity of $+\!\!+$ to make the folded application:

$$matchtail_4\ kp\ (km +\!\!+ ssc\!:\!sss)\ ds$$

In summary, a few algebraic laws are needed on a few occasions. But these are simple properties not subtle theorems, and much of the fold/unfold BTI for the string-matcher is by routine appeal to defining equations.

4.2 Small interpreter

Another example is a small pattern-matching interpreter for recursion equations. For this exercise fold/unfold transformation was used *ab initio* to make binding-time improvements, rather than following a BTI path already established informally. Though small as interpreters go, the interpreter is still much larger than the string-matcher and there is only space here for a brief summary with one or two illustrative extracts.

The original interpreter manipulates environments represented as association lists. Pattern-matching adds the twist that some functions applied to environments may either succeed (with a resulting value, such as a new environment) or fail. In the original interpreter this is accomplished using *Maybe* types for the result (**data** *Maybe a* $=$ *Yes a* | *No*). As an example, Figure 5 shows the definition of a function that matches a pattern against a value v in an environment *env*.

match	*(Var s)*	v	*env* $=$	

$match$ $(Var\ s)$ v $env\ =$
  if *bound env s*
  then if *lookup s env* $==v$ **then** *Yes env* **else** *No*
  else *Yes* $((s,v):env)$
$match$ $(Cons\ f\ ps)$ $(Cons\ g\ vs)$ $env\ =$
  if $f==g$ **then** *matchlist ps vs env* **else** *No*

Figure 5: Pattern-matching in the original interpreter.

The transformation proceeded in four stages:

1. introduce continuation passing style;

2. codify continuations as first order data structures;

3. split continuation structures into static and dynamic parts;

4. split the environments.

Stages 1 and 4 use the heuristics outlined in §3. Stages 2 and 3 were necessary to make the interpreter suitable for a first-order partial evaluator, but no more will be said about them here.

In many transformations there is a choice of working either with function arguments explicitly represented in applications, or in a higher-order style using function-level operators. One style may allow a far more convenient derivation than the other. In Stage 1, it proved convenient to do some of the transformation working with higher-order expressions. For example, with $foldm$ defined by the equations

$$
\begin{aligned}
foldm \ f \ z \ (Yes \ x) &= f \ x \\
foldm \ f \ z \ No &= z
\end{aligned}
$$

after the *eureka* equation

$$
match_2 \ f \ z \ p \ v \ = \ foldm \ f \ z \ \circ \ match \ p \ v
$$

subsequent promotions to achieve recursive calls are by appeal to the distributive law:

$$
foldm \ f \ z \ \circ \ foldm \ g \ y \ = \ foldm \ (foldm \ f \ z \ \circ \ g) \ (foldm \ f \ z \ y)
$$

Stage 4 brought to light a pitfall with the formulation of *eureka* equations for argument splitting. These equations include an application of the function that *combines* the split arguments into an argument of the original kind. In the string-matcher, splitting amounts to chopping a string in two, and so $+\!\!\!+$ is the obvious combining function. When splitting an environment by unzipping it, a *eureka* equation such as

$$
bound_2 \ ns \ vs \ = \ bound \ (zip \ ns \ vs)
$$

may seem equally obvious. But a zip function defined by

$$
\begin{aligned}
zip \ (x{:}xs) \ (y{:}ys) &= (x,y){:}zip \ xs \ ys \\
zip \ \_ \quad \_ &= [\,]
\end{aligned}
$$

will not do. The combining function must be *non-strict in the dynamic argument*. The standard $+\!\!\!+$ is non-strict in its 2nd argument, but zip as defined above is not. All is well if zip is defined instead by:

$$
\begin{aligned}
zip \ (x{:}xs) \ ys &= (x, \ head \ ys){:}zip \ xs \ (tail \ ys) \\
zip \ \_ \quad \_ &= [\,]
\end{aligned}
$$

The explicit formulation of a combining function necessary for fold/unfold argument splitting does have advantages. The definition precisely documents the splitting step, and ensures a consistent interpretation of the split arguments throughout the program.

5 Mechanisation

Various mechanical checkers and assistants have been built for fold/unfold transformation. Darlington built the first such system[3]: it used simple heuristics to control a search for directly recursive re-formulations of *eureka* definitions supplied by a user — who also approved or suppressed possible lines of development as they were encountered in the search. Feather's ZAP [4] interpreted fuller specifications of transformational plans — series of goals (function definitions conforming to given patterns) and alternative tactical combinations by which they might be reached. But few systems have been used routinely as interactive tools alongside an interpreter for developing initial programs, and most do not support characteristics of recently designed functional languages.

The transformations of the previous section were conducted using Starship [7], an interactive fold/unfold checker for higher-order recursion equation programs with non-strict semantics and polymorphic typing. In addition to a repertoire of basic fold/unfold commands used interactively, Starship has a simple inductive proof system for validating laws about defined functions and support for recording, editing and replaying transformations.

The final transcripts for the transformation of the string-matcher and the interpreter run to a little over 50 and 100 commands respectively. Though there is certainly scope for improved abstraction to avoid repeating similar steps, such figures seem acceptable. However, these final scripts do not include various failed avenues, often following the introduction of an unsatisfactory *eureka* equation. For example, because Starship does not permit a transformation to result in a loss of generality, the *eureka* equations for both $prefix_1$ and $prefix_2$ (in Figure 4) cause problems. The equation for $prefix_1$ must specify from the outset that application of the continuation is strict:

$$prefix_1 \; p \; s \; k \;\; = \;\; strict \; k \; (prefix \; p \; s)$$

This is because strictness is needed later as a side-condition both for promotion through a conditional and for pattern instantiation. The difficulty with the *eureka* equation for $prefix_2$ has to do with inferred polymorphic types. The generalisation of Figure 4 introduces auxiliary arguments for *matchtail* unconnected in any way with the existing *prefix* arguments, and this is reflected in the inferred type:

$$prefix_2 \;\; :: \;\; [a] \to [a] \to [b] \to [b] \to Bool$$

But as a result of subsequent transformation steps the types are constrained to be the same

$$prefix_2 \;\; :: \;\; [a] \to [a] \to [a] \to [a] \to Bool$$

and such type-refinement is prohibited in Starship.

To be obstructed by a system's sensitivity to such issues can be a nuisance. On the other hand, it can prevent errors. Starship does successfully shield the programmer from many such technicalities — for example, without exception, the many strictness side-conditions that *were* satisfied in these transformations were validated automatically.

One significant disadvantage of current tools for partial evaluation and transformation is the lack of a common language. In this paper, the examples are presented in a Haskell-like notation, but they were previously processed by a partial evaluator for a subset of LML and a transformation system for the

Glide language! Though Haskell has been designed as a common purely functional language, standardising on Haskell is not without its difficulties. To give just one small example, the law of §4.1 for The Trick does not hold in some Haskell programs: since *any* function of type $t \rightarrow t \rightarrow Bool$ can be specified as the equality test for t there is no guarantee that one can substitute x for y even in a context where $x == y$ evaluates to *True*.

6 Conclusions and Future Work

It seems that typical binding-time improvements can indeed be formulated as fold/unfold transformations, providing a useful discipline at some points and the possibility of mechanical checking. Such checking is within the scope of a fold/unfold system like Starship that supports proofs of simple laws. Using a mechanical system also has labour-saving advantages for many of the operations involved. Without clear guiding objectives to determine an overall strategy only minor gains can be expected from localised fold/unfold transformations. But fold/unfold transformation for BTI *has* a clear objective, to make specific parts of a computation static, and the gains from BTI, though negligible (or even negative) for the "improved" program itself, may be far reaching for residual programs. The partial evaluator acts as a powerful amplifier, delivering large performance gains for small program changes.

On the other hand, the working framework not just provided but enforced by a mechanical fold/unfold system can be artificially constraining. A greater degree of flexibility in automated support is needed — without any loss of security. Fold/unfold systems would offer better support for BTI if they incorporated appropriate binding-time analysis. At present the choice of programming language is also a problem: most if not all pairs of partial evaluators and transformation checkers work on different languages.

State-of-the art partial evaluators are much more sophisticated in their manipulation of binding-times than §2 and §3 might suggest. The two applications of §4 are based on standard exercises that have been used to drive the development of improved techniques, and soon there may be systems that can automatically derive efficient residual programs from the original unmodified specifications for these examples. However, it is widely accepted that the art of effective BTI defies full automation. For some time yet, at least, there will be a need for tools to support interactive BTI.

Finally, in a much wider context, Schumacher[8] has drawn attention to the way that useful intermediate technologies are often lost, leaving a choice only between the most primitive tools (*cf.* text-editor) and the most advanced ones (*cf.* fully automatic partial evaluator). This undesirable phenomenon Schumacher calls "the disappearing middle". Beside interactive fold/unfold systems, what else is there in the disappearing middle of programming technology?

Acknowledgement

John Hughes introduced me to the subject of partial evaluation when I was a visitor at Chalmers and we gave a joint course on partial evaluation and program transformation. The paper is a result of my attempts to use fold/unfold transformation, as supported by Starship, for the BTI exercises in John's notes.

References

[1] RS Bird. The promotion and accumulation strategies in transformational programming. *ACM TOPLAS*, 6(4):487–504, 1984.

[2] RM Burstall and J Darlington. A transformation system for developing recursive programs. *JACM*, 24(1):44–67, 1977.

[3] J Darlington. An experimental program transformation and synthesis system. *Artificial Intelligence*, 16(1):1–46, 1981.

[4] MS Feather. A system for assisting program transformation. *ACM TOPLAS*, 4(1):1–20, 1982.

[5] ND Jones, CK Gomard, and P Sestoft. *Partial evaluation and automatic program generation*. Prentice Hall, 1993.

[6] A Pettorossi and RM Burstall. Deriving very efficient algorithms for evaluating linear recurrence relations using the program transformation technique. *Acta Informatica*, 18(2):181–206, 1982.

[7] C Runciman, I Toyn, and MA Firth. An incremental, exploratory and transformational environment for lazy functional programming. *Journal of Functional Programming*, 3(1):93–115, 1993.

[8] EF Schumacher. *Small is beautiful*. Sphere Books, 1974.

Data Dependent Concurrency Control

Phil Trinder

Glasgow University

Glasgow Scotland *

January 10, 1995

Abstract

In the implementation of many parallel functional languages data dependencies are used to synchronise concurrent tasks. This paper investigates the use of data dependency to synchronise transactions in a transaction-processor implemented in a parallel functional language. Data dependent concurrency control has some interesting properties. It permits an unusual degree of concurrency, and this is exhibited by the implementation. It is automatically provided by the underlying machine and also avoids the granularity and phantom problems raised by conventional locking. The implementation also reveals some serious deficiencies of data dependent concurrency control: it is closely based on the functional task synchronisation model, it relies on creating new versions of the database as differentials, and it enforces excessive serialisation between transactions.

1 Introduction

To prevent concurrent transactions from interfering a database must provide concurrency control. Locking is the most common concurrency control mechanism but optimistic methods have also been proposed [12, 15]. An excellent survey of concurrency control mechanisms can be found in [5]. Data dependency, a new concurrency control mechanism, is investigated here. Data dependency is the task synchronisation mechanism used in many parallel functional languages [14]. A simple transaction-processing component of a database has been implemented in a parallel functional language and is used to investigate the effects of using data dependency to control the interaction of transactions.

Data dependence has some intriguing properties. Most importantly it permits an unusual degree of concurrency between transactions. The functional transaction-processor uses updates that create a new differential version of the database replacing an entity *without first reading the entity replaced*. Section 5 demonstrates that the only restriction between transactions using these updates is that a read-transaction cannot overtake a write-transaction that is creating the entity it is about to inspect. That is, a read-transaction can overtake a preceding read-transaction and a write-transaction can overtake both a preceding read-transaction and a preceding write-transaction on the same entity.

Data dependent concurrency control simplifies the task of database implementation: the task synchronisation mechanism already provided by a parallel graph reducer is utilised. In contrast, the implementors of a conventional

---

*This work was supported by the SERC Bulk Data Types, the EPSRC PARADE and the ESPRIT FIDE projects. Email: trinder@dcs.glasgow.ac.uk

232

database usually need to go to some considerable trouble to implement concurrency control [16]. A disadvantage of such a general-purpose, fine-grained synchronisation mechanism is that it may not fit the database requirements exactly nor be as efficient as a specialised mechanism. Because data-dependence is so closely bound to the execution-model of parallel functional languages, it is not clear that it can be easily used in databases implemented in more conventional languages like C. A transaction mechanism has been implemented and proved to be *correct*, i.e. the transactions are serialisable, deadlock-free and live [18]. Data dependence also avoids the granularity and phantom problems encountered by conventional locking schemes [7].

Some disadvantages of data dependent concurrency control are uncovered by the implementation. It relies on creating a new differential version of the database for each modification, like a shadow-paged transaction mechanism [10]. In contrast to conventional shadow paging, the functional database uses the shadow versions to provide concurrency in addition to the conventional aims of providing recovery and a neat means of reversing aborted transactions. Data dependent concurrency control also enforces excessive serialisation between transactions.

Investigating data dependent concurrency control is part of a wider exploration of the feasibility of implementing transaction-processing in parallel functional languages. This exploration has been under way for some time, and the work is ongoing [2, 17]. These data dependency results were obtained several years ago, but have not been previously published. In related work data dependency has been used to synchronise transactions processed on GRIP [1], a real parallel machine [13]. Because our interpreter is simple and heavily instrumented it is used for the current experiment instead of the GRIP implementation. A similar transaction-processor has been implemented on an interpreter at Imperial College, London [4]. The Imperial transaction-processor uses a slightly different transaction-mechanism from that described in Section 6, but also exhibits the software bound on parallelism observed in Section 4.

The remainder of the paper is structured as follows. Section 2 describes the database architecture. Section 3 describes the hypothetical machine on which the transaction manager is implemented. Section 4 describes data dependent concurrency control and gives results showing its behaviour in the best case. Section 5 demonstrates the unusual degree of concurrency possible between transactions. Section 6 briefly outlines how transactions are constructed and how the mechanism avoids some locking problems. Section 7 describes the disadvantages uncovered by the implementation. Section 8 summarises the results and describes ongoing work.

2 Database Architecture

2.1 Introduction

A *collection* is a homogeneous group of data items, e.g. a collection might represent a set of bank accounts. For simplicity the transaction manager described in this paper supports operations on a single collection of data. The same principles apply for operations on a database containing multiple collections [17]. In most existing languages only certain types of data may be permanently stored.

Much of the effort in writing programs that manipulate permanent data is expended in unpacking the data into a form suitable for the computation and then repacking it for storage afterwards. The idea behind *persistent* programming languages is to allow entities of any type to be permanently stored [3].

In a persistent environment a collection can be represented as a data structure that persists for some time. Operations that do not modify such a bulk data structure, for example looking up a value, can be implemented efficiently in a functional language. However, data structures must be modified non-destructively in a pure functional language, i.e. a new version of the structure must be constructed. At first glance it appears to be prohibitively expensive to create a new version of a bulk data structure every time it is modified.

2.2   Trees

A new version of a tree can be cheaply constructed as a differential. For simplicity the prototype transaction manager uses a binary tree. In a more realistic database a more sophisticated, balanced tree would be used. The effect of tree rebalancing on concurrency is described in [17]. Consider a collection of entities with a key function that, given an entity, will return its key value. If et and kt are the entity and key types then an abstract datatype bdt, for a tree representing the collection can be written

$$bdt = Node\ bdt\ kt\ bdt \mid Entity\ et$$

Using this definition, a function to lookup an entity can be written as follows.

$$
\begin{aligned}
lookup\ k'\ (Entity\ e)\ &= Ok\ e, \textbf{ if } key\ e = k' \\
&= Error, \textbf{ otherwise}
\end{aligned}
$$

$$
\begin{aligned}
lookup\ k'\ (Node\ lt\ k\ rt)\ &= lookup\ k'\ lt, \textbf{ if } k' \leq k \\
&= lookup\ k'\ rt, \textbf{ otherwise}
\end{aligned}
$$

A function to update an entity is similar except that, in addition to producing an output message, a new version of the tree is returned.

$$
\begin{aligned}
update\ e'\ (Entity\ e)\ &= (Ok\ e,\ Entity\ e'), \textbf{ if } key\ e = key\ e' \\
&= (Error,\ Entity\ e), \textbf{ otherwise}
\end{aligned}
$$

$$
\begin{aligned}
update\ e'\ (Node\ lt\ k\ rt)\ &= (m, Node\ lt'\ k\ rt), \textbf{ if } key\ e' \leq k \\
&= (m, Node\ lt\ k\ rt'), \textbf{ otherwise} \\
&\quad \textbf{where} \\
&\qquad (m, lt') = update\ e'\ lt \\
&\qquad (m, rt') = update\ e'\ rt
\end{aligned}
$$

2.3   Efficiency

Let us assume that the tree contains n entities and is balanced. In this case its depth is $\log n$ and hence the update function only requires to construct $\log n$ new nodes to create a new version of such a tree. This is because any unchanged nodes are shared between the old and the new versions and thus a new *path* through the tree is all that need be constructed. This is best illustrated by Figure 2.1 that depicts a tree that has been updated to associate a value of 3 with x.

A time complexity of $\log n$ is the same as an imperative tree update. The cheap versions of the database-tree have several uses. In particular they make reversing an aborted transaction easy: the original database is simply reinstated [2, 17]. A fuller discussion of the efficiency of functional database-tree operations and the uses of the tree versions an be found in [17].

Figure 2.1 An Updated Tree

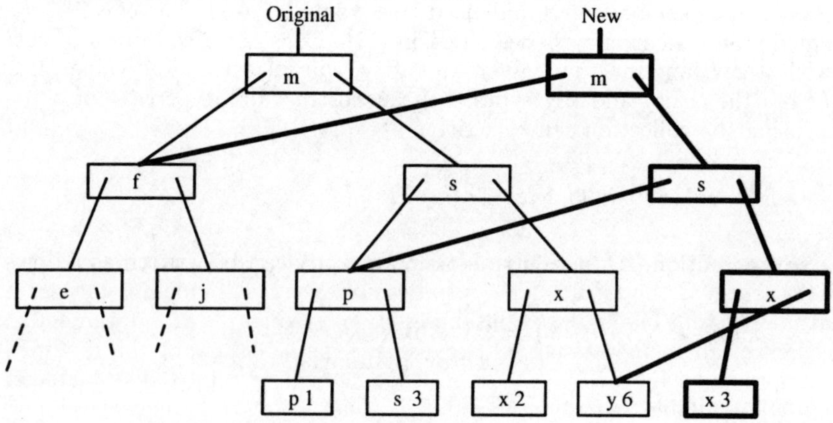

2.4   Bank Account Example

The database-tree used to produce the results reported in the following Sections is a binary tree of 512 bank account entities. Each account entity has an account number, a balance, a class and a credit limit. The database resides entirely in primary memory. Whilst this data structure is small it is sufficient to demonstrate the behaviour of the transaction manager.

Transaction Functions

A transaction is a function that takes the database as an argument and returns some output and a new version of the database as a result. Let us call this type, $bdt \rightarrow (output \times bdt)$, txt. Transactions are built out of tree manipulating operations such as *lookup* and *update*. In the bank database, two functions that prove useful are *isok*, that determines whether an operation succeeded, and *dep* that increments the balance of an account.

$$isok\ (Ok\ e) = True$$

$isok\ out = False$

$dep\ (Ok\ Acct\ ano\ bal\ crl\ class)\ n\ =\ Acct\ ano\ (bal + n)\ crl\ class$

Using *isok* and *dep*, a transaction to deposit a sum of money in a bank account can be written as follows.

$$deposit\ a\ n\ d = update\ (dep\ m\ n)\ d, \textbf{if}\ (isok\ m)$$
$$= (Error, d), \textbf{otherwise}$$
$$\textbf{where}$$
$$m = lookup\ a\ d$$

Note that *deposit* is of the correct type for a transaction-function when it is partially applied to an account number and a sum of money, i.e. *deposit a n* has type $bdt \rightarrow (output \times bdt)$.

Manager

The database-tree is controlled by a manager function that processes a stream of transactions to produce a stream of responses. That is, the manager has type $bdt \rightarrow [txt] \rightarrow [output]$. A simple version can be written as follows.

$$manager\ d\ (f : fs) = out : manager\ d'\ fs$$
$$\textbf{where}$$
$$(out, d') = f\ d$$

The first transaction f in the input stream is applied to the database and a pair is returned as the result. The output component of the pair is placed in the output stream. The updated database, d', is given as the first argument to the recursive call to the manager. Because the manager retains the modified database produced by each transaction it has an evolving state. The manager can be made available to many users simultaneously using techniques developed for functional operating systems [11].

3 Hypothetical Machine

3.1 Architecture

For the purposes of the current experiment the transaction manager is evaluated on a pseudo-parallel interpreter that emulates a hypothetical machine. The architecture of this machine determines the nature of the parallelism. Fuller details of the architecture and instrumentation can be found in [17]. It is assumed that the secondary storage underlying the persistent environment is based on disks. The machine is assumed to have a shared primary memory.

The machine is assumed to be a multiple-instruction multiple-data, or MIMD, machine. Hence each of the processing agents is capable of performing different operations on different data. The machine performs super-combinator graph reduction [14]. The evaluation strategy used in the machine is lazy except where eagerness is introduced by the primitives described in the following Section. In a machine cycle an agent may either

- Perform a super-combinator reduction, or

- Perform a delta-reduction, i.e. evaluate a primitive such as 'plus', or

- Perform a house-keeping activity such as sparking a new task.

The work to be performed by the program is broken into tasks. Each task reduces a subgraph of the program graph. Initially only one task exists. New tasks are sparked by the eager primitives described later. Task synchronisation occurs as follows. A task marks the nodes it is processing as busy. A task encountering a busy node is marked as *blocked*. As soon as the required node is no longer busy the blocked task resumes. A task that is not blocked is termed *active*. The scheduling strategy used in the hypothetical machine is both simple and fair: every active task is assigned to a processing agent and in a machine cycle the next redex in each active task is reduced.

The hypothetical machine is simple, but consistent with existing models of parallelism [6, 13]. The machine is simplistic in having an unlimited number of processors and a uniform machine cycle and in not supporting throttling or granularity control, and in having no task-creation or load-distribution overheads.

3.2 Instrumentation

The hypothetical machine is instrumented to record the following statistics during the evaluation of a program: the number of super-combinator and delta-reductions, the number of graph nodes allocated, the number of machine cycles and the average number of active processes. The number of super-combinator and delta- reductions is a measure of the sequential time-complexity of the program. The number of graph nodes allocated is a measure of a program's memory usage. Under the assumption that machine cycles take constant time, the number of machine cycles is a measure of the elapsed-time taken to evaluate a program, i.e. the parallel time complexity. The average number of active tasks gives the average concurrency available during a program's evaluation. In addition to the above figures, every 10 machine cycles the average number of active tasks during those cycles is recorded. This information is used to plot a graph of the average number of active tasks against time, measured in machine cycles.

4 Data Dependent Concurrency Control

4.1 Description

Data dependent synchronisation, or blocking, occurs when a task evaluating an expression requires, or *demands*, the value of a sub-expression. This occurs, for example, when a function demands its arguments. To introduce parallelism a more eager strategy is required and typically primitives that spark new tasks are used to generate parallelism [14]. Thus in a non-strict parallel language a function-task demanding an argument may find it in one of the three states outlined below. As an illustration let us consider the following program fragment.

$$f \; x \; y \; = \; x + y$$
$$f \; 3 \; (5 * 6)$$

The argument to a function may be

- evaluated, in this case the task evaluating the function body can proceed. In the example above, + demands its left argument and discovers that it is evaluated, to 3, and proceeds to evaluate its right argument.

- unevaluated, like y in the example above , which is bound to the expression $(5+6)$. In this case there are two further alternatives. The argument is either

  - not being evaluated by another task. In this case the task evaluating the function must evaluate the argument before it can proceed.
  - being evaluated by another task. In this case the task evaluating the function can do nothing useful until the value it requires has been computed. The function-task thus becomes *blocked* until the argument it requires is made available by the task evaluating it. *It is precisely this blocking that provides concurrency control in the functional database.*

4.2   Concurrent Manager

The manager from Section 2.4 can be made concurrent simply by making the output list constructor eager. A typical eager list constructor sparks a task to evaluate the head of the list and continues to evaluate the tail of the list. The task evaluating the head of the list, *out*, does so by applying the first transaction-function to the database, $f \; d$. The task evaluating the tail of the list applies the manager to the updated database and the remaining transaction-functions, *manager d' fs*. The recursive call to the manager itself contains an eager list constructor that will spark a new task to evaluate the second transaction and continue to apply the manager to the remaining transactions.

The behaviour of the concurrent manager is now investigated using lookup and update operations. Lookup and update are representative of a richer set of operations, and an experiment using insert and delete operations can be found in [17].

4.3   Lookups

To demonstrate data dependent synchronisation and illustrate the results obtained from the implementation let us consider the best case that arises when the manager processes a sequence of lookups. The invocation resembles:

$$manager \; d \; [lookup \; 1600; \; lookup \; 1760; \; ... \;]$$

The database remains unchanged, i.e. the arguments of the lookup functions are all already *evaluated*. Thus the tasks evaluating the lookups never become blocked. Initially the number of active tasks increases as new lookup-tasks are sparked by the manager. However, once the first lookup completes, earlier lookup-tasks will complete at the same rate as the manager sparks new ones.

238

The manager has reached a state of dynamic equilibrium. If the input stream is finite, then, once the last lookup has been sparked, the number of active processes will decline as the earlier lookup-tasks complete. The active task graph for the manager processing 30 lookups is shown in Figure 4.1.

The first lookup completes after approximately 190 cycles and the maximum concurrency is reached at this point. After the last lookup-task is sparked at approximately 430 cycles the concurrency declines steadily until the output phase is entered at cycle 590. The manager function requires 430 machine cycles to spark all 30 tasks, indicating that it requires approximately 14 cycles to spark a new task. The metrics below are obtained by executing the program lazily, i.e. sequentially, and then eagerly, i.e. in parallel.

30 LOOKUPS

Metric	Lazy	Eager
Number of super-combinator reductions	1923	1923
Number of delta-reductions	1573	1573
Number of graph nodes allocated	32366	32366
Number of machine cycles	5734	681
Average number of active tasks	1.04	8.82

The first three rows in the table indicate that the lazy and eager versions of the program have performed the same amount of work and used the same amount of space. The fourth row indicates that the eager version has taken considerably less time: only 681 cycles. Note that the average concurrency during the lazy evaluation of the program is not 1.00. This is because a strict primitive in the lazy program will spark a sub-task and for a brief period both parent and child tasks are active before the parent task discovers that it is blocked.

Figure 4.1 30 Lookups

To compensate for this calibration error the average concurrency in the eager evaluation can be divided by the lazy average concurrency to give an *adjusted average concurrency* of 8.48 active tasks. Note that the elapsed-time to evaluate the eager program has been reduced by a factor of 8.42. The *elapsed time reduction factor* is reassuringly close to the adjusted average concurrency, indicating that the additional tasks are reducing the elapsed time by performing useful work.

5 Concurrent Transactions

5.1 Introduction

Data dependent concurrency control allows an unusual degree of concurrency between read- and write-transactions. This concurrency is facilitated by the multiple database versions generated under a non-destructive update regime. Consider two transactions that appear adjacent in the manager's input stream. The second transaction is said to *overtake* if, although it is applied to the database after the first, it may complete earlier in real time.

All transactions depend on any preceding write-transaction for at least the root node, and possibly other internal nodes. However, because the entities at the leaves are most likely to be in secondary storage, *the dependence between the entities accessed by two transactions is significant.* Clearly a transaction that does not read or write any entity read or written by a preceding transaction does not depend on the entities of the earlier transaction and can overtake. Let us therefore only consider read- and write-transactions that read and write the *same* entity. For simplicity the transactions are taken to be a single lookup and a single update. An example of concurrency between larger transactions is given in [17, 18]. The invocations of the manager are very simple, for example a read following a write is written:

$$manager\ d\ [update\ (Acct\ 1560\ 345\ 'A'\ 40);\ lookup\ 1560]$$

To emphasise the effect of the concurrency control, lookup and update operations with a 'disk delay' are used and the effects of cacheing are ignored. The effect of disk accesses is difficult to demonstrate in the prototype manager because all of the database-tree resides in memory. To simulate the effect of a disk access to retrieve the leaves of the tree, a delay function has been added to the lookup and update operations so that they wait for approximately 750 cycles on demanding a leaf. The update operations are made slightly more eager to force them to perform the delay-function even when the value of the updated entity at the leaf is not demanded. The additional concurrency this introduces is apparent in the average concurrency for the 'lazy' version of the program in tables 2 and 4 below.

It is extremely important to note that the write-transactions considered here only write entities, they do not read them beforehand. This sort of write-transaction is useful if the new value of the entity does not depend on the existing value. For example, such write-only transactions might be used to maintain a class of personal identity numbers (PINs).

5.2 Read/Write Permutations

Read-transaction following a Read-Transaction

As demonstrated in the previous section, a read-transaction can overtake a preceding read transaction because the database is immediately available for processing by the following read-transaction. The second and third columns of Table 1 give the results obtained when the manager processes two disk-access lookups lazily and eagerly. The adjusted average concurrency assures us that the lookups are occurring in parallel.

Table 1: Transaction Overtaking Results

Metric	R follow R		R follow W		W follow R		W follow W	
	Lazy	Eager	Lazy	Eager	Lazy	Eager	Lazy	Eager
S-comb. reds	757	757	788	788	788	788	819	819
Delta-reds	723	723	767	777	750	750	794	804
Nodes alloc.	20220	20220	20643	20655	20637	20637	21062	21072
Mach. cycles	1913	967	2044	1850	2016	1070	2147	1129
Avg tasks	1.38	2.73	1.39	1.55	1.39	2.62	1.39	2.69
Time redn.		1.98		1.10		1.88		1.90
Avg. concur.		1.98		1.12		1.88		1.94

Read-transaction following a Write-Transaction

A read-transaction cannot overtake a write-transaction. Consider a lookup of an entity following an update to the same entity. The lookup depends on the path through the database that the update is creating and is blocked at each level in the tree until the update has created the new node at that level. In particular, the lookup-task is blocked at the leaf until the update-task has created the entity that the lookup requires. The 4th and 5th columns of Table 1 show that the lookup is delayed until the update has performed the 750 cycle 'disk' delay. As a result the adjusted average concurrency is just 1.10 and the update completes after 1070 machine cycles and the lookup after 1850 cycles.

Write-transaction following a Read-Transaction

In contrast, a write-transaction can overtake a read-transaction because there is no data dependency between them. As the database is unchanged by the read-transaction, the database argument to the write-transaction is always evaluated and it never becomes blocked. The write-transaction can construct a new version of the database without disrupting the preceding read-transaction which is proceeding on its own version of the database. The 6th and 7th columns of Table 1 report the results of the manager processing an update following a lookup. The degree of concurrency and the reduction in elapsed time indicate that the lookup and update occur concurrently.

Write-Transaction following a Write-transaction

Most unusually a write-transaction can overtake another write-transaction. Recall that the write-transactions only write entities, they do not both read and write. An update following an earlier update to the same entity must wait until the new path in the database being created by the preceding update exists. However, once the entity at the leaf has been located, both updates can independently construct a new version. Overtaking at the leaves is significant because they are the part of the database most likely to be on secondary storage. The entity written by the first update will not be visible to transactions after the second update. It will, however be visible to any lookups between the first and second update.

Table 2: Read and Write-only Concurrency

Concurrency Permitted	Locking	Data Dep. Read+Write-only	Data Dep. Read+Read/Write
Read following Read	Y	Y	Y
Read following Write	N	N	N
Write following Read	N	Y	Y
Write following Write	N	Y	N

The 8th and 9th columns of Table 1 report the results of the manager processing two updates directed to the same entity. As before, the degree of concurrency and the reduction in elapsed time indicate that the updates occur concurrently.

Summary and Application

In summary, Table 2 compares the concurrency between read- and write-trans-actions permitted by data-dependency with that permitted by conventional locking schemes. The comparison in the second column of Table 2 isn't entirely fair because a conventional write-lock permits the task in possession of the lock to both read and write the entity locked. In the functional context an operation that *replaces* the entity with a function of itself provides this functionality. As summarised in the third column of Table 2, data dependency permits greater concurrency between lookups and such a Read/Write operations than a locking scheme does. This is because a replace operation can inspect the original version of the entity and construct a new version of it without disturbing a lookup that is proceeding on the original version.

An important use of this extra concurrency is to allow long read-only trans-actions to proceed in the presence of update transactions. Some small examples are given in [17, 18].

6   Data Dependent Transaction Mechanisms

The concurrency permitted by data-dependent concurrency control has been demonstrated by single operations. In contrast a typical transaction performs many operations and may abort. Transactions have been constructed using parallel variants of *if* and executed both on interpreters [4, 17] and on a real machine [1] using data-dependent concurrency control. The correctness, i.e. serialisability, liveness and deadlock-freedom, of a data dependent transaction mechanism is given in [18]. Liveness means that a transaction that terminates in isolation will terminate in the presence of competing transactions.

Data dependent mechanisms avoid some difficult issues that arise with con-ventional locking schemes [18]. Data dependency excludes access to just those parts of the database that are currently being modified. In contrast conven-tional locking schemes must statically choose a granularity, e.g. record or file-level locking. The cost paid for the variable-granularity provided by data dependence is that syncronisation is occurring on many small objects, making it relatively expensive. Phantoms are a locking problem that does not arise if transactions create new versions [17].

7 Disadvantages

Three disadvantages of data dependent concurrency control are uncovered by the implementation. Firstly, because it is closely based on the task synchronisation mechanism of a parallel functional language, it is not clear how to employ data dependent concurrency control in databases implemented in non-functional languages. Secondly, data dependent concurrency control relies on non-destructive update, i.e. each update preserves the original database and creates a new version reflecting the modification. While some data structures can be efficiently modified in this way, many cannot and hence the choice of data structures that can be used in the database is limited [17].

Thirdly, data dependence enforces excessive serialisation because a transaction *depends* on the database constructed by its predecessor. If a transaction may commit or abort, there may be a long delay before it starts producing the result database for the following transaction to consume. To overcome this syncronisation problem, the implementations referenced in the previous section use speculative evaluation to start later transactions on the assumption that preceding transactions complete successfully.

8 Summary and Ongoing Work

The task synchronisation mechanism of parallel functional languages has been used to control concurrency between transactions. An unusual degree of concurrency between transactions has been uncovered. Some advantages of the mechanism have been sketched: it is supported by the underlying machine, easily proved correct and avoids some problems encountered by locking schemes. The disadvantages are that it is closely based on functional task synchronisation, relies heavily on creating new database-versions and enforces excessive serialisation between transactions.

A new project, Parade, will construct a functional transaction-processor on multiprocessor database machines. The immediate targets are the ICL Goldrush and Fujitsu AP1000. The new implementation will be more realistic than the one described here and the GRIP implementation [1] as the hardware is recent, data will be stored on disk and larger numbers of transactions will be processed. On Goldrush it will be possible to compare our implementation with the Oracle relational DBMS, which uses locking. We intend to implement, *inter alia*, benchmarks like TPC/C [9] which exercise the long read-only transactions so elegantly supported by data dependent concurrency control.

Acknowledgements

Simon Peyton-Jones kindly gave me a copy of his LML to FLIC compiler. Murray Cole, John Hughes, Ross Paterson, Simon Peyton-Jones and Phil Wadler all made useful comments on the paper. Sigbjorn Finne, Will Partain, Andrew Partridge and Patrick Sansom all gave useful reviews.

References

[1] Akerholt G. Hammond K. Peyton Jones S.L. Trinder P.W. Processing Transactions on GRIP: A Parallel Graph Reducer. Proceedings of PARLE '93, Springer-Verlag LNCS 694 (1993), 634-647.

[2] Argo G. Fairbairn J. Hughes R.J.M. Launchbury E.J. Trinder P.W. Implementing Functional Databases. Proceedings of the Workshop on Database Programming Languages, Roscoff, France (September 1987), 87-103.

[3] Atkinson M.P. Programming Languages and Databases. Proceedings of the 4th International Conference on Very Large Databases (1978), 408-419.

[4] Bennett A.J. Kelly P.H.J. Paterson R. Derivation and Performance of a Pipelined Transaction Processor. In IEEE Symposium on Parallel and Distributed Processing, Dallas, *to appear* (1994).

[5] Bernstein P.A. Goodman N. Concurrency Control in Distributed Database Systems. ACM Computer Surveys 13,2 (June 1981), 185-222

[6] Darlington J. Reeve M. ALICE: A Multiprocessor Reduction Machine for the Parallel Evaluation of Applicative Languages. Proceedings of the ACM Conference on Functional Programming Languages and Computer Architecture, Portsmouth, New Hampshire (1981).

[7] Eswaran K.P. Gray J.N. Lorie R.A. Traiger I.L. The Notions of Consistency and Predicate Locks in a Database System. Communications of the ACM 19,11 (November 1976), 624-633.

[8] Friedman D.P. Wise D.S. A Note on Conditional Expressions. Communications of the ACM 21,11 (November 1978).

[9] Grey J. *The Benchmark Handbook*. Morgan Kaufmann (1993)

[10] Hecht M.S. Gabbe J.D. Shadowed Management of Free Disk Pages with a Linked List. ACM Transactions on Database Systems 8,4 (December 1983), 503-514.

[11] Henderson P. Purely Functional Operating Systems in *Functional Programming and its Application*. Darlington J. Henderson P. Turner D.A. (Eds) Cambridge University Press (1982).

[12] Kung H.T. Robinson J.T. On Optimistic Methods for Concurrency Control. Carnegie Mellon Technical Report CMU-CS-79149 (October 1979).

[13] Peyton Jones S.L. Clack C. Salkild J. Hardie M. GRIP - a High-performance Architecture for Parallel Graph Reduction. Proceedings of the IFIP Conference on Functional Programming Languages and Computer Architecture, Portland, USA (September 1987), 98-112.

[14] Peyton Jones S.L. *The Implementation of Functional Programming Languages*. Prentice Hall (1987).

[15] Reed D.P. Naming and Synchronisation in a Decentralised Computer System. Ph.D. Thesis, Massachusetts Institute of Technology MIT/LCS/TR-205 (September 1978).

[16] Stonebraker M. Operating Support for Database Management. Communications of the ACM 24,7 (July 1981), 412-418.

[17] Trinder P.W. A Functional Database. D.Phil. Thesis, Oxford University Programming Research Group Monograph PRG-82 (December 1989).

[18] Trinder P.W. Data Dependence - A New Exclusion Mechanism. Fide Technical Report FIDE/91/18, Glasgow University (April 1991).

Type-Checked Message-Passing between Functional Processes

Malcolm Wallace
Colin Runciman
(malcolm,colin@minster.york.ac.uk)
Department of Computer Science, University of York,
York, YO1 5DD, United Kingdom

Abstract

Karlsson introduced the notion of communicating functional processes. It relied on a non-deterministic function, used within the functional program, to implement message-passing between processes. Stoye described a sorting office for inter-process messages which removed the need for non-determinism in the functional language. Turner added a limited form of static type-checking on message traffic passing through the sorting office. This paper describes the use of constructor classes to improve the static type-checking model, with example applications in Embedded Gofer.

1 Introduction

1.1 The problem

Consider a set of functional processes [6]. In order for the processes to communicate with each other, they each have an address, and each can send messages to other addresses through a sorting office, which is part of the runtime support system. Each process therefore generates a stream of address-message pairs as output, and receives a stream of messages as input.

```
type Process = [Message] -> [(Address,Message)]
```

This is essentially the scheme Stoye presented [9]. The typing suffers a major deficiency: there is only one message type, which is global to the entire set of processes. In operation, each process is likely to deal with only a subset of all possible messages. This leads to two things. First, processes can detect "wrong" message inputs only at runtime. Secondly, a local change to one process's set of "valid" messages may necessitate a global change in the Message type, and hence recompilation of other processes. For these reasons, it is difficult to write *re-usable* processes, suitable for inclusion in libraries. The global message type tends to constrain processes to rely too much on the particular context of the program in which they were originally written.

1.2   Some previous solutions

Some refinements to the type scheme above have been proposed. Stoye himself recognised a possible way forward. The first insight is that all messages received by a particular process should be of the same type, but distinct processes may receive different types of message. In other words, a process can be *parameterised on its input message type*. However, a process can *send* messages containing data items of different types, provided that each one is of an appropriate type for its receiver.

```
type Process imsg = [imsg] -> [(Address,Message)]
```

But now what is the type of a *Message*? It must still encompass all the messages in a particular program. Even if this type could be formulated, perhaps as a tagged union, it would be too general. It should not be possible to send an integer to a character-receiving process, or a character to a boolean-receiving process. The process address ought to constrain the type of message that can be attached to it. Stoye states that the usual Hindley-Milner type system is unable to describe the *Message* type. He posits that an *existential* type system would be of benefit.

Under such a scheme, rather than the type *Address*, there would be a type generator *AddressFor x*, being the type of process address to which items of type *x* can be sent.

```
type Process imsg = [imsg] -> [∃omsg.(AddressFor omsg, omsg)]
```

MacQueen et.al. describe a system in which this type is valid [7], but at the time of Stoye's investigation, no automatic checker existed for the system. As a result, Stoye's implementation of functional processes sidestepped typechecking altogether in numerous places. Recent developments in type systems do allow the specification and checking of existential types, but only to a limited degree [1].

Turner points out that *Message* could be an *abstract* type, whose representation is known only to the runtime system [10]. He suggests that a series of *wrapper* functions be created, each of which casts a value of some type to a *Message*:

```
type Wrapper omsg = omsg -> Message
type Process imsg = [imsg] -> [Message]
```

Each process in the system is associated with its own individual wrapper function, provided by the runtime system on the process's creation. A process can send a message to another only by using the *receiver's* wrapper: this neatly avoids any need for addresses at all. The wrapper can be viewed as exactly an address function. The scheme relies on dynamic process creation, because the only way for a process to get hold of another's wrapper is if a parent/child relationship holds between them. This is due to Turner's insistence that messages contain only *data* values: a wrapper cannot be sent inside a message, because it is a function.

The actual mechanism for creating and passing wrappers is a `fork` function. This works just like the UNIX mechanism of the same name. It takes two continuation arguments, the first of which is executed as the parent, and the second as the child.

```
fork :: (Wrapper c->Process p) -> (Wrapper c->Process c)
        -> Process p
```

Both the parent and child are given the new child's wrapper, which can easily be bound to a name for future reference. The child in addition inherits the name bindings of the parent, and hence has access to the parent's wrapper.

Turner's scheme works, but has two drawbacks. First, dynamic process creation may not be desirable, e.g. hard real-time systems require a static process net. Secondly, the wrapper functions are locally bound to each process, which increases the amount of local state they have to manage. The number of wrapper arguments to a process can get very large if it intends to send messages to many other processes!

1.3 A new solution

An addressing function, like Turner's wrapper, ensures that items are sent only to a process which can receive messages of that type. This paper shows how the overloading permitted by type and constructor classes [4] can give every such addressing function the *same name*. For this reason the addressing functions are defined globally, relying on the resolution of overloading rather than on scope rules to ensure that the correct function is used locally at runtime. One advantage is that program clutter is reduced, because the processes do not have to manage a local namespace for the wrappers. The approach also allows static creation of processes.

An additional advantage of the constructor class method is the ability to create *specialised* classes of process: either flat or layered sets of I/O privileges can be granted to a process by the judicious use of class contexts.

The following section re-formulates the problem in terms of recent ideas about functional I/O. Section 3 describes how overloading can be used to make the provision of addressing functions less ad hoc. Section 4 builds specialisation on top of this process mechanism, and section 5 concludes.

2 Modern functional I/O

2.1 Monads

For the remainder of the paper we adopt a *monadic* approach to the expression of I/O, rather than the *synchronised stream* approach used by Stoye, or the *continuations* used by Turner. Monadic I/O is semantically equivalent to both stream and continuation I/O, but arguably provides a cleaner syntax [8]. It is worthwhile rehearsing the basic ideas of monadic I/O here, before we describe how message traffic may be type-checked.

The definitions below follow Jones's characterisation of monads in Gofer [4]. Some of what follows relies in particular on the extended constructor class facilities of Gofer version 2.30 [5]. For an introduction to standard type classes, see [11], [2], or [3].

Some parts of a program can perform I/O actions. A monad encapsulates the actions, ensuring that they are sequenced in a single-threaded manner. This is very similar to the sequencing enforced by the continuation passing style of I/O. The monad additionally ensures that exactly one value is bound forward from each action; for instance, in the following program fragment using the usual I/O monad [8], a value representing the contents of a file is passed forward from the *readFile* action, and the *writeFile* action passes forward *()*, representing success.

```
readFile  ::  Filename -> IO String
writeFile ::  Filename -> String -> IO ()
main = readFile "/foo/bar"             'bind' λcontents ->
       writeFile "/rab/oof" contents 'bind' λ() ->
       etc
```

I/O actions are combined together using the *bind* operator whose result type is an action. Simple values can be lifted into the monad using the *result* operator. The *Functor* class context states that a *Monad* constructor must have a *map* function already defined over it. In this paper, the *join* operation will not be used. For further details on both the *Functor* class and *join*, see [4].

```
class Functor m => Monad m where
      result ::  a -> m a
      bind   ::  m a -> (a -> m b) -> m b
      join   ::  m (m a) -> m a
```

2.2 Processes

A process is simply an I/O action, made up of a combination of smaller actions. However, we define a new type for processes: *Action*. It differs from the standard I/O monad because it is parameterised on the type of message it expects to receive, as well as by the type of value it will pass on. Although the message type does not appear in the concrete representation of *Action*s, it plays an important role in type-checking. For instance, there are occasions where the type of value to pass on must be exactly the message type.

```
data Action imsg val = Value val
instance Monad (Action imsg) where
        result x   = Value x
        f 'bind' g = let Value x = f in g x
```

We can use the class system to describe the basic operations which characterise a process: sending and receiving messages. Later, we shall see how to extend this characterisation to include file I/O and other interaction with the real world.

```
class Monad (act imsg) => Process act imsg where
      send ::  Address -> omsg -> act imsg Bool
      recv ::  act imsg imsg
```

This says that a monadic type, such as *Action imsg*, constitutes a process type if there are operations *send* and *recv* defined, of the appropriate types to send and receive messages. A message *of any type* can be sent to an *Address*, passing forward within the sending process an indication of whether it could be delivered. A message can be delivered only if it has the specific message type allowed in the receiving process's type specification; the input message value is passed forward within the receiving process. *Action imsg* is declared to be an instance of this class by associating the names *send* and *recv* with primitive implementations in the runtime system.

```
instance Process Action imsg where
      send = primsend
      recv = primrecv
```

So far we have simply described the situation as it existed in Stoye's paper, but in a monadic framework. The following section describes how the class system can be used to ensure that the *send* operation only sends a message to the address of a process capable of receiving that message type.

3   Overloading expresses addressing

3.1   Constraints on addresses

At the implementation level, the sorting office requires both an address and a message in order to be able to deliver that message. (The syntax for introducing a primitive function here is Gofer-specific.)

```
primitive primsend "sendmsg" ::
          Address -> omsg -> Action imsg Bool
```

At the level of the source program however, we must disallow processes from making the attachment between address and message. As in Turner's scheme, a process sends just the message, and some *other* part of the runtime system works out what the address should be. But here, a class provides the necessary link between messages and the addresses they can be sent to:

```
class AddressFor omsg where
      address ::  omsg -> Address
```

An appropriate context constraint on the *send* operation is that the message type must belong to this class. That is, when *send* is invoked, it can send a message of any type *provided that an address exists* for that message type.

```
class Monad (act imsg) => Process act imsg where
    send ::  AddressFor omsg => omsg -> act imsg Bool
    recv ::  act imsg imsg
```

It is still the case that although an address is guaranteed to exist for every message accepted by this type schema, that address may not be associated with a process. For example, in a dynamic process network, there must always be "spare" addresses available which can be attached to new processes as they are created. It is for this reason that *send* still passes on an indication of whether delivery was possible or not. Where processes are created statically however, successful delivery can be guaranteed through additional static analysis, in which case the boolean report is redundant.

3.2   Using overloading

Now, we need to ensure that the appropriate address is actually attached to each message as it is sent. The declaration of *Action imsg* as an instance of the *Process* class is where this happens.

```
instance Process Action imsg where
    send x = primsend (address x) x
    recv   = primrecv
```

This says that when a message is sent, the underlying sorting office mechanism is given both an address and a message. The class system provides function-name overloading which guarantees that the right addressing function is used in every actual call.

3.3   Examples

In any particular program, an instance of the *address* function must be declared for every message type used. If every process receives a distinct message type, this is simple. For example, with the following definition of *Address*, there are three addressing functions.

```
data Address = Characters | Booleans | Integers
instance AddressFor Char where address = const Characters
instance AddressFor Bool where address = const Booleans
instance AddressFor Int  where address = const Integers
```

When any process calls, say, *send False*, the value *False* will be delivered correctly to the process *Booleans*.

However, there might be more than one process able to receive messages of a particular type. In this case, the content of the message must be sufficient to distinguish the address for delivery. For example, with the following enumerated address type, every process expects to receive characters. The value of each character message is used to determine which process receives it. A call to *send 'M'* would deliver the character *M* to the process *UpperAlpha*, whilst *send '*'* would deliver to the process *Other* if it exists.

```
data Address = UpperAlpha | LowerAlpha | Numeric | Other
instance AddressFor Char where
        address c | 'A' <= c && c <= 'Z' = UpperAlpha
                  | 'a' <= c && c <= 'z' = LowerAlpha
                  | '0' <= c && c <= '9' = Numeric
                  | otherwise            = Other
```

As a final example, consider a functional program to control two liftshafts. The code for each liftcar process is identical, dealing with exactly the same type of messages, but each copy of the process has a different address. Again, the content of the message must distinguish which process receives it. Here, the request to *GoToFloor B 4*, generated by the *B* set of buttons is delivered to *Lift B*. The request having been serviced, *DoneFloor B 4* is delivered back to *Buttons B*.

```
data AB = A | B
data Address = Lift AB | Buttons AB
data Request = GoToFloor AB Int
data Service = DoneFloor AB Int
instance AddressFor Request where
        address (GoToFloor ab n) = Lift ab
instance AddressFor Service where
        address (DoneFloor ab n) = Buttons ab
```

This example is a simplified fragment from an *Embedded Gofer* program. Embedded Gofer is an extension of Gofer directed at programming embedded systems [12]. Research on embedded applications was the original motivation for the current work on communicating functional processes.

4 Specialised classes of process

4.1 Flat specialisation

Having provided a class which defines the basic process I/O operations, it is possible to go on to define more specialised classes of process. For instance, although it suffices for most processes in a system to communicate solely with other processes, there may be a need for some processes to communicate in addition with an external file system.

```
data FilingReport = OK | Error String
class Process act imsg => FileProcess act imsg where
      readFile   ::  Filename -> act imsg (FilingReport,String)
      writeFile  ::  Filename -> String -> act imsg FilingReport
      appendFile ::  Filename -> String -> act imsg FilingReport
```

A different class of process may be required to interact with terminal screens:

```
class Process act imsg => TermProcess act imsg where
      putChar ::  Char -> act imsg ()
      getChar ::  act imsg Char
```

With these *two* specialised *classes* of process, we now have the possibility of *four* different *types* of process: one which handles files; one which handles a terminal; one which handles both; and one which handles neither. The advantage gained is protection from programmer errors. For instance, if a process is specified to interact with a terminal but not with files, then a programming error in which files are accessed by that process is caught as a static type error. This form of process specialisation should however be used with care, because with n different classes, there are 2^n different possible types.

4.2 Layered specialisation

In addition to flat specialisation, *hierarchies* of subclasses can be layered on top of the basic process class. Each inherits all the operations of its superclasses, whilst adding some new operations. This technique is used in Embedded Gofer, to allow two layers of specialisation in defining device drivers. The first layer permits access to device I/O registers.

```
class Process act imsg => DevProcess act imsg where
      getReg ::  RegAddr -> act imsg Word
      updReg ::  RegAddr -> Word -> act imsg ()
```

The second layer allows a process to receive interrupts as well as messages, provided that it already has device access.

```
class DevProcess act imsg => IntrptProcess act imsg where
      select ::  (Interrupt->act imsg val) ->
                 (imsg->act imsg val) ->
                 act imsg val
```

In effect, this provides a *privilege* mechanism on I/O. The type system can infer the level of privilege for each process by examining what operations are used in its definition. If the programmer does not agree with the inferred class constraint, this signals a static error.

5   Conclusions

We have shown that recent developments in the technology of type systems can bring improved type security to communicating functional processes.

- Parameterisation allows different processes to receive messages of different types.

- The overloading afforded by type classes makes it straightforward for a sending process to address outgoing messages and be sure that the message is of the correct type for the receiver.

- Overloading also eliminates any need to store the addresses in the local state of the process, and is therefore suitable for a system in which processes are statically created.

- Elimination both of a global message type and of the local creation of addresses simplifies the re-use of processes. A process and its associated addressing function can be a self-contained unit suitable for separate compilation and storage in a library.

- Constructor classes enable specialised sets of I/O operations and hierarchies of privilege to be expressed. (Thrift is called for here, however, because of the potential for an explosion in the number of possible process types.)

In summary, the class facilities provided by Gofer, especially in version 2.30, have been found very useful in characterising certain sorts of I/O behaviour. The scheme described here has been applied to example programs in Embedded Gofer giving gains in security and error detection.

6   Acknowledgements

The authors would like to acknowledge support from the Department of Education (Northern Ireland) in the form of a Research Studentship for this work. Mark Jones has always been very helpful in answering questions about Gofer. Phil Wadler inspired the push to convert to monadic I/O which resulted in this line of enquiry.

References

[1] Lennart Augustsson, *Haskell B user's manual v0.999.5*, Chalmers University, Sweden, October 1993.

[2] Paul Hudak and Joe Fasel, *A Gentle Introduction to Haskell*, **SIGPLAN Notices**, 27(5), May 1992.

[3] Mark P Jones, *Computing with lattices: an application of type classes*, **Journal of Functional Programming**, 2(4), pp.475-503, October 1992.

[4] Mark P Jones, *A system of constructor classes: overloading and implicit higher-order polymorphism*, pp.52-61, Proceedings of 6th Conference on Functional Programming Languages and Computer Architecture, Copenhagen, ACM Press, June 1993.

[5] Mark P Jones, *The implementation of the Gofer functional programming system*, YALEU/DCS/RR-1030, Department of Computer Science, Yale University, May 1994.

[6] Kent Karlsson, *Nebula, a functional operating system*, LPM11, Department of Computer Science, Chalmers University, Gothenburg, Sept 1981.

[7] D B MacQueen, G Plotkin, and R Sethi, *An ideal model for recursive polymorphic types*, pp.165-174, Proceedings of 11th Symposium on Principles of Programming Languages, ACM Press, January 1984.

[8] Simon Peyton Jones and Phil Wadler, *Imperative functional programming*, Proceedings of 20th Symposium on Principles of Programming Languages, ACM Press, January 1993.

[9] William Stoye, *Message-based functional operating systems*, **Science of Computer Programming**, 6, pp.291-311, 1986.

[10] David A Turner, *Functional programming and communicating processes*, pp.54-74, Proceedings of PARLE '87, Springer-Verlag LNCS 259, 1987.

[11] P Wadler and S Blott, *How to make ad-hoc polymorphism less ad-hoc*, pp.33-52, Proceedings of the workshop on Implementation of Lazy Functional Languages, Programming Methodology Group, Chalmers University, September 1988.

[12] Malcolm Wallace and Colin Runciman, *Extending a functional programming system for embedded applications*, **Software Practice and Experience**, 25(1), January 1995.

Author Index

Published in 1990–92

AI and Cognitive Science '89, Dublin City University, Eire, 14–15 September 1989
Alan F. Smeaton and Gabriel McDermott (Eds.)

Specification and Verification of Concurrent Systems, University of Stirling, Scotland, 6–8 July 1988
C. Rattray (Ed.)

Semantics for Concurrency, Proceedings of the International BCS-FACS Workshop, Sponsored by Logic for IT (S.E.R.C.), University of Leicester, UK, 23–25 July 1990
M. Z. Kwiatkowska, M. W. Shields and R. M. Thomas (Eds.)

Functional Programming, Glasgow 1989
Proceedings of the 1989 Glasgow Workshop, Fraserburgh, Scotland, 21–23 August 1989
Kei Davis and John Hughes (Eds.)

Persistent Object Systems, Proceedings of the Third International Workshop, Newcastle, Australia, 10–13 January 1989
John Rosenberg and David Koch (Eds.)

Z User Workshop, Oxford 1989, Proceedings of the Fourth Annual Z User Meeting, Oxford, 15 December 1989
J. E. Nicholls (Ed.)

Formal Methods for Trustworthy Computer Systems (FM89), Halifax, Canada, 23–27 July 1989
Dan Craigen (Editor) and Karen Summerskill (Assistant Editor)

Security and Persistence, Proceedings of the International Workshop on Computer Architectures to Support Security and Persistence of Information, Bremen, West Germany, 8–11 May 1990
John Rosenberg and J. Leslie Keedy (Eds.)

Women into Computing: Selected Papers 1988–1990
Gillian Lovegrove and Barbara Segal (Eds.)

3rd Refinement Workshop (organised by BCS-FACS, and sponsored by IBM UK Laboratories, Hursley Park and the Programming Research Group, University of Oxford), Hursley Park, 9–11 January 1990
Carroll Morgan and J. C. P. Woodcock (Eds.)

Designing Correct Circuits, Workshop jointly organised by the Universities of Oxford and Glasgow, Oxford, 26–28 September 1990
Geraint Jones and Mary Sheeran (Eds.)

Functional Programming, Glasgow 1990
Proceedings of the 1990 Glasgow Workshop on Functional Programming, Ullapool, Scotland, 13–15 August 1990
Simon L. Peyton Jones, Graham Hutton and Carsten Kehler Holst (Eds.)

4th Refinement Workshop, Proceedings of the 4th Refinement Workshop, organised by BCS-FACS, Cambridge, 9–11 January 1991
Joseph M. Morris and Roger C. Shaw (Eds.)

AI and Cognitive Science '90, University of Ulster at Jordanstown, 20–21 September 1990
Michael F. McTear and Norman Creaney (Eds.)

Software Re-use, Utrecht 1989, Proceedings of the Software Re-use Workshop, Utrecht, The Netherlands, 23–24 November 1989
Liesbeth Dusink and Patrick Hall (Eds.)

Z User Workshop, 1990, Proceedings of the Fifth Annual Z User Meeting, Oxford, 17–18 December 1990
J.E. Nicholls (Ed.)

IV Higher Order Workshop, Banff 1990
Proceedings of the IV Higher Order Workshop, Banff, Alberta, Canada, 10–14 September 1990
Graham Birtwistle (Ed.)

ALPUK91, Proceedings of the 3rd UK Annual Conference on Logic Programming, Edinburgh, 10–12 April 1991
Geraint A. Wiggins, Chris Mellish and Tim Duncan (Eds.)

Specifications of Database Systems
International Workshop on Specifications of Database Systems, Glasgow, 3–5 July 1991
David J. Harper and Moira C. Norrie (Eds.)

7th UK Computer and Telecommunications Performance Engineering Workshop
Edinburgh, 22–23 July 1991
J. Hillston, P.J.B. King and R.J. Pooley (Eds.)

Logic Program Synthesis and Transformation
Proceedings of LOPSTR 91, International Workshop on Logic Program Synthesis and Transformation, University of Manchester, 4–5 July 1991
T.P. Clement and K.-K. Lau (Eds.)

Declarative Programming, Sasbachwalden 1991
PHOENIX Seminar and Workshop on Declarative Programming, Sasbachwalden, Black Forest, Germany, 18–22 November 1991
John Darlington and Roland Dietrich (Eds.)

Building Interactive Systems:
Architectures and Tools
Philip Gray and Roger Took (Eds.)

Functional Programming, Glasgow 1991
Proceedings of the 1991 Glasgow Workshop on
Functional Programming, Portree, Isle of Skye,
12–14 August 1991
Rogardt Heldal, Carsten Kehler Holst and
Philip Wadler (Eds.)

Object Orientation in Z
Susan Stepney, Rosalind Barden and
David Cooper (Eds.)

Code Generation - Concepts, Tools, Techniques
Proceedings of the International Workshop on
Code Generation, Dagstuhl, Germany,
20–24 May 1991
Robert Giegerich and Susan L. Graham (Eds.)

Z User Workshop, York 1991, Proceedings of the
Sixth Annual Z User Meeting, York,
16–17 December 1991
J.E. Nicholls (Ed.)

Formal Aspects of Measurement
Proceedings of the BCS-FACS Workshop on
Formal Aspects of Measurement, South Bank
University, London, 5 May 1991
Tim Denvir, Ros Herman and R.W. Whitty (Eds.)

AI and Cognitive Science '91 University College,
Cork, 19–20 September 1991
Humphrey Sorensen (Ed.)

5th Refinement Workshop, Proceedings of the 5th
Refinement Workshop, organised by BCS-FACS,
London, 8–10 January 1992
Cliff B. Jones, Roger C. Shaw and
Tim Denvir (Eds.)

**Algebraic Methodology and Software Technology
(AMAST'91)**
Proceedings of the Second International
Conference on Algebraic Methodology and
Software Technology, Iowa City, USA,
22–25 May 1991
M. Nivat, C. Rattray, T. Rus and G. Scollo (Eds.)

ALPUK92, Proceedings of the 4th UK
Conference on Logic Programming,
London, 30 March–1 April 1992
Krysia Broda (Ed.)

Logic Program Synthesis and Transformation
Proceedings of LOPSTR 92, International
Workshop on Logic Program Synthesis and
Transformation, University of Manchester,
2–3 July 1992
Kung-Kiu Lau and Tim Clement (Eds.)

NAPAW 92, Proceedings of the First North
American Process Algebra Workshop, Stony
Brook, New York, USA, 28 August 1992
S. Purushothaman and Amy Zwarico (Eds.)

First International Workshop on Larch
Proceedings of the First International Workshop
on Larch, Dedham, Massachusetts, USA,
13–15 July 1992
Ursula Martin and Jeannette M. Wing (Eds.)

Persistent Object Systems
Proceedings of the Fifth International Workshop
on Persistent Object Systems, San Miniato (Pisa),
Italy, 1–4 September 1992
Antonio Albano and Ron Morrison (Eds.)

**Formal Methods in Databases and Software
Engineering,** Proceedings of the Workshop on
Formal Methods in Databases and Software
Engineering, Montreal, Canada, 15–16 May 1992
V.S. Alagar, Laks V.S. Lakshmanan and
F. Sadri (Eds.)

Modelling Database Dynamics
Selected Papers from the Fourth International
Workshop on Foundations of Models and
Languages for Data and Objects,
Volkse, Germany, 19–22 October 1992
Udo W. Lipeck and Bernhard Thalheim (Eds.)

14th Information Retrieval Colloquium
Proceedings of the BCS 14th Information
Retrieval Colloquium, University of Lancaster,
13–14 April 1992
Tony McEnery and Chris Paice (Eds.)

Functional Programming, Glasgow 1992
Proceedings of the 1992 Glasgow Workshop on
Functional Programming, Ayr, Scotland,
6–8 July 1992
John Launchbury and Patrick Sansom (Eds.)

Z User Workshop, London 1992
Proceedings of the Seventh Annual Z User
Meeting, London, 14–15 December 1992
J.P. Bowen and J.E. Nicholls (Eds.)

Interfaces to Database Systems (IDS92)
Proceedings of the First International Workshop
on Interfaces to Database Systems,
Glasgow, 1–3 July 1992
Richard Cooper (Ed.)

AI and Cognitive Science '92
University of Limerick, 10–11 September 1992
Kevin Ryan and Richard F.E. Sutcliffe (Eds.)

Theory and Formal Methods 1993
Proceedings of the First Imperial College
Department of Computing Workshop on Theory
and Formal Methods, Isle of Thorns Conference
Centre, Chelwood Gate, Sussex, UK,
29–31 March 1993
Geoffrey Burn, Simon Gay and Mark Ryan (Eds.)